Studies in Immigration and Culture

Royden Loewen, series editor

11 *The Showman and the Ukrainian Cause*
Folk Dance, Film, and the Life of Vasile Avramenko
Orest T. Martynowych

10 *Young, Well-Educated, and Adaptable*
Chilean Exiles in Ontario and Quebec, 1973-2010
Francis Peddie

9 *The Search for a Socialist El Dorado*
Finnish Immigration to Soviet Karelia from the United States and Canada in the 1930s
Alexey Golubev and Irina Takala

8 *Rewriting the Break Event*
Mennonites and Migration in Canadian Literature
Robert Zacharias

7 *Ethnic Elites and Canadian Identity*
Japanese, Ukrainians, and Scots, 1919–1971
Aya Fujiwara

6 *Community and Frontier*
A Ukrainian Settlement in the Canadian Parkland
John C. Lehr

5 *Storied Landscapes*
Ethno-Religious Identity and the Canadian Prairies
Frances Swyripa

4 *Families, Lovers, and Their Letters*
Italian Postwar Migration to Canada
Sonia Cancian

3 *Sounds of Ethnicity*
Listening to German North America, 1850–1914
Barbara Lorenzkowski

2 *Mennonite Women in Canada*
A History
Marlene Epp

1 *Imagined Homes*
Soviet German Immigrants in Two Cities
Hans Werner

THE SHOWMAN AND THE UKRAINIAN CAUSE

FOLK DANCE, FILM, AND THE LIFE OF VASILE AVRAMENKO

OREST T. MARTYNOWYCH

UMP
University of Manitoba Press

University of Manitoba Press
Winnipeg, Manitoba
Canada R3T 2M5
uofmpress.ca

Printed in Canada
Text printed on chlorine-free, 100% post-consumer recycled paper

18 17 16 15 14 1 2 3 4 5

Cover design: Frank Reimer
Cover photo: Vasile Avramenko doffing his hat during dance sequence in film Natalka Poltavka (1936). Avramenko Collection, LAC, Ottawa: MIKAN 3592708, PA-210201, Accession No. 1991-259, envelope no. 23.
Interior design: Jessica Koroscil

Library and Archives Canada Cataloguing in Publication

Martynowych, Orest T., author
The showman and the Ukrainian cause : folk dance, film, and the life of Vasile Avramenko / Orest T. Martynowych.

(Studies in immigration and culture ; 11)
Includes bibliographical references and index.
Issued in print and electronic formats.
ISBN 978-0-88755-768-2 (pbk.)
ISBN 978-0-88755-470-4 (pdf)
ISBN 978-0-88755-472-8 (epub)

1. Avramenko, Vasylª. 2. Dancers—Ukraine—Biography. 3. Dancers—Canada—Biography. 4. Motion picture producers and directors—Canada—Biography. 5. Folk dancing, Ukrainian. 6. Folk dancing, Ukrainian—Canada. I. Title. II. Series: Studies in immigration and culture ; 11

GV1785.A87M37 2014 792.802'8092 C2014-903279-X
C2014-903280-3

The University of Manitoba Press gratefully acknowledges the financial support for its publication program provided by the Government of Canada through the Canada Book Fund, the Canada Council for the Arts, the Manitoba Department of Culture, Heritage, Tourism, the Manitoba Arts Council, and the Manitoba Book Publishing Tax Credit.

FOR TANIA AND ALANA

CONTENTS

LIST OF PHOTOGRAPHS

12. Vasile Avramenko, Leon Sorochynsky and Andrii Kist (top row, centre-right), publicity photo for tour of the Prairie provinces, Winnipeg, 1927.
Source: Avramenko Photo Collection, UCECA (Oseredok), Winnipeg.

13. Vasile Avramenko (top left), Pauline Garbolinsky (middle centre) and Andrii Kist (top right) with junior dance class, Winnipeg, 1928.
Source: Avramenko Photo Collection, UCECA (Oseredok), Winnipeg.

14. Vasile Avramenko with dance pupils, probably in New York City, c. 1930.
Source: Avramenko Collection, LAC Ottawa, MIKAN 3592705, PA – 210198, accession no. 1994-296, item no. 103.

15. Julian Stechishin, 1928.
Source: Ivan Bobersky Photo Collection, UCECA (Oseredok), Winnipeg.

16. Alexander Koshetz with chorus and dancers, Washington Bicentennial tour, May 1932.
Source: Koshetz Photo Collection, UCECA (Oseredok), Winnipeg.

17. Vozny (Mathew Vodiany) flirts with Natalka (Thalia Sabanieva) in *Natalka Poltavka* (1936).
Source: Avramenko Photo Collection, UCECA (Oseredok), Winnipeg.

18. Vyborny (Michael Shvetz) offers matrimonial advice to Vozny (Mathew Vodiany) in *Natalka Poltavka* (1936).
Source: Avramenko Photo Collection, UCECA (Oseredok), Winnipeg.

19. Petro (Dmitri Creona) pines for Natalka while working as an agrarian labourer in *Natalka Poltavka* (1936).
Source: Avramenko Photo Collection, UCECA (Oseredok), Winnipeg.

20. Vozny (Mathew Vodiany) and Palamar (Vladimir Zelisky) inebriated and belligerent in *Natalka Poltavka* (1936).
Source: Avramenko Photo Collection, UCECA (Oseredok), Winnipeg.

21. Vyborny (Michael Shvetz) and Vozny (Mathew Vodiany) flanked by wedding guests in *Natalka Poltavka* (1936).
Source: Avramenko Photo Collection, UCECA (Oseredok), Winnipeg.

22. Edgar G. Ulmer, c. 1940.
Source: Academy of Motion Picture Arts and Sciences/Margaret Herrick Library, Beverly Hills, California.

23. Vasile Avramenko (standing) with Antin Rudnytsky, 1938.
Source: Avramenko Collection, LAC, Ottawa, e002712690.

24. Odarka (Maria Sokil) and Ivan Karas (Michael Shvetz) ponder their uncertain future in *Cossacks in Exile* (1938).
Source: Canadian Ukrainian Youth Association (SUMK) Collection, University of Manitoba Archives, Winnipeg.

25. Extras dressed as eighteenth century Ukrainian Cossacks on the set of *Cossacks in Exile* (1938).
Source: Canadian Ukrainian Youth Association (SUMK) Collection, University of Manitoba Archives, Winnipeg.

26. Young people dance while elders look on in *Cossacks in Exile* (1938).
Source: Canadian Ukrainian Youth Association (SUMK) Collection, University of Manitoba Archives, Winnipeg.

27. Oksana (Helen Orlenko), Odarka and Ivan's teenaged ward in *Cossacks in Exile* (1938).
Source: Canadian Ukrainian Youth Association (SUMK) Collection, University of Manitoba Archives, Winnipeg.

28. The sultan (Nicholas Karlash) and Ivan (Michael Shvetz) visit the harem in *Cossacks in Exile* (1938).
Source: Canadian Ukrainian Youth Association (SUMK) Collection, University of Manitoba Archives, Winnipeg.

FOLLOWING PAGE 116

29. Vasile Avramenko in his New York City office c. 1940.
Source: Avramenko Collection, LAC, Ottawa, MIKAN 3592707, PA -210200, accession no. 1994-296, item no. 60.

30. Souvenir program of "Glory to Canada" pageant, Winnipeg, 1946.
Source: Avramenko Photo Collection, UCECA (Oseredok), Winnipeg.

31. Cast of "Glory to Canada" pageant, unidentified city, 1946.
Source: Avramenko Collection, LAC, Ottawa, accession No. 1991-259, envelope no. 28, e002712642.

32. Vasile Avramenko, Hollywood actor John Hodiak, and Michael J. Gann, New York City, 1954.
Source: Avramenko Collection, LAC, Ottawa, e002712637.

33. Paul Yuzyk, Fr. Stefan Semczuk, Mayor Steve Juba, Vasile Avramenko, Metropolitan Ilarion (Prof. Ivan Ohienko), Michael Hryhorczuk MLA Manitoba Attorney General, and unidentified man, Winnipeg, 1957.
Source: Avramenko Collection, LAC, Ottawa, e002712638.

34. Vasile Avramenko and Paul Yuzyk, London, 1960.
Source: Avramenko Collection, LAC, Ottawa, e002712665.

35. Vasile Avramenko presented with flowers and a special certificate at the Ukrainian Free University, Munich, West Germany, 1970.
Source: Avramenko Collection, LAC, Ottawa, accession no. 1991-259, envelope no. 33, e002712670.

36. Bishop Isidore Borecky, Vasile Avramenko, Metropolitan Maxim Hermaniuk, Bishop Ivan Bukatko and filmmaker Yaroslav Kulynych, Vatican City, c. 1964-65.
Source: Avramenko Collection, LAC, Ottawa, accession no. 1991-259, envelope no. 32, e002712659.

37 Vasile Avramenko kisses the ring of Pope Paul VI, Vatican City, 25 February 1965.
Source: Avramenko Collection, LAC, Ottawa, accession no. 1991-259, envelope no. 32, e002712704.

38 Vasile Avramenko, holding miniature Ukrainian, American and Israeli flags, with unidentified man, c. 1970.
Source: Avramenko Collection, LAC, Ottawa, MIKAN 3592704, PA – 210197, accession No. 1994-296, item no. 89.

39. Vasile Avramenko with Israeli teenagers in Ukrainian costumes, Jerusalem, 1971.
Source: Avramenko Collection, LAC, Ottawa, accession no. 1991-259, envelope no. 34, e002712661.

40. Vasile Avramenko and Prime Minister Pierre Trudeau, Ottawa, mid-1970s.
Source: Avramenko Collection, LAC, Ottawa, accession no. 1991-259, envelope no. 35, e002712680.

41. Vasile Avramenko, inveterate traveller, mid-1970s.
Source: Avramenko Collection, LAC, Ottawa, accession no. 1991-259, envelope no. 34, e002712656.

42. Vasile Avramenko's card, c. 1972.
Source: Author's private collection.

WORLD PREMIERE AT THE ORPHEUM

PROLOGUE

It was Saturday evening, 3 December 1938, and the Orpheum Theatre in downtown Winnipeg was filled to the rafters. Those in attendance included Manitoba lieutenant governor W.J. Tupper; J.T. Thorson, member of Parliament for the Manitoba Interlake district; Ukrainian Catholic bishop Basil Ladyka; and countless other dignitaries. They had all come to see the world premiere of *Cossacks in Exile,* a motion picture that had been produced and financed by a Winnipeg-based Ukrainian-Canadian company and featured at least a dozen local singers and dancers in several choral and dance scenes.

"The Theatre," according to the *Winnipeg Free Press,* "was appropriately decorated for the occasion with the blue and gold colours of the Ukraine and the Union Jack and Canadian ensign flanking each side of the proscenium arch." On the stage, 150 young people "garbed in folk costumes of varied harmonizing bright hues" performed a program of Ukrainian folk dances. "To say these dances were skilfully and happily done is understating their triumph. Here was a contribution to Canadian life by Canadians of a nature to make one feel like climbing a tree and singing a song." When the performance was over, the film was finally screened.

Almost 4,000 people saw the film on the first day, and local movie critics were generous with their praise. "Compliments may sincerely be extended to the … film company, whose head offices are in Winnipeg, for the excellent production, *Cossacks in Exile,*" declared the *Free Press.* "It is a Ukrainian opera, filmed artistically with very attractive settings and with sound re-production which does full justice … to the voices of principals and chorus. … Romance is there too, but this is subordinated to the general trend of the story, and comedy is so cleverly introduced that it forms one of the most pleasing features of the bright and entertaining narrative." The *Winnipeg Evening Tribune* added that "the picture brims with good humour and good music, striking at times almost a Gilbert and

Sullivan vein. Hollywood experts were wisely employed to handle the technical end. As a result the photography is outstanding.... This is not the first Ukrainian film produced on this side of the Atlantic but the third. But this, so sprightly, interesting and well-executed, shows finally that Ukrainian-language films as a means of cultural expression of the race [sic] have definitely 'arrived.'"

Free Press columnist Francis H. Stevens was even more emphatic in his praise. He told his readers that "right now you can climb up on the roof, throw your hat in the air and shout 'Hooray for the Ukrainians' and there'll be nothing the matter with you if you do.... They have gone and produced the first full-length motion picture opera ever put out by an all-Canadian company, and have made a first class job of it."

The man responsible for the spectacular stage performance at the premiere and for the film itself, Stevens informed his readers,

> is a versatile, well-nigh incredible person named Vasile Avramenko who does so many things there's no use trying to classify him. They tell me he has got the Ukrainians in all parts of the Dominion to dancing like one grand nation-wide ballet. He wrote the screenplay of *Cossacks in Exile,* he is the general production director of the company, and it is named after him. At the premiere Saturday night, he not only did a solo dance of his own, he made a speech that raised the roof, a rousing patriotic Canadian speech in the course of which he announced he had been asked by Ottawa to help arrange entertainment for the King and Queen during their forthcoming visit to Canada.

Vasile Avramenko was not a typical Ukrainian immigrant. Unlike most of his countrymen who immigrated to North America from western Ukrainian lands in the Austro-Hungarian Empire, Avramenko was born near Kyiv in the Russian Empire. A migrant labourer in his youth, he finally found his calling as an actor and a dancer while serving with the Imperial Russian and the Ukrainian National Republican Armies. After the Revolution of 1917, he fought for Ukrainian independence and immigrated to North America, where he attempted to draw attention to his people's political struggle by showcasing their vibrant folk culture. A quixotic figure who promoted impossible projects with little regard for the financial and human costs involved, he was a whirlwind of energy, unforgettable, often aggravating, and always larger than life. In his prime, between 1925 and 1940, Avramenko emerged as the most charismatic and energetic champion of Ukrainian folk dancing outside the homeland and the only person in North America with the drive and audacity to undertake the production of feature-length Ukrainian-language motion pictures. His dance pupils included future Ukrainian-Canadian parliamentarians, a budding Hollywood actor, and a nine-year-old who would become ballet master at the New York City Ballet. Avramenko collaborated and fought with Alexander Koshetz, a renowned choral conductor and authority on liturgical music, and he had a hand in reviving the career of ostracized Hollywood director Edgar G. Ulmer, the "king of B movies" and a cult figure for many independent filmmakers in Europe and North America. His projects galvanized large numbers of Ukrainian immigrants, generated a great deal of positive publicity for their community, and managed to transform "Ukrainian dance" into a respectable activity in what was still a very puritanical and WASPish Canada. At the same time, Avramenko made promises that he failed to honour, and he borrowed large sums of money from ordinary Ukrainian immigrants that he never repaid, alienating many supporters with his erratic behaviour.

More than thirty years after his death, and almost seventy-five years after the last of his noteworthy accomplishments, Avramenko remains unknown to the public at large and to mainstream historians in particular. At the same time, he has become a mythical and highly idealized figure in parts of the Ukrainian diaspora and in Ukraine. Historians of North American dance, film, and popular culture have yet to mention him in their works—even in notes. Ukrainian admirers continue to recycle hoary legends about Avramenko—the world-famous ballet master who showcased Ukrainian dance on Broadway, the Hollywood director who made the first two Ukrainian talkies, and the selfless champion of Ukrainian performing arts who saved generations of Ukrainian youth from assimilation into a vacuous and homogenizing North American mass culture.

This book examines Avramenko's rise and fall as a producer of ethnic folk dance spectacles and motion pictures by placing his career within the context of Canadian and North American popular culture. It tries to give Avramenko his due while at the same time separating the man from the myths that still hold some in thrall. It also explores the origins of the Avramenko myth in Canada, and it attempts to present a nuanced and balanced picture of a deeply flawed but fascinating character, one who deserves a place in the history of interwar Canadian and North American popular culture.

Historians who want to get at the unvarnished Avramenko can be grateful that modesty and perspicacity were not the maestro's (as he liked to be called) strongest traits. Convinced that his work was more important than that of any other Ukrainian in North America, Avramenko amassed and guarded an enormous archive of more than 150 large boxes of documents of every kind. The collection, consisting almost entirely of Ukrainian-language materials, was deposited at the National Archives of Canada (now Library and Archives Canada) with the aid of influential supporters shortly before his death even though

Avramenko—a frequent visitor to and a sporadic resident of the country—was never a Canadian citizen. This massive collection contains virtually every piece of personal correspondence (no matter how unflattering) that Avramenko received or produced, along with professional records, newspaper clippings, leaflets, posters, photographs, film footage, and thousands of unsold tickets, and it provides a fascinating look at every part of the life of this extraordinary showman. This book is the result of intensive research in the Avramenko collection at Library and Archives Canada, supplemented by work at the Ukrainian Cultural and Educational Centre Archives in Winnipeg, where the papers of some of Avramenko's closest collaborators and severest critics are held.

THE MAN AND HIS MISSION

CHAPTER 1

Vasile Avramenko was born on 22 March 1895 in the village of Stebliv 140 kilometres south of Kyiv. He was one of seven children in the household of Kyrylo and Paraskevia (Dovbush) Avramenko.[1] Like most Ukrainian peasants in the district, the Avramenkos eked out a living tilling a tiny plot of land and working on the large sugar beet plantations that dominated the countryside west and south of Kyiv and were owned by some of the wealthiest landowners in the Russian Empire.

At the time of Avramenko's birth, Stebliv had a population of 5,750. In contemporary terms, it was an "agro-town" rather than a simple village. It had a sugar refinery that employed 650 workers, a cloth factory, a rolling mill, a cast iron foundry, six watermills, and many more windmills. A small clinic and pharmacy manned by one physician and a semi-professional assistant provided the residents of Stebliv and fifty smaller villages in the district with medical services. An Orthodox church, a Roman Catholic chapel, five small synagogues, two one-room schools, and no fewer than thirteen taverns rounded out Stebliv's roster of institutions. Although Ivan Nechui-Levytsky, one of the most important nineteenth-century Ukrainian novelists, had been born and raised in Stebliv, at the turn of the century only 10 percent of the population was literate.[2]

Stebliv and the Ukrainian lands west of the Dnieper River had been incorporated into the Russian Empire in the 1790s during the last two partitions of Poland. By the time of Avramenko's birth, the Russian tsars had been appropriating Ukrainian lands for almost two-and-a-half centuries. They had subordinated the local Orthodox church to the Patriarch of Moscow; abolished all vestiges of self-government and autonomy; stationed Russian garrisons and tax collectors throughout the land; destroyed the Zaporozhian Sich, the fortress below the Dnieper rapids that represented the last bastion of Ukrainian Cossack liberty; assimilated the Cossack officer elite into the Russian nobility; and enserfed those peasants who had managed to retain their freedom. Although serfdom had been abolished in 1861, emancipated peasants like Avramenko's parents and grandparents had received tiny plots of land, and they had been burdened with huge redemption payments that inhibited their ability to earn a living and forced them to toil on the estates of the nobility. Prior to 1905, the Russian Empire, unlike neighbouring Austria-Hungary, which controlled the westernmost Ukrainian lands, remained an autocracy unconstrained by an appointed noble assembly or an elected parliament. Per capita spending on education was among the lowest in the world, and the number of schools in central Ukraine had actually declined for much of the eighteenth and nineteenth centuries. Ukrainian villagers who managed to spend a year or two in school were taught in Russian because the Ukrainian language was classified as a dialect of the former and rejected as a medium of instruction. Since imperial bureaucrats also regarded Ukrainians as the "Little Russian" branch of the Russian people, efforts to study and highlight the distinctive nature of Ukrainian culture or to promote the use of Ukrainian as a medium of popular enlightenment were suspect as manifestations of "separatism." In the aftermath of the 1863 Polish insurrection against Russian rule, tsarist officials also cracked down on the nascent Ukrainian movement. They banned the publication of Ukrainian religious and instructional books (but not *belles-lettres*), closed Ukrainian adult education Sunday schools, and exiled Ukrainian activists to remote corners of the empire. A decade later anxious tsarist officials reacted to cultural contacts with Ukrainians in the more liberal and tolerant Austro-Hungarian Empire by outlawing the publication and importation of all Ukrainian books and the use of Ukrainian on the stage (though the latter restriction was rescinded in 1881). Only during the Revolution of 1905, which destabilized the old order and ushered in a semi-constitutional tsarist regime, did the first Ukrainian-language newspapers, cultural societies, and legal political parties emerge in the Russian Empire, though most of these gains were reversed or curtailed after the government suppressed the revolution and tried to return to its old ways.[3]

Childhood and Youth

Avramenko always spoke fondly of his native village even though his childhood in Stebliv during these turbulent times was anything but idyllic. Writing to his older sister Liuba in the 1930s, he recalled the incessant reproaches with which their father had tormented their mother and the many occasions on which their mother had taken him by the hand and fled into the countryside, hiding out until their father's rage had subsided. When Avramenko was not quite four, his mother died, and his father remarried within a year. Relations with his stepmother were strained, and Avramenko seems to have turned for emotional support to Liuba, already married and the mother of four children not much younger than Vasile. He also found an escape from his anxieties, and from the toil and drudgery of peasant life, in tales of Cossack uprisings, many of which had transpired within walking distance of Stebliv and survived in the memories of his grandfather and other aged villagers.[4]

Nor did Avramenko receive any formal schooling during his childhood in Stebliv. He remained illiterate well into his teens. Like many peasants, he spent his childhood working. At first, he worked for his sister Liuba and her husband, doing odd jobs and threshing wheat with a flail, and then he sought out work in more affluent peasant and Jewish households. About a quarter of the population of Stebliv was Jewish, and years later Avramenko would recall that he had always been treated well by his Jewish employers.[5] By the age of fifteen, he had also worked in a distillery on the landowner Warwarski's estate adjacent to Stebliv, in a warehouse in the working-class Demievka quarter of Kyiv, and in a mine owned by Princess Yusupov in what is now the Donetsk region of southeastern Ukraine.

A few years before the First World War, probably around 1910, Avramenko embarked on a forty-five-day 9,000-kilometre journey that took him from Kyiv to the Russian port of Vladivostok on the Sea of Japan. Several years earlier his older brothers Andriian and Oleksandr had followed in the footsteps of some 2 million Ukrainian peasants and migrant labourers who sought a brighter future in the Russian Empire's Siberian hinterland, particularly in the Far Eastern Amur region. After finding his brothers, Avramenko worked in a brewery, as a dockhand and stevedore in the port, and finally in a printing shop. When not working, he was drawn to the taverns frequented by sailors whose vessels docked in Vladivostok; to the movie theatres, where he saw his first motion picture (a comedy starring French slapstick comedian Max Linder); and to the theatre, where, one day in 1912, he chanced upon a production of the Ukrainian operetta *Natalka Poltavka*.[6] The spectacle, set in a Ukrainian village, featuring familiar songs and dances, and populated by Ukrainian-speaking characters who reminded Avramenko of himself and his siblings, moved him to tears and made a profound and lasting impression on the teenaged wanderer. The play triggered the first glimmerings of a Ukrainian national consciousness in Avramenko, and he realized that he would have to learn to read and write if he was to fulfill his new ambition of performing on the stage in Ukrainian plays.

Natalka Poltavka had been penned in 1818 by Ivan Kotliarevsky, the author of the first literary work in the Ukrainian vernacular two decades earlier. Written in colloquial language, enlivened by the playwright's knowledge of local folk songs and customs, and infused with his compassionate interest in the lives of common people, the play won widespread popularity. It became a cornerstone in the repertoire of the Ukrainian amateur and touring theatre groups that had emerged by the 1850s, survived the tsarist regime's efforts to ban the use of Ukrainian in scholarship and on the stage, and was transformed into an operetta by the composer Mykola Lysenko in 1889.

The first professional Ukrainian theatre troupe was established by the playwright Marko Kropyvnytsky in 1881 after the government grudgingly permitted the use of Ukrainian on the stage if a Russian play appeared on the same bill.[7] Although serious drama and foreign classics would remain the exclusive preserve of the Russian-language theatre, and the Ukrainian repertoire would be restricted to comedies and village melodramas for another twenty-five years, Ukrainian theatre grew in popularity and managed to attract many talented artists because it was the only form of Ukrainian cultural expression that could develop in relative freedom in the Russian Empire.

The revival of Ukrainian theatre at the end of the nineteenth century was led by four siblings from the talented and dynamic Tobilevych family. Born near Yelysavethrad (currently Kirovohrad), Kherson province, in central Ukraine, they performed, directed, produced, and wrote plays under the stage names Ivan Karpenko-Kary, Mykola Sadovsky, Panas Saksahansky, and Maria Sadovska-Bariolotti. During the early 1880s, all four, including Mykola Sadovsky, who would be a lifelong source of inspiration for Avramenko, had become prominent members of Kropyvnytsky's company, which also included the playwright and director Mykhailo Starytsky and the renowned actor Maria Zankovetska.

Restricted to romantic and ethnographic themes from village life, the Ukrainian theatre of Sadovsky and his contemporaries broadened its appeal by combining acting with singing and dancing. In particular, it drew on folk rituals that featured songs and dances to produce a more convincing representation of Ukrainian life and to add to the play's aesthetic appeal. By the 1890s, the folk dance had become an intrinsic component of the Ukrainian theatre and took on a special importance in comedies and melodramas of everyday life and in operettas such as Kotliarevsky and Lysenko's *Natalka Poltavka* and Hulak-Artemovsky's *Zaporozhets za Dunaiem* (Cossacks beyond the Danube/ Cossacks in Exile). To the dismay of its founders, the Ukrainian theatre's popularity and success stimulated the formation of dozens of troupes, many of them established by small-time impresarios eager to make a quick and easy profit. They staged second-rate peasant melodramas and vaudevilles featuring vulgar comedy routines, scenes of prodigious drinking, highly stylized and inauthentic peasant costumes, and mongrel "folk dances" that introduced acrobatic tricks and parodied village dances.[8] By the turn of the century, this "Little Russian" theatre had become synonymous with vulgar frivolity and comic buffoonery, and it was increasingly identified with Ukrainian theatre per se.

Yet, for all the restrictions placed upon it by the tsarist regime, and despite its many limitations, turn-of-the-century Ukrainian theatre had an indisputable impact. It helped to preserve and improve the Ukrainian language, it kept Ukrainian culture alive, and, as historian Orest Subtelny has observed (and as Avramenko's experience confirms), "many Ukrainians felt their first spark of national pride and consciousness upon seeing a well-performed play in their often-denigrated native language."[9]

The Revolution of 1905 opened up new opportunities for popular cultural expression in the Russian Empire. Sadovsky, who had acquired a national reputation for his heroic roles and emerged as the premier Ukrainian theatrical impresario, had relocated to Lviv, the largest city in the Austro-Hungarian crownland of Galicia, where he directed the Ukrainian Ruska Besida Theatre that had been organized in 1864 under Austria's more tolerant and liberal regime. After the revolution, he returned to central Ukraine, where he established the first resident Ukrainian theatre in Poltava, and then, in 1907, moved it into Kyiv's newly constructed Troitsky People's Home.

During the twelve years preceding the Revolution of 1917, Sadovsky's theatre represented "an important transitional step from the populist ethnographic to a modern Ukrainian theatre."[10] Sadovsky hired choreographers such as Vasyl Verkhovynets to study and preserve the integrity of folk dances. He placed Ukrainian opera on firm ground by engaging Alexander Koshetz to serve as his choir director and by staging Ukrainian and European operas, among them Mascagni's *Cavalleria Rusticana,* Smetana's *Bartered Bride,* and Moniuszko's *Halka.* And he attempted to introduce a more modern and cosmopolitan repertoire, though the public did not welcome this departure. Ultimately, the decision to abandon "musty folkloristic plays with their singsongs and national dances" and replace them with "plays from the world repertoire" would be made by Sadovsky's young western Ukrainian colleague Les Kurbas in the years after 1917.[11]

Motivated and invigorated by his unexpected encounter with the Ukrainian theatre, Avramenko was determined to become an actor. He continued to work in the port and in the printing shop during the day and took private lessons from a student named Trysviatsky in the evening. First he learned to read and write; then he prepared for certification as a village primary school teacher. By the time he passed his teacher's exams at the Vladivostok men's gymnasium in 1915, Russia had entered the First World War, and within a matter of weeks Avramenko was drafted into the Russian Imperial Army and assigned to the 4th Heavy Artillery Regiment.[12]

Immediately, the modest education that he had obtained began to pay dividends. After two months of basic training, Avramenko was reassigned to the Irkutsk military school for ensigns (second lieutenants) on the strength of his teacher's certificate. Those admitted to the school in Irkutsk, and to the thirty-three other hastily constructed institutions of its kind established in each of the Russian Empire's military districts, were all between twenty and twenty-five years old and drawn from the ranks of skilled, literate workers, prosperous peasants, and the best graduates of village schools.[13] Upon completion of the ensigns' school, Avramenko was assigned to the 35th Siberian Infantry Regiment in Tiumen and advanced with this unit from Irkutsk to Briansk and finally to the Russian western front. He saw action at the front and was wounded and hospitalized, first in Minsk, then in Petrograd, where he had an opportunity to see the imperial capital and visit some of its theatres. Back in Minsk, he became active in a troupe of military actors led by Yasha Vavrak, a Jew who realized that Avramenko had a real flair for the stage.[14]

Self-Discovery

It was at this point, in February 1917, that the Russian Revolution toppled the tsarist regime and ushered in a period of rapid and profound change. Out of this exciting and turbulent period, Avramenko emerged conscious of his Ukrainian identity, committed to the Ukrainian cause, and with a sense of purpose and mission that would sustain and drive him for the rest of his life. In March 1917, he was a soldiers' delegate at a meeting in Minsk convened by the Ukrainian Social Democratic activist Symon Petliura (then an employee of the All-Russian Zemstvo Union). The meeting resolved to establish a local Ukrainian council (*rada* or *soviet*), and for the first time in his life Avramenko learned which provinces (*gubernias*) of the Russian Empire were populated by Ukrainians and destined to become part of a new Ukraine "without Tsars and Muscovites." Apparently, he also became conscious of the fact that he was not a "Little Russian" but a Ukrainian "whose fate it was to live and struggle for Ukraine." During the next few months, he was assigned to organize a Ukrainian *rada* in the town of Orsha, situated midway between Minsk, Mogilev, and Smolensk, and in June 1917 he was present at the Second All-Ukrainian Military Congress in Kyiv, which delegated him and many others to mobilize youth in Kyiv province.

The spring and summer of 1917 were a period of unprecedented optimism and anticipation for the young people who found themselves at the forefront of the Ukrainian national movement in the newly democratic Russian Empire. Avramenko, who spent much of this brief interlude in Kyiv attending political meetings and frequenting theatres in which Mykola Sadovsky, Panas Saksahansky, and Ivan Marianenko performed, thought, as did many others, that he was present at the dawn of a new and brighter era. According to Avramenko, at some point during the summer of 1917, he went to see Petliura, now the Ukrainian Central Rada's general secretary of military affairs, concerning the resumption of his military service. Instead of offering him a military commission, the general secretary, who might have seen Avramenko on the stage in Minsk, told him that he could do more for Ukraine as an artist than as a soldier. Then, with the aid of Liudmyla Starytska-Cherniakhivska, Mykhailo Starytsky's daughter, Petliura found a place for Avramenko at the Lysenko School of Music and Drama.[15] There the aspiring actor had an opportunity to attend lectures read by Mykola Sadovsky; art historian Dmytro Antonovych; poet, playwright, and critic Liudmyla Starytska-Cherniakhivska; and, most notably, choreographer Vasyl Verkhovynets, the first serious student of the Ukrainian folk dance. It appears that Avramenko attended only three of Verkhovynets's rare and irregularly scheduled lectures, which included theory and practical demonstrations, but they made a profound and lasting impression on him. Henceforth it was the Ukrainian folk dance, its choreography and performance on stage, that fascinated and preoccupied Avramenko.

Vasyl Verkhovynets, responsible for transforming Ukrainian folk dancing into a performing art, became Avramenko's second source of inspiration. He was born Vasyl Kostiv in Stary Mizun, a picturesque village in the foothills of the Carpathian Mountains near Stanyslaviv (now Ivano-Frankivsk), in the Austro-Hungarian Empire.[16] His father was a village church choir conductor with an avocation for collecting the songs and folklore of the local peasantry, while his mother had an excellent voice and sang the songs to young Vasyl. A teacher by profession, Kostiv took up a position in 1899 in the county of Kalush, from where the first Ukrainians had immigrated to Canada less than a decade earlier. Then, after studying voice at the Cracow Conservatory of Music, he joined the Ukrainian Ruska Besida Theatre as an actor-singer and choral director shortly before Mykola Sadovsky and Maria Zankovetska came to Lviv in 1905.

During his year in Lviv, Sadovsky took a liking to the young and talented Kostiv (whom he nicknamed Verkhovynets or Highlander), and when he returned to central Ukraine the impresario invited Verkhovynets to join his new company. In Kyiv, the two men collaborated on several operas, including Moniuszko's *Halka*. When the latter was finally produced in Kyiv in 1909, Verkhovynets introduced the *Arkan*, a western Ukrainian highland warrior dance hitherto unknown in central and eastern Ukraine, into the opera. It caused a sensation.

In 1917, when Avramenko first met him, Verkhovynets was a recognized authority on the Ukrainian folk dance. Because Sadovsky's theatre continued to tour even after 1906, Verkhovynets had ample opportunity to see all parts of Ukraine, visit countless villages, and diligently study the folk dance in its social context and natural habitat. What he learned he applied in his theoretical writings and practical activities as a choreographer. In 1912, he published his first study, *Ukrainske vesillia* (The Ukrainian Wedding), a thorough description and analysis of the traditional Ukrainian wedding and its many rituals. No less significantly, on 21 April 1912 in Kyiv, he participated with a small group of amateur dancers in the first successful public performance devoted exclusively to Ukrainian folk dance. On that occasion, the *Arkan* from *Halka*, as well as a *Hopak* and several folk dances from the Kherson region, were performed on their own rather than within a play or opera. In no time, similar folk dance performances were being staged by students interested in the folk dance in many Ukrainian cities.

Verkhovynets worked with Sadovsky's theatre until 1915, when he joined a new company led by Saksahansky, Zankovetska, and Marianenko. Having completed a course of studies at the Mykola Lysenko School of Music and Drama, he became the new company's musical and choral director, and he choreographed its dance numbers. He remained with this company until 1919, when he published *Teoriia ukrainskoho narodnoho tantsiu* (The Theory of the Ukrainian Folk Dance). Determined to establish "the beauty, richness, and diversity" of the Ukrainian folk dance and to discredit the vulgar parodies presented on the "Little Russian" stage, Verkhovynets had produced the first and most important textbook on the subject. In the slender volume, which became one of Avramenko's prized possessions, he provided a detailed description and analysis of various dances, steps, and gestures with accompanying illustrations; developed a notational system for transcribing folk choreography; offered suggestions to help dancers develop their techniques; made recommendations on how to do field research; and proposed that folk dances should be recorded on film. After the revolution, Verkhovynets introduced elements of classical ballet into some of the folk dances that he choreographed for the stage. In the process, he helped to inspire the formation of the first professional state folk dance ensembles in Soviet Ukraine and Russia, before falling victim, as did so many others of his generation, to Stalin's terror.

Only months after Avramenko's studies with Verkhovynets commenced, they were interrupted and then terminated. The Bolshevik seizure of power in Petrograd in October 1917, the Red Army's invasion and occupation of the newly proclaimed Ukrainian National Republic (UNR) in January 1918, the arrival of German armies in March, and the installation of Hetman Pavlo Skoropadsky's German-backed regime put an end to the hopes and dreams of a liberal and democratic Russia and an autonomous or even independent Ukraine that had been born and nurtured in the spring of 1917. Avramenko studied sporadically during this period, and he might have performed small roles in Sadovsky's theatre, which by this time was clearly in decline. When the Hetman's regime was toppled late in 1918 and the UNR restored under the Directory headed by Petliura, Avramenko once again entered military ranks.

During the ensuing struggle against Bolshevik and White Russian Armies, Avramenko served in the Central Telegraph Administration of the UNR. When UNR forces retreated westward in February 1919, he was posted to a military administrative unit. In February, he was in the precincts of Proskuriv, where a fierce pogrom took the lives of several thousand Jews. Although historians now agree that the Directory's otaman-led irregulars perpetrated the massacre, Avramenko always believed that Petliura was not responsible for the atrocity and that a Bolshevik unit had provoked the pogrom.[17] By the spring of 1919, Avramenko was in Stanyslaviv, where he briefly became a member of Yosyf Stadnyk's western Ukrainian theatre. He next joined Mykola Sadovsky's troupe, which had made its way from Kyiv to Kamianets-Podilsky and then to Stanyslaviv before turning back. Working with Sadovsky, Avramenko was able to broaden his knowledge of Ukrainian folk dancing and choreography, and he had an opportunity to apply some of the lessons that he had learned in the Lysenko School of Music and Drama. When UNR forces retreated westward again in the winter of 1919–20, Avramenko remained in Soviet-occupied territory, working with some of the Ukrainian troupes that continued to travel from town to town. Only after the Bolsheviks had executed several acquaintances did Avramenko decide to flee westward into Polish-occupied eastern Galicia. After performing with yet another troupe of itinerant actors, led by Orel Stepniak, Avramenko and a few friends were interned in Kalisz, 210 kilometres west of Warsaw.[18]

The internment camp in Kalisz was one of many established at the conclusion of the Russo-Polish war to hold UNR Army veterans who had entered Poland while retreating from advancing Soviet armies in November 1920. By 1921, there were almost 30,000 refugees from the UNR in Poland, and most of them were interned soldiers. In February 1921, "his interest aroused in Ukrainian folk dancing as a patriotic expression," Avramenko established a school of Ukrainian folk dancing in the Kalisz camp.[19] This was the first of more than 100 folk dancing schools (more accurately folk dancing courses) organized by Avramenko over the next twenty years in Europe and North America. About 100 rank-and-file soldiers and officers, as well as their wives and children, enrolled. Instruction was provided in a corridor with an uneven cement floor next to a chapel in one of the buildings. Armed with a copy of Verkhovynets's *Teoriia ukrainskoho narodnoho tantsiu*, Avramenko was especially eager to impress upon his pupils that Ukrainian folk dancing could be a recreational activity and art form completely divorced from the "sausages and whiskey glasses" (*kovbasa i charka*) and "the howling and whistling of village youths" with which it was often associated in the popular imagination.[20]

During the spring and summer of 1921, after some three or four months of instruction, Avramenko's pupils made their stage début. The first performance, on 24 May 1921, received standing ovations from the internees in attendance. On 22 July 1921, Petliura and the highest-ranking officers of the interned UNR Army attended a performance at which Avramenko unveiled a "ballet" called *Za Ukrainu* (For Ukraine) that commemorated the recent struggle against the "Muscovite communists." Then, on 30 August 1921, Avramenko improvised a special performance when the Polish head of state, Marshal Józef Piłsudski, visited the Kalisz camp with Petliura. Legend has it that at the end of the performance Piłsudski shook hands with Avramenko and congratulated him on a job well done. When Avramenko launched a second dance course several weeks later, enrolment increased exponentially. In addition to the general dance course, he now also held special classes for talented pupils destined to become instructors.

It was at this point, in the fall of 1921, that Avramenko met Alexander Koshetz, the last of the three men whom he would try to emulate for the rest of his life. Almost three years earlier, in January 1919, the victorious Allies had convened the Paris Peace Conference to redraw the map of Europe. Keenly aware that the restoration of an independent Polish state was at least partly attributable to propaganda and goodwill generated by the celebrated pianist Ignacy Paderewski in the West, the leaders of the Ukrainian National Republic decided to dispatch a "musical mission" of their own. Thus was born the Ukrainian Republican Cappella (subsequently renamed the Ukrainian National Chorus), a mixed choir of about sixty voices sent to Europe as goodwill ambassadors to bring Ukrainian concerns and aspirations to the attention of the Western public and its leaders. Koshetz, the pre-eminent choral conductor in Ukraine, was selected to lead the Cappella.

Alexander Koshetz was born in the village of Romashky and raised in Tarasivka near Kaniv, 150 kilometres south of Kyiv and only seventy kilometres northeast of Avramenko's Stebliv. The son of an Orthodox priest, he had graduated from the Kyiv Theological Seminary and earned a graduate degree from the Kyiv Theological Academy before turning full time to music, first as a collector of folk songs in various ethnographic expeditions and then as a choir conductor. Between 1904 and 1917, Koshetz conducted choirs and served as musical director at the Kyiv Theological Seminary, the Mykola Lysenko School of Music and Drama (where he also studied composition), the Imperial Conservatory of Music, the St. Vladimir University Students' Choir, Mykola Sadovsky's theatre, and the Kyiv Opera. By January 1919, he was chief of the Music Section in the Directory's Ministry of Education.[21]

The first leg of the Cappella's goodwill and propaganda tour lasted from April 1919 until May 1921. During this two-year period, Koshetz and his singers gave more than 210 concerts in Czechoslovakia, Poland, Austria, Germany, Switzerland, France, Belgium, Holland, Great Britain, and Spain. They performed in major cities and in provincial towns, in the finest concert halls and in workingmen's clubs. In every country, they staged benefit concerts for local charities and special performances at reduced prices for the working people. Everywhere their audiences were wildly enthusiastic, and music critics searched for superlatives to describe their singing. One of their most popular numbers, Mykola Leontovych's *Shchedryk,* became a popular European and North American standard under the name *Carol of the Bells.*

Representatives of all strata of European society could be found among the choir's enthusiastic admirers. In Brussels, Queen Elizabeth of Belgium and her ministers attended a benefit concert for Belgian students in March 1920. Emil Vandervelde, one of the leaders of the Second Socialist International, was also an admirer. In Paris, fans included one of French prime minister Georges Clemenceau's daughters; the Princesse de Polignac, a patron of Ravel and Stravinsky; and Isadora Duncan and her dancers, several of them natives of Kyiv. The Princesse de Polignac asked the Cappella to sing in her famous salon (which they did), while Isadora Duncan invited Koshetz for tea and expressed a desire to choreograph and perform a dance to the accompaniment of the *Vesnianky,* pre-Christian, springtime ritual folk songs sung by girls in conjunction with ritual dances (which Koshetz declined). Other fans included Weimar Germany's president Friedrich Ebert; Sir Bernard Pares, professor of Russian history at the University of London; and Lord Aberdeen, who had served as Canadian governor general during the 1890s.[22]

The second leg of Koshetz's triumphant tour took place between October 1922 and May 1924. Having recruited new singers, including the Moscow Opera star Nina Koshetz, a niece, and renamed his choir the Ukrainian National Chorus, Koshetz embarked on a tour of North, Central, and South America arranged by the very successful Jewish-American impresario, Max Rabinoff. This time the chorus performed in Canada, the United States, Mexico, Cuba, Uruguay, Brazil, and Argentina. Once again audiences at several hundred concerts applauded and cheered wildly, while music critics wrote of "a human symphony orchestra,"[23] "a revelation in choral singing," and "the foundation of a new art movement."[24] In Mexico City, no fewer than 32,000 people attended a Christmas concert in 1922. Following December 1923 concerts in Winnipeg, the *Manitoba Free Press* hailed them as red-letter events: "Basses that sounded like the drone of double basses of an orchestra, tenors that cropped up with viola richness and a penetrating soprano section that was like none other, made them entirely different from anything ever heard here."[25] Were it not for political unrest in Mexico and Cuba in the spring of 1924, the tour might have gone on much longer.

In November 1921, while recruiting new singers for the second leg of his concert tour, Koshetz visited Kalisz and witnessed one of Avramenko's performances. Shocked by the terrible living conditions in the camp, he was nevertheless highly impressed by the virtuosity of the dancers led by the "young, lean blond boy with the face of a village shepherd." In his diary, Koshetz made the following observations:

> I was invited to attend a ballet performance by Avramenko's school. The ballet was marvellous: it was simply impossible to believe that such an exacting and artistic work could be created out of our dance! I wanted to see all of this in a spacious, well-illuminated concert hall filled to the rafters with cheerful people capable of appreciating, in their hearts, the joy of life. … But here, in this barrack, which seemed to have been built for victims of cholera, it struck one as a dance in front of an open coffin. I wanted to weep and cry out so they would stop. … It was terrifying to watch these marvellous and absolutely talented people and to know that … only death awaited them. Better that I had not seen this.[26]

As his dancing and teaching began to earn accolades from rank-and-file internees and prominent individuals, Avramenko's sense of mission grew. Driven relentlessly to popularize Ukrainian folk dancing, which Avramenko regarded both as an art form and as a propaganda weapon, he hoped to secure permission for a tour of Ukrainian-populated eastern Galicia and Volhynia from the Polish authorities. In the meantime, he assembled a group of dancers and set off on a tour of neighbouring internment camps in the environs of Kalisz, Strzalków, and Ałeksandrów-Kujawski. His ensemble also visited the industrial city of Łódz and Ostrów Poznanski at the invitation of an American YMCA mission that had filmed his dance school in Kalisz. At these performances and in the future, Avramenko or one of his associates delivered lectures based on *Teoriia ukrainskoho narodnoho tantsiu* by Verkhovynets. After permission to tour Poland's Ukrainian territories was denied and camp authorities decided to disband the dance school, Avramenko left Kalisz and moved to Cracow, where an orchestra offered him a contract to perform as a solo artist in the city's cabarets.

The Politics of Folk Dancing

For the first few months of the year, Avramenko performed in cabarets in Cracow, Biała-Bilsko, Bydgość, and Warsaw. A crowd favourite, he was frequently billed as a "Russian" by his handlers, who hoped to capitalize on the mystique that had surrounded Russian dancers since the appearance of the Ballets Russes on the eve of the First World War. This outraged Avramenko, as did the drunkenness in the cabarets and the prospect of entertaining Polish officers. By the spring of 1922, he had left the cabaret circuit and moved from Warsaw to Lviv. There he hoped to establish a professional dance ensemble that could some day tour European centres and demonstrate the beauty of Ukrainian folk dance to the world in the way that Alexander Koshetz and the Ukrainian National Chorus were revealing the beauty of Ukrainian folk songs and choral music.

At first, few if any members of the western Ukrainian intelligentsia could be persuaded that Ukrainian folk dancing was an artistic endeavour worthy of being performed on stage. Only after performances by Avramenko and sixteen pupils (primarily university students) at the Mykola Lysenko Hall in May and in the Ukrainska Besida Theatre in June did he gain credibility in the eyes of local Ukrainian opinion makers and popularity among Lviv's Ukrainian population. Encouraged by this newfound celebrity, Avramenko toured eastern Galicia with a small group of dancers and the bandurist Danylo Shcherbyna, a virtuoso from central Ukraine who had worked with Mykola Sadovsky. Between July and October, the troupe gave seventy-two performances in most towns and in some of the larger villages of eastern Galicia.[27]

The tour came to an end in October when Avramenko and several members of his troupe were arrested by Polish authorities in Drohobych. Having secured eastern Galicia by force of arms in 1919, the Polish administration coexisted with the Ukrainian population in what historians have described as a state of "mutual negation."[28] Ukrainians refused to recognize the legitimacy of the Polish government and boycotted elections, while extremists such as the underground Ukrainian Military Organization (UVO) resorted to sabotage and terrorism. Polish authorities, on the other hand, ignored Ukrainian concerns, violated the civil liberties of the Ukrainian inhabitants, and treated these territories as if they were an integral component of Poland. Prior to the decision of the Council of Ambassadors, in March 1923, to recognize Poland's claims to eastern Galicia, the Polish authorities were especially jittery and wary of anyone capable of stimulating nationalist sentiment among the Ukrainian population.[29] This was precisely what Avramenko, in Poland at the sufferance of the Polish administration, had set out to do, so it was hardly surprising that he would be arrested for brief periods on at least six occasions between 1922 and 1924.

Never one to overestimate obstacles that stood in his way, Avramenko was on the road again in December 1922. He would spend much of the next year performing and offering dance courses in Volhynia, Chełm, and Brest-Litovsk. These Ukrainian-populated territories had been ceded to Poland by Soviet Russia in 1921, and Avramenko, accompanied by only two dancer-instructors and the bandurist Shcherbyna, probably calculated that he would be less conspicuous and vulnerable there. Between December 1922 and July 1923, Avramenko and his associates gave sixty-five performances and organized dance schools in Lutsk, Rivne, Kremianets, Aleksandriia, and Mezhyriche. In each centre, the schools were established in the local Ukrainian Prosvita (Enlightenment) Society building. They attracted about forty to 100 pupils and continued to function under local instructors, who had been trained by Avramenko, after his departure. Once again, with missionary zeal, Avramenko tried to impress upon his pupils that Ukrainian folk dancing had nothing in common with drinking and buffoonery, that it had the potential to become a sophisticated art form.

Important performances were staged in Volodymyr Volynsky at a Peasant Congress attended by 10,000 delegates; in Kovel; in Lutsk; and in the Czech colonies in Teremne and Ivanchytsi. The most successful performances were in Rivne in May 1923, where fifty dancers from the Rivne and Lutsk schools participated, and in some of the smaller towns in the district. The highlight of most performances was Avramenko's frenetic solo dance *Gonta,* which celebrated the martyred leader of a peasant uprising in 1768, when the Orthodox Ukrainian Haidamakas had massacred Polish nobles, as well as their perceived Jewish and Ukrainian Uniate (Eastern rite Catholic) allies, before being crushed themselves by Russian armies. Yet, at a February 1923 performance in Lutsk, Avramenko also premiered his solo dance *Hore Izraielia* (Woe of Israel). The dance attempted to evoke the centuries-long plight of the Jewish Diaspora and to demonstrate to the local Jewish inhabitants, in the aftermath of the recent pogroms that had devastated countless Jewish communities, that the Ukrainian people wanted to live in harmony with the Jews, that the pogroms had been provoked by outsiders, and that Ukrainians understood the plight of Jews because they shared a similar historical experience.[30]

From Volhynia, Avramenko and his instructors moved north in August, performing in Chełm, Włodawa, Brest-Litovsk, and the major centres of Polissia and Podlachia. One-month dance courses, which attracted from twenty to sixty pupils, were offered in Chełm and Brest-Litovsk in September and October, once again with the aid of local branches of the Prosvita Society.

By November 1923, Avramenko was in Lviv once again. The city would remain his base for the next year while he and his associates established folk dancing schools there and then, in the spring and summer of 1924, in the major provincial centres—Stryi, Przemyśl, Stanyslaviv (Ivano-Frankivsk), Kolomyia, Deliatyn, Ternopil, and Drohobych—of eastern Galicia. Two schools that attracted about 150 pupils each were organized in Lviv. The first consisted primarily of secondary and university students; the second provided free instruction to orphans under the care of the Basilian Sisters. His instructors provided much of the instruction in Lviv because Avramenko had sustained a leg injury while dancing *Gonta* at a special St. Nicholas feast day performance in December. To raise funds for the ailing and hospitalized "ballet master" (as Avramenko was beginning to call himself), a number of performances and social evenings (*vechernytsi*) were sponsored by the school during the winter of 1924 in Lviv. In any event, by mid-March, his health had been restored to the point where he could offer a special two-month course for Ukrainian folk dance instructors and then organize dance schools and stage recitals in provincial centres in the spring and summer. The grandest of these spectacles were mounted in June on the Sokil-Batko athletic society grounds in Lviv and at the Great Hutsul Festival in Mykulychyn in the Carpathian Mountains. Leaflets for many of these spectacles, especially those held in larger urban centres, were usually printed in Ukrainian, Polish, and Yiddish, and two performances in Lviv, in late August, featured Avramenko's *Hore Izraielia* and other dance numbers based on Jewish history.

Less than a fortnight later, on the day that Avramenko and his pupils were scheduled to give a farewell performance sponsored by Prosvita and Sokil-Batko at the Mykola Lysenko Hall, he was arrested on orders of the Polish police chief of Lviv, Kajdan. This time Avramenko was incarcerated for a month and released only after it was strongly suggested that he consider working as a secret police agent. Once safely out of jail, a secret farewell dinner attended by many prominent Galician Ukrainians was held, and the following day, 13 October 1924, Avramenko was spirited across the Polish border into Czechoslovakia by his Ukrainian friends.

Czechoslovakia, and in particular Prague and the picturesque spa town of Poděbrady, forty-five kilometres east of the capital, were the primary and most vital centres of Ukrainian émigré life in interwar Europe. In addition to thousands of displaced war veterans and students, Prague and Poděbrady had a number of Ukrainian academic and research institutions established by émigré scholars. And in Subcarpathian Ruthenia at the easternmost tip of Czechoslovakia, there was a Ukrainian-speaking population approaching 500,000.

When Avramenko arrived in Czechoslovakia, the administration issued a visa that specifically denied him the right to visit Subcarpathia. As a result, he made his way to Prague and opened his first school of Ukrainian folk dancing in Josefov (Josefstadt), the old Jewish quarter of Prague located between the Old Town and the Vltava River. There, in the shadow of one of the oldest synagogues in Europe, Avramenko taught Ukrainian war refugees and veterans of the Sich Riflemen's Battalion how to dance. The new course was barely off the ground when, in December 1924, Avramenko injured his leg once again and had to be hospitalized for a second time. After several months of convalescence in Prague, he opened a second school of Ukrainian folk dancing at the Ukrainian Technical and Husbandry Institute in Poděbrady. There, in addition to students and war veterans, his classes and performances were attended by a number of prominent émigrés, including philanthropist and publisher Yevhen Chykalenko, pedagogue Sofia Rusova, poets Olena Teliha and Mykhailo Obidny, and Avramenko's mentor, the aging actor and impresario Mykola Sadovsky, who had served as artistic director of the Prosvita Society's Ruthenian Theatre in Uzhhorod and would soon return to Soviet Ukraine.

Early in 1925, while Avramenko was convalescing in Prague, Reverend Paul Crath (Pavlo Krat), a Ukrainian-Canadian Presbyterian missionary working in east-central Europe, requested permission to film his dance school in Josefov.[31] Avramenko consented, and soon he was corresponding about prospects in the New World with a number of Ukrainians who had recently immigrated to Canada. Although he had been applauded by the Ukrainian public, encouraged by community leaders, and reviewed enthusiastically by Ukrainian critics, his schools and performances had rarely yielded a profit in the war-ravaged and economically depressed Ukrainian communities in which he had worked. Two lengthy sojourns in hospital had also drained his scant resources, saddled him with debts, and obliged him to issue fruitless public appeals for financial assistance. Not unexpectedly, then, Canada, and especially the United States, with their large and relatively affluent Ukrainian immigrant communities, attracted Avramenko. Not only did the New World offer a way out of his financial predicament, but it also represented a new mission field where the Ukrainian folk dance might be propagated for the "Ukrainian cause."

And so, after corresponding with Winnipeg residents Ivan Bobersky, founder of the Sokil-Batko athletic society, and Ladislaus (Vladyslav) Biberovich, the son of prominent western Ukrainian actors, as well as with Ivan Hassan, a friend from Kalisz living in Toronto after touring the Americas with Koshetz and his chorus, Avramenko resolved to try his luck in the New World like so many Ukrainians before him.[32] On 18 October 1925, he gave a farewell performance in Poděbrady, and two days later he was in Delmenhorst, Germany, a suburb of Bremen, waiting for a Canadian visa. As it took some time to obtain the visa and to raise money in Canada for his ocean passage, Avramenko organized one more dance course for the Ukrainian labourers in Delmenhorst and staged one final performance on 28 November. Several days later the local German paper published a glowing review.

On 2 December, Avramenko left Hamburg, Germany, aboard the *Andania* bound for Liverpool. From Liverpool, he travelled to Halifax on the Cunard liner *Aurelia*. On 12 December, the *Aurelia* docked in Halifax, and Avramenko took his first steps on North American soil.

When he arrived in Canada, he was brimming with confidence and purpose. During the preceding decade, he had learned to read and write, experienced war and revolution, entered the world of the Ukrainian theatre, and gained entry into the highest echelons of émigré Ukrainian society. More importantly, Avramenko the homeless wanderer had emerged from the struggle for Ukrainian independence with a sense of belonging and a commitment to the Ukrainian cause that would drive him relentlessly for the rest of his life. Impressed with, attracted to, and eager to emulate the work of Mykola Sadovsky, Vasyl Verkhovynets, and Alexander Koshetz, Vasile Avramenko was already formulating plans to tour North America with an ensemble of dancers, singers, actors, and instrumentalists in imitation of Sadovsky, to teach Ukrainian folk dancing in accordance with the precepts laid down by Verkhovynets, and to win respect and glory for the Ukrainian people and their cause, just as Koshetz had done.

DANCE MASTER

CHAPTER 2

On 27 February 1926, the *Toronto Evening Telegram* published a review of a Ukrainian dance recital at the Standard Theatre on the corner of Spadina and Dundas: "When the Ukrainians dance they dance as the winds that wave the grasses of the steppes," the reviewer wrote:

> … No nigger acrobatics. No hugging matches. Hands and arms are used sparingly. They dance with their feet, which, after all, seems a natural way to dance. But how they can dance. … This ballet festival was not a ceremony in which blasé youth looked on at the performance of grown-ups. … Everyone took part. … There was much vigour and no vulgarity. Suggestion was a million miles away. They danced as David might have danced before the Lord. Some of the best dancing was like the best Ukrainian singing, done by groups of men, or by girls singly or in pairs. … Old Ukraine will live forever in new Canada while such good work continues.[1]

Such reviews marked a sharp departure in the popular Canadian perception of Ukrainians. The first wave of Ukrainian immigrants had reached Canadian shores at a time when the British Empire was at the height of its power, covering one-fifth of the Earth's land surface and embracing almost one-quarter of its population. Most Canadians of British origin gloried in this achievement, regarded the empire as "the greatest secular instrument for good in the world," and saw Canada as the empire's new "centre of gravity," its "connecting link" between Asia and Europe.[2] Some even believed that Canada's place in the empire imposed upon its citizens the duty to bear "a larger share of 'the white man's burden' … [and] take a larger part in the moral elevation and spiritual betterment of the whole human race."[3] The arrival of Ukrainians (or Ruthenians, as they were still called) from the remote and previously unknown Austrian crownlands of Galicia and Bukovyna appeared to imperil Canada's lofty imperial destiny. Poorly educated and often illiterate, barely a generation removed from serfdom, with little or no experience of electoral politics, the exotic "men (and women) in sheepskin coats" appeared to lack the qualities of mind and spirit that would make them good nation-building material. Congregating in urban enclaves and rural bloc settlements where they clung to their language and culture, the newcomers struck their hosts as an "undigested, unassimilated, ... foreign, unsympathetic, unhealthy element"[4] that would have to be "Canadianized" with proper dispatch. Ukrainian popular culture and especially Ukrainian dancing were singled out for opprobrium because they appeared to threaten lofty British and Protestant moral standards. Protestant missionaries and earnest public school teachers bent on Canadianizing immigrants were scandalized by dancing on the Sabbath, and they routinely lamented that, at Ukrainian weddings and other festive occasions, "the attitudes and poses of the dancers are anything but elevating."[5] Now, suddenly, Ukrainian folk dancing was being touted by the mainstream press as a socially and culturally acceptable activity, as a pastime capable of upholding rather than destroying the moral standards on which British and Canadian civilization rested. Ukrainian Canadian community leaders were ecstatic, and the man whom they hailed was Vasile Avramenko, who had just made his Canadian debut.

When Avramenko arrived at Halifax in December 1925, Canada did not have an indigenous professional theatre: the stage was still dominated by American touring companies, and a vibrant amateur theatre movement was just getting under way.[6] There were only two symphony orchestras in the country, and dance in particular was an unknown quantity. Audiences in some of the large urban centres had seen the Los Angeles–based Denishawn touring company perform its modern dance spectacles, garbed in exotic oriental costumes, and the Russian ballerina Anna Pavlova had toured Canada on several occasions, performing *Giselle* and *The Dying Swan*. But most Canadians, including arts critics employed by major urban newspapers, knew very little about ballet or modern dance. For someone with Avramenko's raw talent and drive, a cultural backwater such as Canada held out limitless possibilities.

In 1925, Avramenko was a man with a mission. He was determined to tour North America with an ensemble of dancers, singers, and instrumentalists to focus attention on the Ukrainian people and their struggle for independence. Never one to underestimate his own abilities, Avramenko announced that it was his intention "to tear down the wall of disdain that surrounded Ukrainians [by] creating a Ukrainian ballet for the glory and liberation of our people!"[7]

This was a daunting agenda that would have caused a more reflective individual to think twice, but during the 1920s and 1930s Avramenko's artistic aspirations and optimism were boundless. In speeches delivered in every city and town that Avramenko visited, he was not shy about linking himself and his accomplishments in the field of dance with the names and achievements of Koshetz in choral music, Sadovsky and Kropyvnytsky in theatre, and Kotliarevsky, Shevchenko, and Franko in literature.[8] Indeed, during these years, the need to win recognition and respect for the "Ukrainian cause," and to establish himself as one of its champions, came to obsess and dominate Avramenko. It would cause him to sacrifice his private life, his friends, and even his family, and in the end it would overwhelm and destroy him. But in 1925 his greatest triumphs still lay ahead.

West Toronto

Avramenko's first Canadian sojourn, from December 1925 until May 1928, began in Toronto, where his friend Yuri Hassan, who had come to North America with Alexander Koshetz, was transforming the Ukrainian People's Home chorus into one of Toronto's finest amateur choirs. Hassan had put up the money to finance his friend's ocean crossing, recruited Volodymyr Kukhta (P.W. Koohtow) to publicize Avramenko's arrival in southern Ontario, and persuaded J.S. Atkinson, director of the Canadian Bureau for the Advancement of Music, to facilitate the dancer's entry into Canada.[9]

By the mid-1920s, there were over 200,000 Ukrainians in Canada. Although more than 85 percent of Ukrainian Canadians were concentrated in the three prairie provinces, Avramenko had been told that his prospects would be best in Toronto. The city's Ukrainian labourers and tradesmen had more disposable cash than prairie homesteaders, and southern Ontario was close to the American states with the highest concentrations of Ukrainian immigrants. Toronto also seemed to offer Avramenko the brightest prospects because Ukrainian factional disputes were relatively muted in the city. Unlike Winnipeg, with its 20,000 Ukrainian Canadians, Toronto was only beginning to divide into warring Catholic, Orthodox, pro-Soviet, and militant nationalist factions.

The dance schools in southern Ontario were launched during the first week of January 1926. For the next three months, instruction was offered in St. Mary's Roman Catholic hall at the corner of Bathurst and Adelaide in Toronto, in St. Josaphat's Ukrainian Catholic parish hall on Franklin Street in West Toronto, and in the Hrushevsky Society hall on Albert Street in Oshawa.[10] Several weeks later, against the advice of his closest associates, Avramenko opened a fourth venue in Toronto for members of the pro-Soviet Ukrainian

Labour-Farmer Temple Association (ULFTA) who did not wish to attend classes with their nationalist adversaries.[11] Enrolment totalled about fifty adults and eighty children in Toronto, while another fifty to seventy pupils attended classes in Oshawa. The classes attracted Ukrainians of all political and religious persuasions, including the children of many influential and well-connected community leaders. The latter included the daughters of Reverend Paul Crath, who had filmed Avramenko's dance classes in Prague the previous year, and most members of the Humeniuk family, including Theodore Humeniuk, Toronto's only Ukrainian lawyer and a leading Ukrainian Orthodox lay activist.[12] Having Crath and Humeniuk among his supporters was a godsend for Avramenko. Crath was a close acquaintance of and collaborator with the poet and journalist Florence Randal Livesay (the mother of poet Dorothy Livesay), whose *Songs of Ukraina and Ruthenian Poems,* published in 1916, had been the first North American translation of Ukrainian verse. When Avramenko arrived in Toronto, Crath and Humeniuk were helping Livesay translate *Marusia,* a classic of nineteenth-century Ukrainian romantic literature, into English. Within weeks, references to and photographs of Avramenko would appear in Livesay's articles and provide the new dance master with instant credibility.[13]

In Canada, as in western Ukraine and central Europe, Avramenko's dance schools focused on the inculcation of Ukrainian pride and identity. Consisting of twenty-five two-hour lessons at a cost of five to ten dollars for preschoolers and up to fifteen to thirty dollars for adults, they promoted national sentiment and were conducted in a disciplined, almost military, fashion. As Alexandra Pritz has observed, "Avramenko ... would begin the class by relating how the Cossacks used to improvise the *hopak* at the Zaporizhian Sich. He would fill the heads of his youthful students with tales of brave Cossack deeds and dances, and when he saw that he had captured their imagination, he would go down into a *prysiadka* (a virile dance step executed from a squat position)."[14] Rules and regulations governing the courses stipulated that Ukrainian was the only language of instruction. Regular, punctual attendance and disciplined behaviour were mandatory. Gum-chewing, smoking, appearing at lessons in an inebriated state, wearing hats, using foul language, discussing politics, drinking cold beverages, challenging the instructor's decisions, and talking during lessons were strictly prohibited. Any pupil who violated one of these regulations could be expelled and would forfeit his or her tuition fees.[15]

Avramenko and his instructors usually taught their pupils ten to twelve dances from several regions of Ukraine, including those that had not sent immigrants to North America. More complex and stylized than any of the folk dances that Ukrainian immigrants might have danced on social occasions, they included *Velykodna haivka,* a spring or Easter ritual dance for girls; *Kozachok podilskyi,* a Cossack courtship dance, native to the Podillia region, for one to four couples; *Kolomyika,* a lively Carpathian highland dance for two or more couples (it should not be confused with the circle dance that has become a staple of contemporary weddings); *Zhuravel,* a wedding dance for four or more couples; *Kateryna,* a salon dance from the Kherson region of southwestern Ukraine; *Hopak kolom,* a vigorous dance of Cossack origin for one or more couples native to the Kyiv region; *Zaporozhskyi herts,* a historical Cossack sword dance; *Arkan,* a Carpathian warrior circle dance traditionally performed around a bonfire before Verkhovynets adapted it for the stage; *Hrechanyky,* a joyful central Ukrainian dance for four couples; *Zhenchychok,* a spring dance, imitating the flight of a bird, performed by two little girls; *Metelytsia,* a dance for ten or more couples that depicted the onset of a winter blizzard; *Honyviter,* a Carpathian solo or group dance for girls that evoked a whirlwind; and *Chumachok,* the dance of itinerant eighteenth-century Black Sea salt merchants performed by boys brandishing whips and dressed in white cotton outfits and straw hats.[16] The purpose of this repertoire, as ethnographer Andriy Nahachewsky has argued, was to promote a select few dances as symbols of Ukrainian identity. Avramenko "dreamed that a Ukrainian from Winnipeg, who met a Ukrainian from Toronto, Melbourne, Curitiba or New York, should be able to dance the same dances together." Ukrainians were "one people and Ukrainian culture should be one," he maintained.[17]

Upon completion of a dance course, every pupil was obliged to pass a theoretical and practical examination before receiving a certificate (*svidotstvo*). After graduating, students could perform dances publicly on two conditions: the dances were billed as Ukrainian dances, and Avramenko was credited as their arranger and choreographer. Anyone wishing to open a school of Ukrainian folk dancing could do so with his permission only after taking and passing a special instructor's course. Unqualified instructors would be called to account for compromising the reputation of the Ukrainian national dance and Ukrainians in general.

From the outset, Avramenko was champing at the bit, eager to select the most talented dance pupils, stage performances, assemble a dance troupe, recruit a few singers and instrumentalists, and tour central Canada and the northeastern United States. A mere seven weeks after offering his first dance class, he had his pupils go through their paces in front of 1,600 spectators in two recitals on the stage of the Standard Theatre, where Yiddish vaudeville was the usual fare. The reviews, as already noted, were very enthusiastic. The

Toronto Evening Telegram marvelled at the colourful and beautiful embroidered costumes, the complicated ensemble dances, the exotic and "oriental" motifs that characterized Ukrainian folk dances, the virtuosity of five-year-old female soloists, the "fire and fervour" of the male sword dances, and especially the "wonderful agility and pantomimic grace" of Avramenko when he performed his solo dances. Even when they noted the "tedious rhythm of the music" and observed that "the dancers were at times a little irregular," critics invariably concluded that the "dance was always beautiful." "It is a wonderful thing that Mr. Avramenko has done to bring his people together in this way, and especially to bring out the talent of the little boys and little girls so pleasantly and naturally."[18] Encouraged, Avramenko scheduled almost a dozen performances in Toronto, Oshawa, and Hamilton.

At this point, just as his luck seemed to be improving, fate intervened once again and scuttled his plans. On 20 March 1926, while performing a *hopak* at Toronto's Alhambra Hall on Spadina Avenue for the benefit of the ULFTA, Avramenko twisted his right leg for a third time. The leg was placed in a cast for four weeks, and, when this did not help, surgery ensued several months later. As a result, Avramenko was unable to teach until the fall and incapable of performing on stage for almost one year. When classes in his first four dance schools came to an end, some of his most talented pupils dispersed across Canada and the United States. Victor Moshuk, a young Bukovynian immigrant and one of Avramenko's best local graduates, taught a new course, launched at the Ukrainian People's Home in May. Simultaneously, as if to rub salt into his wounds, the ULFTA appointed Ivan Grekul, who had just graduated from Avramenko's dance school, to run dance courses in ULFTA halls all across Canada. Recriminations and competition for spectators and revenues followed.[19]

Plans to tour central Canada and the northeastern United States had to be put on hold. Nevertheless, while convalescing, Avramenko continued to keep theatres and Ukrainian community halls busy staging dance school performances and graduation recitals, mounting a *tableau vivant* of Repin's famous painting *The Zaporozhian Cossacks Write a Letter to the Sultan,* and producing Kotliarevsky's *Natalka Poltavka.* In all of these endeavours, he benefited from the talented assistance of Hassan, Kukhta, and Leon (Lev) Sorochynsky, another veteran of Koshetz's Ukrainian National Chorus who was conducting a Ukrainian choir in Rochester, New York, and commuting frequently to Toronto.

The highlight and finale of Avramenko's stay in Toronto were an appearance by dancers from his Ukrainian People's Home school at the Canadian National Exhibition (CNE). From 30 August through 11 September, accompanied by an orchestra and choir, they gave twelve eight-minute performances on the CNE grandstand, each witnessed by up to 25,000 spectators. This performance, in particular, had all the earmarks of a Ukrainian historical pageant or even a secular nationalist liturgy. An article in the *Toronto Evening Telegram,* penned by one of Avramenko's associates, revealed that the performance would recapitulate Ukraine's historical struggles:

> The trumpets sound a call. On the square before the grandstand come in a long snake-like formation men and women, boys and girls. They hold the formation—they gather for a battle with the oncoming Tartar horde! ... Everything seems lost—The little "Tchumak," from the time of Catherine the Great, comes out with his funny newly born steps, representing the fate of the Cossacks, who because of overrunning of their country by the horde of Muscovites, had to take up a trade of a free merchant—a "Tchumak." His dance brings about a will of the besieged people to fight again, and they form into another group, and with the steps called "Metelitza" form a sort of a fort; backs to backs, they stand ready to fight again. A salvo of cannon, and around them come ... the Ukrainian knights, the Cossacks. Like a hurricane they fly into the fray and protect their people from the horde! They do the famous sword dance called "Zaporoshetz." After this, the people kneel and give praise to the Almighty for deliverance from the foe (Easter *khorovod*). The Cossacks form a sort of a protective column, and the people joyfully fly back to their homes, in a festival dance called "Juravelle."[20]

When the dancers gave a special performance at the women's pavilion, Florence Randal Livesay was on hand to speak about Ukrainian folk dancing, explain its intricacies, and suggest that Ukrainian music and dancing had the potential to inject Canada, which was "so gray, so drab," with colour, laughter, and happiness.[21] Not unexpectedly, in the aftermath of the CNE performances, the Ukrainian-Canadian press began to couple the names of Vasile Avramenko and Alexander Koshetz, who at that moment was assembling the Ukrainian National Chorus (including Hassan and Sorochynsky) in New York City for one last tour of North America.

By the fall of 1926, articles about Avramenko and his dancers had appeared in every major Ukrainian-Canadian weekly as well as in the *Toronto Evening Telegram,* the *Toronto Daily Star,* the *Toronto Globe,* the *Toronto Mail and Empire, Saturday Night, Maclean's Magazine, Canadian Magazine,* and *Musical America.*[22] As Ukrainian Canadians all across the dominion now began to take notice of him and seemed ready to welcome him into their communities, Avramenko changed his plans. Instead of leaving Toronto for the United States and making his way toward New York City with a troupe of dancers, he decided to head west, toward the prairie provinces, where most Ukrainian Canadians lived. There he would teach, select and train a troupe, and tour western Canada, and then, when the troupe was ready, he would tour central and eastern Canada and the northeastern United States in preparation for his New York City début. Avramenko also decided to visit western Canada to pre-empt incursions into his turf by local interlopers such as ULFTA instructor Ivan Grekul and newcomers such as Mykhailo Darkovych. The latter had graduated from Avramenko's dance school in Brest-Litovsk in 1923. Since immigrating to Canada in the spring of 1926, he had been performing Avramenko dance solos, including *Chumak* and *Za Ukrainu*, offering private dance lessons, and preparing to open a Ukrainian dance school in Winnipeg. In Ukraine, Avramenko had encouraged his graduates to follow his example by teaching and performing his folk dances and solos wherever an opportunity presented itself, but he was unwilling to brook competition from such upstarts in North America.[23]

By the second week of October, Avramenko, his manager Volodymyr Kukhta, and his assistant dance instructor Victor Moshuk were at the lakehead. There they proceeded to open Ukrainian dance schools in Prosvita Society halls and one ULFTA hall in Fort William, West Fort William, and Port Arthur. Although total enrolment, which surpassed 250 pupils, was substantially higher than it had been in Toronto, Avramenko was not prepared to rest on his laurels or linger in these isolated northern Ontario port and pulp-and-paper towns.[24] From European acquaintances, he had learned that Ukrainian newspapers and magazines in Lviv, Kyiv, and Kharkiv were publishing articles about him, and there were rumours abroad that Soviet Ukrainian authorities were thinking of inviting Koshetz and Avramenko to return to the Ukrainian Soviet Socialist Republic.[25] This undoubtedly provided added incentive for Avramenko to make a name for himself in North America, the sooner the better.

In late November, Avramenko and Kukhta visited Winnipeg to attend a performance by Alexander Koshetz and the Ukrainian National Chorus at the Walker Theatre, Winnipeg's most luxurious and prestigious venue. After the performance, Avramenko met with Hassan and Sorochynsky, exchanged cordialities with Koshetz, and posed for photographs with the renowned choir director. He also used the trip to promote the dance schools that he hoped to launch in Winnipeg in the new year by delivering a lecture on "The Rebirth of the Ukrainian National Dance" in Ukrainian Catholic and Orthodox halls. When he spoke at St. Mary the Protectress Ukrainian Orthodox Church in the city's North End, Koshetz, still in Winnipeg, attended the lecture and duly noted it in his diary.[26] It would be more than five years before Avramenko finally realized his ambition of touring with Koshetz. However, the outcome would be unlike anything that he or Koshetz had anticipated.

Returning to the lakehead, Avramenko staged three dance school recitals in early December, including one at the Orpheum Theatre in Fort William. Then he moved on to Kenora, a small resort and pulp-and-paper town on the shores of Lake-of-the-Woods. There he and Moshuk spent the next month instructing up to fifty local dance pupils, preparing a production of *Natalka Poltavka,* and assembling a group of dancers from all parts of Ontario that would accompany Avramenko to Winnipeg.[27] By the third week of January 1927, he and his entourage were ready to make their début in the city with the largest Ukrainian population in Canada.

North End Winnipeg

In 1927, Winnipeg was the "Gateway to the West," western Canada's largest urban metropolis and still the third most populous city in the dominion. It was the centre of Canada's agricultural industry, one of the most important international grain markets, and one of the largest railway hubs in the world. To accommodate and divert thousands of businessmen and salesmen who passed through the city, Winnipeg's business and entertainment district was dotted with more than sixty hotels, fourteen theatres, and several of the new and opulent motion picture palaces then under construction all across North America. Since the turn of the century, the best London and New York travelling stage shows had been visiting Winnipeg to feed the hunger of its inhabitants and visitors for drama and opera. By 1914, the city had also emerged as a major stop on the Considine and Sullivan, Pantages, and Orpheum vaudeville circuits. Many vaudevillians, including Fred Astaire, Fatty Arbuckle, Lon Chaney, Buster Keaton, W.C. Fields, and Stan Laurel, to name but a few, had visited Winnipeg and performed at the Strand, Pantages Playhouse, and Orpheum Theatres. The Marx Brothers first saw Charlie Chaplin perform in Winnipeg, in 1912, and befriended the young British vaudevillian.[28] By the time Avramenko arrived in the city in January 1927, the Marx Brothers were preparing to leave Broadway for Hollywood, while Chaplin had become the greatest motion picture star in the world.

Unlike Koshetz and the Ukrainian National Chorus, Avramenko and his dancers did not make their Winnipeg début in the Walker Theatre or in one of the theatres that had hosted so many famous vaudevillians. Avramenko's Ontario dance pupils, the first Ukrainian entertainers from eastern Canada to perform in the west, took to the stage in the decidedly less sumptuous and more austere premises of the Canadian-Ukrainian Institute Prosvita hall at the corner of Pritchard and Arlington in Winnipeg's North End, the immigrant quarter where most of the city's Ukrainians, Jews, Poles, and Germans lived. Nevertheless, the two performances on 22 January, mounted to publicize his arrival in the city and to promote enrolment in the dance classes that Avramenko proposed to launch on 1 February, introduced him and his repertoire to the city's Ukrainian community. Reviews in the local Ukrainian press observed that many of the dances were completely unknown to the audience and reported that Avramenko, still unable to perform on stage himself, had delivered a brief speech and a rousing appeal calling on all in attendance to work for the greater glory of Ukraine.[29] Within a week, at least 296 pupils had enrolled in Avramenko's School of Ukrainian National Dance, and on 1 February classes commenced on the third floor of Steiman's Hall at the corner of Selkirk and Andrews. Two weeks later a second, smaller school attended by about fifty pupils opened at the Taras Shevchenko Prosvita hall in Brooklands, a district in the city's West End populated almost exclusively by Ukrainian railyard workers.[30] Because the rivalry between Avramenko and ULFTA dancers trained by Ivan Grekul had become increasingly acrimonious during the past few months, special courses for members of the pro-Soviet organization were not offered in Winnipeg and would not be offered in the future.[31]

The decision to rent the third floor of Steiman's Hall, an establishment owned by Jewish immigrants and situated on the North End's major commercial artery, allowed Avramenko to maintain the "diplomatic neutrality" so vital for success in Winnipeg's highly factionalized Ukrainian community. It also provided him with a very convenient central location for his school. Two of the largest Ukrainian Catholic parishes in Canada, a Ukrainian Catholic day school, a Ukrainian United Church congregation, the Ukrainian Reading Association Prosvita, the Ukrainian National Home Association, the national headquarters of the Ukrainian Labour-Farmer Temple Association, the city's only Ukrainian-owned pharmacy, and most of its Ukrainian physicians, dentists, lawyers, and tradesmen could be found within a five-block radius of Steiman's Hall. The Ukrainian Orthodox congregation, the Canadian Ukrainian Institute Prosvita, and virtually all other North End Ukrainian institutions and businesses were located within a one-kilometre radius. Soon every Ukrainian in Winnipeg knew that Avramenko had arrived in the city and was offering dance classes and preparing to perform on the stage after a one-year hiatus. To make sure that no one forgot, a special "Bulletin of the Avramenko School of Ukrainian Dance" appeared in the local Ukrainian press for the duration of the dance master's stay in the city. Not unexpectedly, Avramenko's pupils represented all religious and most political persuasions and included the children of every prominent Ukrainian businessman, professional, and politician in the city.

Because his leg had not healed, Avramenko was not in a rush to stage performances in Winnipeg prior to the conclusion of the first dance school in April. He passed the time teaching, collecting information on Ukrainian folk dances, and preparing a new stage spectacle entitled *Dovbusheva Nich* about Oleksa Dovbush, the legendary eighteenth-century western Ukrainian outlaw who robbed wealthy Polish and Hungarian nobles and avenged injustices committed against poor Ukrainian highlanders. Prominent Ukrainian-Canadian community leaders of all persuasions and several non-Ukrainians, including public school teachers and administrators who were contemplating the introduction of folk dancing classes into the school curriculum, also visited Avramenko during this interval.[32] Most significantly, in February 1927, he added a new dance instructor to his entourage. A student activist at the University of Chernivtsi in Bukovyna and the editor of a literary monthly, Ivan Pihuliak had completed Avramenko's dance course in Fort William, where he had been teaching in a private Ukrainian evening school since immigrating to Canada in 1924. For the next seven years, the educated, well-organized, and highly disciplined Pihuliak would be the dance master's most important and efficient collaborator.

Concerns about his injured leg meant that Avramenko's return to the stage would be gradual and tentative. During the last week of February, Avramenko travelled to Port Arthur and performed his solo *Hore Izraielia* at a recital in the Lyceum Theatre that also featured 120 local dancers. The reviews of his first stage performance in more than eleven months were promising.[33] Two months later, on 30 April, Avramenko and 275 of his Winnipeg pupils presented a Pageant of Historical and Festival Dances before 3,000 spectators at Winnipeg's Amphitheatre, a venue usually reserved for hockey games and political conventions. Prior to the main spectacle, Avramenko, perched on a raised platform in front of his pupils, conducted a demonstration of the fundamental techniques and gymnastics employed to teach basic dance moves and steps. For the finale, he performed his solo *Chumak,* a dance celebrating the eighteenth-century salt merchants who had plied their trade in southern Ukraine.[34] A month later, on 3 and 4 June, three weeks after modest graduation recitals at Steiman's Hall and the Shevchenko Prosvita in Brooklands, Avramenko mounted a much more lavish and ambitious production at the Pantages Playhouse Theatre. This time, in addition to festive Easter dances and a suite of six traditional folk dances, the performance included Avramenko's solo *Gonta* and, for the first time in Winnipeg, a presentation of the *tableau vivant* based on Repin's painting *The Zaporozhian Cossacks Write a Letter to the Sultan.* Also on the bill was the 150-voice Ukrainian National Home Association Choir, which performed six traditional songs a cappella.

The performance made a positive impression on the city's critics. The *Manitoba Free Press* arts critic reported thus:

> Flashing colours of native costumes, some of them handed down from mother to daughter for generations, movement well-ordered, a view that was kaleidoscopic, now advancing, now receding, now slow, now quick, but never still, a veritable riot of colour and romance. Then the performers burst into song and while they danced they sang. How they could sing! While words were indistinguishable to ears attuned to the English language, the music was there, a mighty volume of rushing sound, at times like a gentle zephyr stirring the tops of the wavelets, again like a huge torrent tearing its way through rocky passes occasionally barbaric but always in harmony with the dance.
>
> The event as intimated, brought to the Playhouse stage much that was artistic and beautiful in the realm of folk songs and folk dances. By presenting this imposing Ukrainian ballet last night and tonight the Playhouse management certainly provided for its patrons a veritable feast of song, colour, grace and rhythmic gorgeousness. Vasile Avramenko, the director of the ballet, is a past master in the training of students and of the native dances of the Ukraine and he seems peculiarly successful in instilling in his pupils all the sparkle, fire and symbolism of those very wonderful dances.[35]

During the first week of May, immediately after the Amphitheatre performance in Winnipeg, Avramenko, Pihuliak, and Moshuk travelled to Saskatoon and Edmonton, where they delivered lectures, showed slides, and established Schools of Ukrainian National Dance. Within ten days, Avramenko was back in Winnipeg, where he conducted final examinations, prepared the best dancers for the Pantages Playhouse performance, and launched a second set of "advanced" dance classes at Steiman's Hall. This time more than 100 pupils enrolled, though many soon dropped out to prepare for high school examinations. Pihuliak remained in Saskatoon, where he taught 130 pupils at the city's Ukrainian National Home and Prosvita Society halls and another forty pupils at the Petro Mohyla Institute, a student residence affiliated with the Ukrainian Orthodox Church. Meanwhile, Moshuk managed to attract about 100 pupils to dance classes in Edmonton. By the end of June, recitals featuring Avramenko and local choirs had been staged in major venues in both cities. On 1 July 1927, Ukrainian folk dancers under the guidance of Avramenko, Pihuliak, and Moshuk performed in massive celebrations marking the Diamond Jubilee of Canadian Confederation at Winnipeg's Assiniboine Park, Saskatoon's Exhibition Grounds, and Edmonton's Victoria Park.[36] During the next few weeks, Moshuk and Pihuliak also performed in a number of rural Ukrainian colonies with small groups of their best pupils. A performance in Vegreville, Alberta, on 1 July was especially successful, with some Ukrainian farmers travelling eighty miles to see the show. The audience was very enthusiastic, and their only regret was that Avramenko had not been there to perform. While there were few Anglo-Canadians in attendance, those who were present stated that they had never enjoyed themselves so much.[37]

Avramenko had been waiting impatiently to tour with a troupe of dancers, singers, and instrumentalists since coming to Canada eighteen months earlier. After injuring his leg for a third time in Toronto, these plans had been postponed indefinitely. Now, in the summer of 1927, everything finally fell into place. His leg had healed and been tested on the stage. Most Ukrainian Canadians and many Canadians without Ukrainian roots had heard or read about him and his dancers in the press. A number of prairie communities had even expressed interest in seeing Avramenko and his Ukrainian dancers perform in their theatres or community halls. Moreover, the personnel required to form a troupe were now available. Winnipeg, Avramenko discovered, had its share of talented Ukrainian singers, dancers, and instrumentalists. Even more fortuitously for him, Alexander Koshetz's final tour of North America had come to a premature conclusion in Kansas City in December 1926, and the remnants of the Ukrainian National Chorus had dispersed in May 1927 after a four-month engagement in Grauman's Egyptian Theater in Hollywood. As a result, Yuri Hassan and Leon Sorochynsky were taking any work they could find. Hassan had been working with choirs in Edmonton since May, while Sorochynsky had been in Winnipeg preparing musical arrangements of Avramenko's most popular dances for publication. Both men were persuaded to tour with Avramenko. Finally, early in July, Andrii Kist—the last important member of Avramenko's entourage—came to Canada from Czechoslovakia. Close friends since 1917, Kist and Avramenko had served in the army of the Ukrainian National Republic, toured with Yosyf Stadnyk's western Ukrainian theatre, and crossed paths again in 1924 in Poděbrady, where Kist had been studying agricultural economics. Blessed with a good voice, able to play the bandura, a traditional Ukrainian stringed instrument, and gifted with pen and ink and a typewriter, Kist had been admitted into Canada, on the recommendation of J.S. Atkinson and with Hassan's financial assistance, to work for the School of Ukrainian National Dance as a secretary, administrator, singer, and instrumentalist.[38]

Consequently, when the spring and summer dance classes in Winnipeg, Saskatoon, and Edmonton came to an end in late July, Avramenko decided to focus all of his energy on touring for the remainder of the year. A trial tour was undertaken during the first two weeks of August, and then, after reorganizing and fine-tuning his troupe in Winnipeg, a second and much more ambitious tour was launched in late September. Prior to both tours, the prairies were flooded with leaflets, handbills, and posters that attempted to entice prospective spectators with promises of "girls that whirl and spin before their partners as the winds that wave the grasses of the steppes." These would be Avramenko's first and last tours of Canada and the longest and most successful tours of his career.

By 1927, the prairie provinces were covered by an extensive network of Ukrainian-Canadian communities and institutions. The year 1914 had marked a turning point in the cultural life of Ukrainian Canadians, especially those in rural areas. Schools, which could serve as venues for concerts and dramatic performances, had been constructed in most Ukrainian districts, and they employed almost 200 Ukrainian public school teachers, who acted as local cultural animators. The centennial of Taras Shevchenko's birth, which took place in 1914, provided the teachers with an impetus to stage concerts and plays in countless rural communities. Economic prosperity also encouraged greater cultural activity. Already prior to 1914, some Ukrainian homesteaders had made the transition from subsistence to commercial farming and were enjoying a measure of wealth and leisure. During the First World War, bumper crops, European demand for Canadian farm products, and skyrocketing agricultural prices put money into the pockets of Ukrainian farmers.[39] This allowed many to redirect at least some of their energies into cultural and recreational activities, including the performing arts.

Nothing reflected these new interests better than the proliferation of community halls or *narodni domy* (literally "people's" or "national homes") after 1914. Before the war, these wood-frame structures existed in only four rural Ukrainian colonies, in Vegreville and Lanuke, Alberta, and in Ethelbert and Tolstoi, Manitoba. Each had an elevated stage, painted backdrop and curtain, wooden benches, and a small office and library near the entrance. By 1920, their number had grown to at least fifty, and by the 1930s there were no fewer than 110 in Alberta and probably more in each of Saskatchewan and Manitoba. Often affiliated with a Ukrainian Catholic or Ukrainian Orthodox parish, with the ULFTA, or with a nationalist association, the community halls served as centres of recreational, educational, and cultural activity. Dances, wedding receptions, bazaars, picnics, public readings, lectures, English-language classes, and political meetings were held there. But it was the choral and orchestral concerts and especially the plays—melodramas, comedies, and historical pieces—performed by amateur drama circles that attracted the largest crowds and defined the *narodni domy* during the interwar years.[40]

While most North Americans were succumbing to the blandishments of mass culture, Ukrainian Canadians continued to make their own entertainment. Indeed, the 1920s witnessed an "explosion of theatrical activity" that has been described as a "golden age" in the history of Ukrainian theatre in Canada.[41] The sheer volume of theatrical activity in Ukrainian colonies during these years was impressive. In rural towns and hamlets and in major urban centres all across Canada, Ukrainian choral and drama societies staged hundreds of plays and concerts during the war and interwar years. Four major amateur drama societies staged 215 plays and sixty-nine concerts in one Winnipeg venue alone between 1919 and 1924, while Toronto's Shevchenko Reading Society produced fifty-seven plays between 1916 and 1926 and then, after purchasing a building with a 475-seat auditorium and renaming it the Ukrainian People's Home, proceeded to stage up to forty-eight plays, including several operettas annually, some of them reviewed in the pages of the *Toronto Telegram*.

The repertoire of rural and urban drama circles ranged "from farces and sketches to five-act tragedies and operettas, ... some poorly written and badly performed, others quite sophisticated and ambitious in presentation." Well into the 1930s, the same nineteenth-century central Ukrainian classics that had been staged by troupes led by Mykola Sadovsky and his siblings retained their popularity. At the same time, the large audiences drawn to theatrical performances from the 1910s through the 1930s spawned the emergence of a small but active group of Ukrainian-Canadian playwrights, whose original works began to be featured with increasing frequency during the 1920s and 1930s.

Ukrainian amateur theatre appealed to and was largely sustained by the Ukrainian-born segment of the immigrant population. This segment included homesteaders and urban labourers who had arrived prior to 1914 and remained geographically isolated, unfamiliar with the English language, and often illiterate in Ukrainian. It also included new interwar immigrants who had not had time to learn English and were often politically engaged, be it in nationalist or communist circles. For this segment of the Ukrainian-Canadian population, amateur theatricals satisfied nostalgic longings, provided entertainment and diversion, and might even have served as a manifestation of resistance to the pressures of assimilation. As a result, amateur theatricals would thrive until the mid-1930s, when the Depression undermined local confidence, sapped financial resources, and stimulated migration to eastern Canada in search of employment.

For their first tour of the prairie provinces, which lasted from 1 to 13 August, Avramenko and Pihuliak assembled a troupe that included two five-year-old soloists, Halia Tychowecka and Pavlyk Trach; twelve adult dancers; a female vocal quartet, made up of young women who were also part of the dance ensemble; several male singers, including Hassan, Sorochynsky, Kukhta, and Kist; and three instrumentalists: Andrii Kist on bandura, Volodymyr Pylypchak on guitar, and Ivan Pasichniak on mandolin. Two-hour performances were staged in Brandon, Regina (where three shows were mounted in one of the city's better theatres), Melville, Yorkton, Sheho, Canora, Arran, Dauphin, and Oakburn. The local mayor and physician, and several other English-speaking guests, attended the Yorkton performance and expressed their admiration for the troupe. Reports in the Ukrainian press stressed the newfound respect that Ukrainian performing arts and culture were acquiring among non-Ukrainians as a result of Avramenko's work.[42]

The fall tour, which began on 28 September and lasted for seventy days, included fifty-two performances in forty-eight prairie centres (see Table 1), a hectic schedule but not unusual in an age when live entertainment still overshadowed radio and cinema in rural districts.[43] With the exception of Portage la Prairie, Saskatoon, Prince Albert, Edmonton, Calgary, and Moose Jaw, all of these were small railway towns in the middle of remote rural Ukrainian bloc settlements. Because Hassan, Kukhta, and Sorochynsky had left Winnipeg to pursue other opportunities, the second troupe consisted primarily of Winnipeggers, many of whom had already toured in August. They included female dancers Pauline Garbolinsky, Olga Kowbel, Anna Kharysh, and Evdokia Pavliukevych; male dancers Vasile Avramenko, Ivan Pihuliak, Ivan Pasichniak, and Volodymyr Pylypchak; child soloists Halia Tychowecka and Pavlyk Trach; and instrumentalists Ivan Fil on violin, Ihnatii Gronitsky on dulcimer, and Andrii Kist, who used the pseudonym A. Wasilko, on bandura. In one segment of the performance, Pasichniak and Pylypchak also played the mandolin and guitar, while the women, featuring vocal soloist Evdokia Pavliukevych, sang Ukrainian folk songs. In small rural Ukrainian communities, some of the performances created a veritable sensation because the local people had never seen folk dances performed on stage and were unfamiliar with many of the dances presented.[44] Nevertheless, Ukrainian press reports again praised the good public relations and the respect for Ukrainian performing arts and culture that Avramenko was promoting. A Smoky Lake correspondent stressed the "high moral quality" of the dances and Avramenko's oratorical and declamatory abilities, which moved old men to tears.[45] The *Edmonton Journal* reported that "the dancers made a colourful picture and their dancing was a revelation. Grace of movement, poise and skill were evidenced in a high degree. They seemed to live the rhythm of the music, and from the beginning to the end of the dances, never missed a beat. The music for the dancing was supplied by a violin and dulcimer, and was full of life and fire."[46]

TABLE 1. *Avramenko's Fall 1927 Tour of the Prairie Provinces*

September	***November***	***December***
28 – Portage la Prairie MB	1 – Prince Albert SK	1 – Moose Jaw SK
29 – Shoal Lake MB	2 – Krydor SK	2 – Melville SK
30 – Russell MB	3 – Hafford SK	3 – Yorkton SK
	4 – Radisson SK	5 – Canora SK
October	6 – Whitkow SK	
1 – Rossburn MB	7 – Lloydminster SK	
2 – Rossburn MB	8 – Vermilion AB	
4 – Donwell SK	9 – Innisfree AB	
5 – Calder SK	10 – Vegreville AB	
6 – Kamsack SK	11 – Mundare AB	
7 – Roblin MB	12 – Lamont AB	
8 – Sifton MB	13 – Zawale AB	
10 – Ethelbert MB	14 – Bruderheim AB	
11 – Pine River MB	15 – Edmonton AB	
12 – Swan River MB	19 – Redwater AB	
13 – Norquay SK	20 – Egremont AB	
14 – Goodeve SK	21 – Bellis AB	
15 – Ituna SK	22 – Radway Centre AB	
17 – Theodore SK	23 – Smoky Lake AB	
18 – Foam Lake SK	24 – Leduc AB	
20 – Saskatoon SK	26 – Edmonton AB	
24 – Saskatoon SK	29 – Calgary AB	
25 – Vonda SK	30 – Moose Jaw SK	
26 – Meacham SK		
27 – Wakaw SK		
28 – Tarnopol SK		
29 – Cudworth SK		
30 – Cudworth SK		

On 6 December, Avramenko's "Ukrainian Ballet" returned to Winnipeg. After a few days off to rest and assess their finances, Avramenko, Pihuliak, and Kist decided to organize a second round of dance schools in Saskatoon, Yorkton, and Edmonton. It was resolved that Avramenko and Kist would go to Saskatoon and teach there and in Edmonton, while Pihuliak would move to Yorkton and offer dance classes in that town and in nearby Canora. By 20 December, Avramenko and Kist were in Saskatoon, where they found accommodation at the Mohyla Institute. During the week of 10 January 1928, dance classes commenced at the Regent Hall in Saskatoon, with 107 pupils signing up, and in Edmonton, where enrolment fluctuated between eighty-five and ninety-five. Simultaneously, Pihuliak launched dance classes in Yorkton and Canora, having attracted fifty pupils in each town.[47] Unfortunately, enrolment in both schools declined during the next two months. A special course at the Ukrainian Catholic St. Joseph's College in Yorkton had to be cancelled when one of the Christian Brothers who taught in the school forbade male students from having any physical contact with girls during dance classes. In Canora, controversy erupted in February when parents of Ukrainian Orthodox pupils took exception to rehearsals and a recital during Lent.[48]

For Avramenko, the winter of 1928 was an extremely hectic and stressful period. Although Kist now took care of the school's administrative matters and handled all of Avramenko's correspondence, including personal letters to family and friends, Avramenko still had more work than he could handle. For more than two months, he commuted between Edmonton and Saskatoon while occasionally visiting Pihuliak in Yorkton and Canora. He helped to prepare Ukrainian Independence Day (22 January) commemorations in Edmonton and participated in productions of two popular comedies at the Hrushevsky Institute. Since some twenty Ukrainian rural public school teachers were attending his Edmonton classes, Avramenko gave them extra lessons so that they could teach Ukrainian folk dancing when they returned to their schools.[49] For their benefit, as well as for all graduates, Avramenko, Pihuliak, and Kist compiled and then published in March a fifty-page illustrated volume, *Ukrainski natsionalni tanky* (Ukrainian National Dances), describing all of the dances taught by Avramenko. On top of everything, he had to prepare, coordinate, and perform at recitals scheduled for March, and then examine pupils, in all four communities. As a result, by February he was ill, suffering from fatigue, and extremely high strung. Acquaintances reported that he was very nervous, extremely argumentative, and rapidly acquiring a reputation as an eccentric.[50]

Rumours about his personal life were also beginning to take a toll on Avramenko. Since the spring of 1927, his name had been linked romantically with that of eighteen-year-old Pauline Garbolinsky, a Winnipeg native educated in Catholic schools and one of his star dance pupils. Avramenko had given her private lessons, asked her to help teach his youngest pupils, included her in both of the troupes that toured the prairie provinces in 1927, and invited her to accompany him and Kist to Saskatoon in December 1927. In no time, Winnipeg gossipmongers, who had speculated that Avramenko and Pauline cohabited when they were on tour, were writing to Saskatoon for news of Pauline and asking who roomed with whom at the Mohyla Institute. By February 1928, when Pauline accompanied Avramenko to Edmonton to assist him with his children's classes, Winnipeg was abuzz with rumours that she was no longer safely ensconced at the Mohyla Institute but now living in sin with Avramenko in Edmonton. To complicate matters, when his friends got wind of the rumours, they began urging him to stand by Pauline, to act honourably, and to marry her because, whether the two of them had been living together or not, her reputation had been ruined. They also pointed out that, should Avramenko abandon Pauline, he would embitter and alienate her and many like her from the "holy" cause of Ukraine. Although Avramenko insisted that his conduct was beyond reproach, that he would never dishonour Pauline, and that he hoped to marry her, he insisted that for the present he simply wanted to help her rise above the lot of most Ukrainian girls. His answer seemed to satisfy no one, and when Pauline, Avramenko, and Kist returned to Winnipeg in April malicious tongues continued to wag about the couple.[51]

During these hectic winter months, Avramenko and his former manager Volodymyr Kukhta also began to plan a tour of eastern Canada and the United States. They hoped to offer dance classes in Winnipeg in the spring, commission artists to make props and stage decorations, and put together a new troupe of at least twenty-five dancers, singers, and instrumentalists that would be ready to tour. The tour would focus on the northeastern United States, and after it had aroused interest in Ukrainian folk dancing Avramenko proposed to establish dance schools in major American cities, choreograph new dances, publish handbooks on Ukrainian folk dancing, and produce a film celebrating the beauty of the Ukrainian folk dance. Unfortunately, when he returned to Winnipeg in the spring, things did not go according to plan. Although he scheduled the commencement of beginners', advanced, and special performers' classes for 2 April in Minuk's Hall on Dufferin Avenue, the response was less than enthusiastic. By the end of April, the special performers' classes had been cancelled, and the beginners', advanced, and instructors' classes were moved to the much smaller Ukrainian Reading Association Prosvita hall at the corner of Flora and McKenzie.

By the time the classes got under way, Avramenko was considering a new option. In mid-April, a Ukrainian women's committee in Chicago had invited him to perform at the Chicago Woman's World's Fair.[52] The committee indicated that it was already advertising his dancers as "one of the most famous old-world dancing troupes on this continent."[53] This was an offer that Avramenko could not refuse. He had been itching to move to the United States and appear on New York's legendary Broadway. Because he was not a Canadian citizen, American immigration officials asked for guarantees that Avramenko would be readmitted into Canada and demanded that a $500 bond be posted.[54] Within a month, all of the formalities had been ironed out, and on 23 May 1928 Avramenko and Kukhta left Winnipeg and entered the United States on a six-month artist's visa.[55] Although he was unable to take any of his dance pupils with him to Chicago, Avramenko still hoped that Kist and Pihuliak, who remained in Canada, could assemble a troupe and finance an American tour. On 26 May, the day after Avramenko's solo performance at the Woman's World's Fair, Pauline Garbolinsky left her parents' home and joined the man of her dreams in Chicago. Three weeks later, on 16 June 1928, Vasile Avramenko and Pauline Garbolinsky were married in a Ukrainian Orthodox ceremony in Chicago. Their only daughter, Oksana, would be born in March 1929 in New York City.[56]

Several weeks after the performance in Chicago, Avramenko, Pauline, and Kukhta moved to Hamtramck, a suburb of Detroit with a large Ukrainian colony, including many Ukrainian Canadians drawn to the city's booming economy. During the next two months, they tried but failed to put together a troupe of Canadian dancers for a tour of the United States.[57] By the fall, Avramenko was offering Ukrainian folk dancing classes to 130 pupils in Detroit and an equal number in Cleveland, all the while commuting from one city to the other.[58] When the classes came to an end, he obtained permission to remain in the United States for another six months, and in December 1928 he and Pauline decided to try their luck in New York City.

In the meantime, Avramenko's School of Ukrainian National Dance continued to operate in Canada. While the school's administrator, Andrii Kist, remained in Winnipeg, where Ivan Pasichniak was offering dance classes, Ivan Pihuliak spent the spring and summer of 1928 teaching in Vegreville, Innisfree, and Shandro, Alberta. Simultaneously, Victor Moshuk was teaching in Toronto, Stefan Yemchuk in Fort William, and Sam Hancharyk in Kenora. In addition, at least a dozen prairie public school teachers, who had taken classes in Saskatoon and Edmonton during the previous two years, were giving instruction in Ukrainian folk dance in rural Saskatchewan and Alberta. Still others probably taught without Avramenko's authorization. In September, Pihuliak and Kist moved to Windsor, where at least fifty pupils attended dance classes until December.[59] When Kist joined Avramenko and Pauline in New York City in December 1928—replacing Kukhta, who had decided to return to Canada—Pihuliak proceeded to Montreal.

By 1929, Montreal was the only major Canadian urban centre with a large Ukrainian population not to have been visited by Avramenko or one of his authorized instructors. From January through March, Pihuliak taught more than 100 pupils in two venues, one Ukrainian Catholic, the other Ukrainian Orthodox.[60] The recital that he staged at the Princess Theatre on 14 April 1929 constituted one of the high points of Ukrainian folk dancing in Canada. Not only did he have to contend with opposition from the local ULFTA, also offering dance classes in Montreal, but Pihuliak also had to scramble when the Princess Theatre booked the Isadora Duncan Dancers (featuring the late Isadora's adopted daughter, Irma Duncan) for a one-week engagement immediately following his recital. The arrival of such a celebrated company, which had been based in Moscow for the past few years, earned rave reviews in New York City, and enjoyed the active support of many ethnic and leftist organizations in Montreal, threatened to stifle ticket sales for Pihuliak's recital. At the least, it would confuse the non-Ukrainian public on whose attendance Pihuliak counted.[61] In the end, a concerted publicity campaign saved the day. Pihuliak almost filled the house, a majority of the spectators were non-Ukrainians, he broke even financially, and the reviews were very good.

The Montreal *Gazette* was especially sympathetic:

> A programme of rare sincerity and charm was presented by the Ukrainian Ballet ... at the Princess Theatre last night. Dressed in brilliant national costume, the dancers, who have been recruited from the local schools, performed the dances of their old homeland as though they were celebrating their time-honoured festivals on their Ukrainian village greens. The complete absence of artiness or staginess made the programme a most refreshing change from the usual type of terpsichorean entertainment, which is provided by the theatre. The spontaneity of the dancers quickly infected the audience and the patter of applause was almost as continuous as the beat of the drum that marked the Slavic rhythm of the dances. New Canadians, like last night's dancers, who are keeping alive in their new home the beauty of the land from which they came, are making a very real contribution to

> the life of the country and thoroughly deserve the warm reception that was accorded them. While the members of the ballet range in age from four-year-olds to adults, their work was throughout distinguished by a whole-hearted abandon, a remarkably sure sense of rhythm, and that concentrated seriousness which is characteristic of folk dancing the world over. The actual steps of their numbers were those typical of all Russian [sic] dances—spirited, quick in tempo, and often exceedingly difficult physical feats. The skill with which they were performed, by even the youngest members of the troupe, was of a very high order. The programme modestly refrained from mentioning the soloists' names, stating merely: "By four-year-old girl" or by "two couples of children" so that it is impossible to single out individual performers for praise. In any case, all were equally deserving of honour.[62]

Pihuliak did not have time to celebrate his achievement. Avramenko was preparing for his New York début and desperately needed Pihuliak's assistance and moral support. When Pihuliak crossed the border and entered the United States on 29 April 1929, the first sojourn of Avramenko and his School of Ukrainian National Dance in Canada came to an end.

It seems that his first Canadian visit had been an unqualified success. In three years, Avramenko and his instructors had established Schools of Ukrainian National Dance in five provinces and the three largest cities, and they had offered instruction to more than 2,000 pupils, toured the prairies, and demonstrated that Ukrainian folk dancing could become not only a popular recreational activity but also a serious performing art. At the same time, they had generated a great deal of press coverage and publicity for Ukrainian folk arts and Ukrainian Canadians in general, all of it favourable, much of it flattering, and some of it extremely laudatory. In fact, in terms of sheer quantity and consistency, Avramenko had generated much more positive publicity for the Ukrainian-Canadian community than had Alexander Koshetz and the Ukrainian National Chorus. While Koshetz and his chorus had received nothing but rave reviews, they had performed in Canada on but two occasions, in 1923 and 1926, and then only in Toronto and Winnipeg. Avramenko had managed to generate good reviews in five provinces for almost three years.

By the time he made New York City his new home, Avramenko had become something of a phenomenon in the Ukrainian-Canadian community. He was an object of longing for teenaged girls, the idol of community leaders, and an example of how the folk arts could be used to preserve Ukrainian identity and mobilize and promote the community. Seventeen-year-old Olena Serdechna, clearly smitten with the dashing dance master, wrote to Avramenko that she thought every day about him and dreamt every night about attending his classes and dancing with him. Her heart had stopped beating when she heard that he was ill, and she prayed for his success every day. His classes had opened up a whole new world for her, and though they would probably never meet again she implored Avramenko to take greater care of himself.[63] Petro Bilon, a Ukrainian Orthodox priest, compared Avramenko to Koshetz and insisted that among Ukrainians both were unique geniuses.[64] Ivan Bodrug, a Protestant pastor, believed that God, in his infinite wisdom, had sent Avramenko to Canada to save "the Ukrainian spirit from drowning prematurely in the great English sea." Avramenko had been sent by providence "to renew the spirit of Ukraine among Ukrainian immigrants in North America." He was the harbinger of an independent Ukraine who would be followed by a new generation of leaders and the emergence of a Ukrainian nation ruled by God.[65] Nykyfor Hryhoriiv, an émigré Ukrainian Socialist Revolutionary publicist based in Prague, who travelled across Canada during these years, maintained that there was not one rural Ukrainian home that did not display a memento of Avramenko and his dancers.[66] While reports of this kind might have exaggerated his impact, they were a testament to the success of the advertising and public relations campaigns that had transformed Avramenko into a Ukrainian-Canadian cultural icon by the late 1920s.

To understand the emergence of the Avramenko phenomenon in Canada during these years, it is necessary to realize that he arrived at a crucial juncture in the history of both the Ukrainian-Canadian community and North American popular culture. As a result, his career received the kind of impetus that might not have been available under different circumstances.

When Avramenko arrived, almost 60 percent of Ukrainian Canadians had been born in Canada, and 30 percent lived in urban centres. Apart from ULFTA-sponsored mandolin orchestras and youth groups, there were few Ukrainian clubs or organizations for Canadian-born teenagers because community leaders had been preoccupied with disputes about religion and old-country politics. Urban youth, in particular, were losing fluency in the Ukrainian language, and young people, fed up with their elders bickering about religion and events back in the homeland, were becoming alienated from the immigrant community and attracted to the pervasive new mass culture that swept across the United States and English-speaking Canada after the Great War.

The new mass culture that conquered and transformed the United States and Canada during the "Roaring Twenties" was a product of unprecedented postwar prosperity. By 1924, the recession had come to an end, and new consumer goods industries and the mass production of automobiles fuelled economic growth. Per capita income rose, prices fell, young women entered the labour force, the work week was reduced to forty-eight hours, and unemployment fell to an all-time low. For the first time, middle- and working-class North Americans had the disposable income and the time to indulge in consumption and the pursuit of leisure activities. Rather than make their own entertainment at home or in local organizations, Americans and Canadians increasingly purchased mass-produced entertainment in the form of records, radios, or inexpensive movie theatre tickets. Songs and dances popularized by the recording industry, radio broadcasts of music and sporting events, and above all motion pictures, accessible to even the newest immigrants, provided common shared experiences that cut across social and ethnic boundaries, diminished cultural differences, and helped to Americanize and Canadianize immigrants and especially their children.[67]

By the late 1920s, most middle-class and many working-class and farm families owned a gramophone and records. The 300,000 radios in Canada were usually tuned to one of the 612 American radio stations, many of which had powerful transmitters and could offer a much broader variety of popular programming than the seventy-five Canadian stations.[68] Only hockey games, first broadcast in February 1923, were able to draw Canadian listeners away from American stations, which featured musical stars such as Rudy Vallee, the Paul Whiteman Orchestra, and Bing Crosby, not to mention talk shows, boxing matches, baseball games, and the first sitcoms. Most influential of all, though, were motion pictures.

Filmmaking was a $2 billion industry in the 1920s that produced hundreds of feature-length films annually and promoted a galaxy of star actors to guarantee that fans would pay to see any film starring their idol. Palatial theatres were erected in every city and town, where they became centres of community life, frequented at least once a week by most young people. Weekly attendance, which totalled 46 million in the United States in 1925, doubled by 1930 after Warner Brothers introduced sound (*Don Juan*) and talking (*The Jazz Singer*) pictures in 1926–27.[69] In Canada, where the feature film industry, driven by Ernest Shipman's efforts to produce Canadian stories filmed on location, had some success between 1914 and 1922, more than 1,100 theatres sold 2 million tickets every week in 1929, but almost all of the pictures screened had been produced in the United States.[70]

The music most prominently disseminated by all these new powerful media was jazz. During the 1920s, the best-selling records, the most popular radio programs, and the first talking motion picture all featured jazz. With jazz came a new kind of dancing. The most popular jazz dances were watered-down versions of black social dances and included the Cakewalk, the Turkey Trot, the Shimmy, and the Black Bottom. All of these dances eliminated the rigid formality of ballroom dancing and involved sensuous and rhythmic movements. The Cakewalk introduced exaggerated strutting steps; the Turkey Trot involved "birdlike movements with the shoulders and upper body";[71] in the Shimmy, the body "was held straight and shaken rhythmically and rapidly from the shoulders down"; and the Black Bottom consisted of sticking out, shaking, and slapping one's backside. However, the greatest jazz dance craze was the Charleston, which could be danced solo, with a partner, or in a group by "kicking the feet out sideways and keeping the knees together" while in a semi-squat position. Although it had been noticed in dance halls by 1913, the Charleston soared in popularity in 1923, and it was in its heyday between 1924 and 1926, conquering North America and Europe, including Paris, where Josephine Baker launched her career with a wild rendition of the Charleston in *La Revue Nègre*. Because dancing was the most popular social diversion and recreation during the 1920s, the Cakewalk, Turkey Trot, Shimmy, Black Bottom, and Charleston became especially popular among North American youth, including urban Ukrainian-Canadian high school and university students, drawn precisely to the dances criticized by parents, teachers, and other authority figures.

Indeed, a sense of moral panic engulfed the more conservative segments of the North American middle class during the 1920s. Prosperity and good times, they believed, were undermining and destroying moral standards. Consumerism, promoted in press and radio advertisements and on the silver screen, encouraged youth to abandon thrift and seek fulfillment in clothes, cigarettes, cosmetics, and hedonistic pleasures. Evidence of declining moral standards seemed to be visible everywhere. Supervised courting was being subverted by young couples who made automobiles into "getaway" vehicles and "brothels on wheels."[72] Young female "flappers" flaunted their freedom by dancing with reckless abandon, smoking, wearing loose and skimpy dresses that revealed their knees, and caking as much makeup on their faces as only prostitutes would have done a generation earlier.[73] Jazz, associated with red light districts, gambling, booze, marijuana, and nightclubs owned by gangsters, struck middle-class moralists as particularly scandalous and dangerous. Jazz music was unwholesome because it expressed "hysteria, incited idleness, revelry, dissipation, destruction, discord and chaos." Jazz dances were dangerous because they encouraged "youths of both sexes [to] mingle in close embrace—with limbs intertwined and torso in contact," the *Ladies Home Journal* lamented.[74] Municipal officials, school administrators, and women's clubs expressed their offended respectability by banning dances such as the Shimmy, described as an "insult to our whole moral code." Auto manufacturer and multi-millionaire Henry Ford, who saw jazz dancing as a particularly insidious example of the growing influence of African Americans, Jews, and recent immigrants, started a crusade to introduce demure and chaste American folk and square dances into the public schools and the workplace.

By the mid-1920s, jazz—with its rhythmic and throbbing music and spontaneous and sensuous dances—had managed to penetrate the handful of small and rather exclusive student organizations that catered to Ukrainian-Canadian youth.[75] Ukrainian-Canadian community leaders, beginning to realize that something had to be done for the Canadian-born, also experienced the moral panic that had been provoked by the Jazz Age among guardians of middle-class morality all across North America.

On 30 April 1927, Julian Stechishin, rector of the Mohyla Institute, attended a student dance in Edmonton. After the dance, Stechishin wrote in his journal that the students at the Edmonton branch of the institute were a "lost cause":

> Jazz and jazz and nothing else. I tried to initiate a Ukrainian dance, but it was absolutely impossible. They move about the floor just as if they were all insane. I admonished one of them to dance in a more decent fashion, but he just stared me down.... When he started making excuses, I told him I would return his fifty-cent admission and throw him out. Later I had to admonish another one. That put an end to the trouble on this occasion, but they could not be persuaded to entertain themselves after our fashion or even try one of our dances.[76]

As fate would have it, a week later, on 8 May, Avramenko, about to launch his first dance school in Saskatoon, gave a public lecture. It was the same homily that he delivered in every community he visited. Dance, Avramenko insisted, had the power to raise national consciousness; it could vanquish hopelessness and despair and harden national resolve. It had the power to galvanize the Ukrainian people, currently oppressed and divided among four foreign states, and to awaken their determination to fight. In fact, Ukrainian folk dancing and the struggle for liberation went hand in hand. This was the reason, Avramenko suggested, why the Poles and Czechs had been so frightened when he performed *Gonta* and *Zaporozhets:* "When we put on our national costume and dance the *Kolomyika* our enemies ... begin to worry." Moreover, Ukrainian folk dancing and the Ukrainian national costume were the greatest barriers to the alienation and assimilation of youth: "If your little boy, who is growing up in a foreign land, learns to dance the *Zaporizkyi kozak,* he will know for the rest of his life that he is a Ukrainian." Avramenko concluded by vowing to use Ukrainian folk dancing and folk arts to awaken the elemental love for Ukraine dormant deep within the hearts of Ukrainian youth in North America.[77]

His speech offered a quick fix, an activity around which young people could be rallied and mobilized. Stechishin was fascinated by the lecture and concluded that here was at least part of the answer to the problem posed by Ukrainian-Canadian youth. Avramenko's thoughts on dance and its relation to national consciousness, and his unambiguous rejection of "all kinds of modern dances and ... jazz music," were especially welcome. After the lecture, Stechishin endorsed Avramenko's plans and appealed to those in attendance to enrol in Avramenko's school. For the rest of his life, Stechishin would be one of Avramenko's staunchest supporters.

Nor was concern about the dangers posed by jazz and the Shimmy confined to middle-class Ukrainian-Canadian community activists. In January 1928, Avramenko received several letters from the aging Ukrainian émigré philanthropist and publisher Yevhen Chykalenko, whom he had last seen in Poděbrady, near Prague. Chykalenko cautioned Avramenko to avoid arguments with pro-Soviet Ukrainians in Canada and then explained why he wanted him to remain on good terms with supporters of a regime that had driven both of them into exile: "It is absolutely imperative that you return to Ukraine, conquer all of our youth between the Zbruch and the Kuban rivers with your dances, and thereby reclaim them from all kinds of 'Shimmies' for our own native (*ridni*) dances." If Avramenko quarrelled with pro-Soviet Ukrainian Canadians, then he would not see Ukraine as long as the Bolsheviks remained in power, and as a result traditional Ukrainian folk dancing would be swept aside by modern social dances.[78]

If we want to grasp Avramenko's popularity among Ukrainian Canadians, then it is also important to remember that some of the most ringing endorsements of Avramenko dance school recitals published in the English-language press praised Ukrainian folk dances precisely because they were so unlike the modern popular dances—especially the Charleston and the Shimmy—that scandalized conservative middle-class Canadians. Reviews of Avramenko dance school performances featured headlines such as "High Steppers from the Steppes ... Outdo the Charleston"[79] and, like the one in the *Toronto Evening Telegram* cited at the beginning of this chapter, suggested that Ukrainian dancing was pure, virtuous, decorous, and worthy of absorption into the fabric of Canadian life: "None of your 'cake-walk' or 'Charleston' or 'Valencia,' none of your passionate 'fox trots' and 'tangos' but a dance that will say: 'We are in sorrow' or 'we are gay and jolly,' or 'we shall fight our way to freedom.' etc."[80]

Ukrainian-Canadian community leaders such as Julian Stechishin, who yearned for positive recognition, welcomed such reviews and cheered Avramenko. After the 25 June 1927 performance at the Pantages Theatre in Edmonton, Stechishin was absolutely delighted. His journal contains the following observations:

> I was extremely satisfied because I sensed that the public, which included many English people, enjoyed the performance. Perhaps this will improve their perception of us at least partly. After the performance, Avramenko spoke to his pupils. He spoke with great passion and delivered a very patriotic speech. He stated that our people must do everything to gain glory for our nation. He introduces our culture to foreigners, thereby acquainting them with us through the medium of the dance, which is a unique Ukrainian art form. He concluded his speech by appealing to his pupils not to forget their dances and to reject foreign jazz and unaesthetic contortions.[81]

A week later, in the aftermath of the Dominion Day performance at Victoria Park, Stechishin could barely contain himself: "Our dances during the finale were so good that the English shouted 'Good for Ukrainians. Last and best!' ... We represented ourselves in a manner that made us proud. We sensed that we had performed so well that the English, had they not been embarrassed [by their own inadequacies], would have praised our numbers much more than their own. That day, in the evening, everyone was happy."[82]

By the late 1920s, Avramenko had emerged as a genuine icon for many Ukrainian Canadians because, for a brief moment, he had managed to make many of them feel proud of their heritage. Nevertheless, there were already signs that the dance master's success and future prospects rested on shaky foundations. Forthright friends and colleagues observed that Avramenko spent little if any time perfecting his craft and, by 1928, was no longer preparing any new material for the dance ensembles that he hoped to lead on triumphant tours. Concerned that this approach would prove to be self-defeating, they urged Avramenko to pay more attention to his craft. Ivan Bobersky remarked that Avramenko's *Gonta* solo, for all its bravura and complexity, was an incomplete work that desperately needed a much more subtle and nuanced musical arrangement.[83] Shortly before they left for the United States in 1928, Kukhta warned Avramenko that his repertoire was primitive and contained little more than the kernel of a ballet.[84] Bobersky also observed that Avramenko's dance schools focused on producing good Ukrainians rather than skilled dancers, and as a result many of his pupils were ponderous and inflexible when they appeared on stage. Such ensembles might promote Ukrainian identity among the Canadian-born, and their performances might stir nostalgia in Ukrainian audiences, but they were of little interest to non-Ukrainians who valued dance for its aesthetic qualities. He also suggested that, if Avramenko really wanted to captivate more sophisticated audiences with the beauty of Ukrainian dance, he would have to put together an ensemble composed of accomplished dancers with beautiful faces, attractive figures, supple bodies, and refined movements and provide them with sophisticated choreography and musical arrangements.[85] Both men also urged Avramenko to choreograph at least a few dances with North American content that might resonate with non-Ukrainian audiences and make them more open and receptive to Ukrainian dance.[86] Avramenko listened but never acted on any of these suggestions.

Of greater immediate concern was the woeful state of his financial affairs. Convinced that he was working for the glory of the Ukrainian people and their cause, Avramenko saw no reason to pinch pennies. Denying himself all but the most vital necessities of life, he spent very liberally to promote his school, rent attractive venues, and advertise performances. Rehearsal halls, accommodations, instructors' salaries, costume storage fees, and incessant travel from one school to another drained much of his income. There were also expenditures on publicity photos, newspaper advertisements, stationery, certificates, diplomas, posters, window cards, handbills, leaflets, librettos, sheet music, and the illustrated handbook published in March 1928. The last two items cost almost $1,000 to produce and publish but failed to yield any income. And, instead of putting on one quality performance at high admission prices in a good theatre, Avramenko always put on second and third performances and appeared in every Ukrainian community and parish hall available. As a result, much of the income from his dance schools was lost because more performances were scheduled than the public was willing or able to attend.

By the spring of 1927, largely as a result of his lack of business acumen and inability to take advice even from the best of friends, Avramenko had debts totalling more than $1,000.[87] The two tours of the prairie provinces only added to his financial woes. Because he ignored warnings about the great distances; the costs of halls, theatres, performers' salaries, transportation, food, and accommodation; and the likelihood that harvest and post-harvest farm work and inclement weather would hurt attendance, the tour yielded a $700 deficit, and by January 1928 Avramenko had debts totalling more than $2,000.[88] When he left Canada in May 1928, his personal debts were in excess of $3,000, a heavy burden at the time.[89]

New York City's Lower East Side

New York City, with a population of almost 7 million, was the world's largest urban centre, busiest port, and most important financial and commercial hub when Vasile Avramenko, Pauline Garbolinsky, and Andrii Kist arrived in December 1928. Reflecting the city's new global pre-eminence were the countless skyscrapers clustered on Manhattan Island. The most frenzied burst of construction had started during the 1920s and would culminate between 1928 and 1932 when the Bank of Manhattan, Chrysler, Empire State, and RCA Victor Buildings were erected. With its museums and galleries, and its publishing, recording, and radio broadcasting industries, New York was also the cultural capital of the United States and the media capital of the world. The city's "Great White Way," the largest concentration of theatres in the world, extending along Broadway from 42nd to 50th Streets, exerted a special attraction for performers who wanted to prove themselves. Avramenko yearned for success on Broadway because he believed that it would bring the Ukrainian cause to the attention of the American public and the world at large.

In 1929, New York was home to more actors, playwrights, lyricists, musicians, and dancers than any other North American city. Its theatre district boasted sixty-six theatres and produced more plays during the 1920s than at any other time, peaking at 264 in 1928. While the work of playwrights such as Eugene O'Neill and Maxwell Anderson earned critical laurels, most Broadway plays, especially comedies such as *Gentlemen Prefer Blondes* (1926) or the Marx Brothers vehicle *Animal Crackers* (1928), catered to popular tastes. Musicals remained the most popular fare on Broadway, with up to fifty new offerings each season. A new generation of talented composers and lyricists, including Jerome Kern, George and Ira Gershwin, and Cole Porter, were creating more sophisticated musicals. A turning point was Kern's and Oscar Hammerstein's *Show Boat* (1927), which pioneered the introduction of adult themes such as racism in musicals.[90]

Modern dance was represented in New York by the Denishawn School of Dance and touring company, which had been popularizing the art form in the United States since 1915. Its founders, Ruth St. Denis and Ted Shawn, based their choreography on the dance styles of Egypt, India, and Japan, as well as on Native American, folk, and popular culture. Their dances highlighted the physical beauty of dancers and relied on exoticism, romanticism, and sentimentality for mass appeal. In the mid-1920s, three Denishawn alumni rejected their mentors' penchant for sentimentality and spectacle and launched the first avant-garde movement in American modern dance. Martha Graham, who opened her school of contemporary dance in midtown Manhattan in 1927, and Doris Humphrey and Charles Weidman, whose school and company were launched in 1928, believed that dance could be more than light entertainment. They thought that it could reflect a wide spectrum of human emotions and address contemporary social issues. Abandoning ballet and modern dance conventions, they introduced violent and repetitive movements, falls, and foot stompings to express themes ignored by their predecessors. Just before the Depression, Graham premiered several protest works, including *Immigrant* (1928) and *Heretic* (1929), which reflected on intolerance and scapegoating in American society, and a solo *Lamentation* (1930) that portrayed a grieving woman. Humphrey and Weidman, whose tours during the 1930s would establish an audience for modern dance, unveiled *The Shakers* (1931), a dance that used drums, accordions, and incoherent utterances to portray ecstatic religious fervour.[91]

The world's finest jazz musicians and dance bands performed at the Roseland Ballroom on 52nd Street and farther uptown in Harlem's booming nightclubs. The most alluring of them was the Cotton Club, where every important jazz singer, dancer, and musician performed. From December 1927, the Duke Ellington Orchestra was the house band. In 1929, the world's foremost jazz musician, trumpeter Louis Armstrong, appeared at the club for the first time. When Ellington and his orchestra left the club in 1931, they were succeeded by Cab Calloway. The Savoy Ballroom, just a few steps away, was Harlem's biggest, most attractive, and most popular dance hall, where many new jazz dance crazes originated.[92]

During their first year in New York, Vasile and Pauline Avramenko lived far from its entertainment centre, in rented rooms at 6903 8th Avenue in Brooklyn. From the outset, however, Avramenko spent most of his time at his dance school headquarters located in "Little Ukraine" on Manhattan Island, a district inhabited by Ukrainians since the 1870s. It was there, between Houston and 14th Streets and 3rd and A Avenues, that the Ukrainian Catholic and Ukrainian Orthodox parishes, the Ukrainian National Home, the Ukrainian Labour Home, the Surma Music and Book Store, and a variety of other Ukrainian businesses, fraternal associations, and community organizations were located. Two of New York's most famous neighbourhoods, Greenwich Village to the west and the Lower East Side to the southeast, flanked the small Ukrainian enclave.

Writers, political radicals, and avant-garde artists had found a haven in Greenwich Village, just west of Little Ukraine, where Avramenko established his dance headquarters, since the birth of the American republic. Virtually every famous American writer, from James Fenimore Cooper to Eugene

O'Neill, lived there at one time or another. During the First World War, Max Eastman and John Reed published *The Masses,* a radical cultural journal, in the Village; anarchists gathered at the offices of Emma Goldman's *Mother Earth;* and, for a few months in the winter of 1917, Leon Trotsky worked for the Russian socialist newspaper *Novyi mir* (New World) at 77 St. Mark's Place in the East Village.[93] Greenwich Village was also the place where indigenous American art movements such as the Ashcan school of urban realism were nurtured. The famous 1913 Armory show, held a few blocks north of the Village, promoted modernism in the United States by exhibiting the work of Picasso, Cézanne, Matisse, Gauguin, Seurat, and Duchamp. After the war, Edward Hopper, whose paintings of seedy rooms and diners, desolate urban landscapes, and disconnected human beings exerted a major influence on American popular culture, particularly film, lived and worked in the Village.[94]

The Lower East Side, south of Little Ukraine, was home to immigrants from southern and eastern Europe, including more than half a million Jews. By 1900, it had become the most densely populated urban quarter in the world. During the next three decades, the Lower East Side gained notoriety for producing popular entertainers and gangsters in equal measure. A remarkable number of composers, singers, dancers, and comedians—many of them Jewish—came out of the Lower East Side. They included George and Ira Gershwin, Irving Berlin, Fanny Brice, Eddie Cantor, Artie Shaw, George Burns, Jimmy Durante, and James Cagney.[95] For those lacking talent and moral scruples, organized crime offered an alternative career path. Because of immigrant poverty, the Lower East Side became a breeding ground for gunmen and racketeers. Meyer Lansky, Lucky Luciano, Bugsy Siegel, Vito Genovese, Louis "Lepke" Buchalter, and Giuseppe "The Boss" Masseria started their criminal careers on the Lower East Side. At the time of Avramenko's arrival, a struggle between the old mafia bosses represented by Masseria and a new generation of mobsters represented by Luciano and Siegel had just erupted.[96]

Avramenko's first five years in New York were a period of incessant and frenzied activity. Avramenko established as many dance schools as possible, staged small, local performances whenever there was an opportunity, and prepared for his assault on Broadway.[97] During these years, he also dreamed of establishing a Ukrainian performing artists' colony in rural New York State and a dance school on Broadway complete with a choir, an orchestra, and a theatre specializing in the traditional Ukrainian folk and historical repertoire. There he hoped to choreograph folk ballets and produce popular operettas. In some of his private letters, he revealed that he wanted to attract a broader cross-section of the public to his spectacles. Ultimately, he dreamed of leading a troupe that could perform and hold its own in the best American theatres.[98]

In January 1929, Avramenko began to promote his dance schools by lecturing on "The Rebirth of Ukrainian Dance" in every Ukrainian hall in New York City and in those on the west side of the Hudson River in New Jersey. On 1 February 1929, he opened his first school in the Stuyvesant Casino at 140 2nd Avenue, a venue notorious as a focal point of criminal activity prior to the First World War.[99] During the next three months, having engaged Peter Smook and Ivan Zablotsky as instructors, he organized ten more dance classes (attended by a total of 515 pupils, including eighty-one orphans) in lower Manhattan, Brooklyn, Staten Island, and Yonkers, New York; in Perth Amboy, Carteret, Elizabeth, Passaic, and Newark, New Jersey; and in Philadelphia, Pennsylvania. After Ivan Pihuliak joined Avramenko in the spring, he and Kist were dispatched to organize schools among Ukrainian immigrants in the small mining towns of Pennsylvania. Then, during the next five years, Avramenko, Pihuliak, and a handful of instructors, including several natives of rural Manitoba, who had attended Avramenko's classes in Detroit, organized and taught dance courses in over sixty Ukrainian communities in the states of New York, New Jersey, Pennsylvania, Connecticut, Rhode Island, Massachusetts, New Hampshire, Maryland, West Virginia, Ohio, Michigan, Illinois, Wisconsin, Missouri, Minnesota, and North Dakota.[100]

From time to time during the early 1930s, Pihuliak and his pupils also offered dance classes in southern Ontario and Quebec. In western Canada, the most active promoters of Ukrainian folk dancing during the 1930s were Hryhorii Tyzhuk, who had studied with Avramenko in Mezhyriche, Volhynia, in 1923, and Paul Yavorsky. Both men were employed as national organizers by SUMK, the youth association affiliated with the Ukrainian Orthodox Church, and they would do much to sustain interest in Ukrainian folk dancing in western Canada.[101]

It was easier for Avramenko and his instructors to offer dance courses after 1930 because they were no longer dependent on live musicians. A thriving ethnic recording industry had emerged in the United States during the 1920s, and Avramenko had twelve of the dance tunes on his repertoire recorded by violinist Paul Humeniuk, the leader of a small folk orchestra and the most popular Ukrainian recording artist in North America. An album of six 78 rpm recordings was released in short order by Columbia Records and sold for five dollars.[102] Dance instructors were no longer required to find accompanists for lessons and rehearsals, while pupils and recent graduates could practise dance steps at home. By 1940, Avramenko could claim that his School of Ukrainian Folk Ballet had introduced 10,000 pupils in North America to Ukrainian folk dancing.

Money, however, continued to elude Avramenko in the United States as it had in Canada. Offering courses in a number of widely dispersed communities at the same time meant hiring several dance instructors and paying them monthly salaries. Peter Smook, a native of Senkiw, Manitoba, earned from $100 to $125 a month for teaching in the New York–New Jersey region; John Ewanchuk, a native of Gimli, Manitoba, who taught and managed Avramenko's dance school in Detroit in 1929, might have earned slightly more.[103] By 1931, Avramenko had at least five instructors on his payroll at any one time. Moreover, because he frequently operated schools in Pennsylvania, New Jersey, upper New York State, Detroit, and Chicago at the same time, he spent a great deal of money commuting from one city to another, supervising his instructors, examining pupils, and preparing performances. Hall rentals, substantially higher than in Canada, were another major expense. In January 1930, when he moved his dance school headquarters into the Ukrainian National Home at 217–219 East 6th Avenue, Avramenko had to pay a $300 caution fee and was saddled with rent of $300 per month for the use of the concert hall, a rehearsal studio on the second floor, and a tiny office.[104] Problems with United States Immigration also cost Avramenko dearly. Because he was a man without a country, without property, and without a profession, he had been admitted into the United States on a six-month artist's visa after posting a $500 bond. For several years, until he finally qualified for permanent resident status, Avramenko was obliged to return to Canada every six months, apply for readmission into the United States, and find a sponsor to post the $500 bond. If he failed to leave the United States in time, he would forfeit the bond. Apparently, this happened to Avramenko and Kist on at least one occasion, when they forfeited their bonds and had to borrow money, hire lawyers, and find new sponsors. The whole misadventure cost Avramenko almost $2,000.[105] Finally, his commitment to the Ukrainian struggle for independence also depleted his financial resources. On 7 July 1929, his dance pupils were featured performers at a "military picnic" sponsored by supporters of the émigré underground Ukrainian Military Organization (UVO) in Clinton Park on Long Island. Those in attendance included Colonel Yevhen Konovalets, leader of the UVO and of the Organization of Ukrainian Nationalists (OUN), travelling across North America incognito and speaking about the armed liberation struggle in occupied Ukrainian territories. At the conclusion of his number, Avramenko issued an appeal for more donations to the UVO, and he continued to raise money for the organization at select performances during the next few years.

He also hosted UVO emissaries and assured its leaders that he would do all in his power to support their "Holy and Heroic work."[106]

Incessant travel, the need to coordinate the work of numerous dance schools and instructors, and the preparation of an endless round of performances—at least thirty-five between the fall of 1929 and the spring of 1930—meant that Avramenko taught less, had little contact with dance pupils, and had no time to choreograph new dances or the Ukrainian folk ballet that he had hoped to create. It also meant that he became more irritable, anxious, and generally difficult. He quarrelled with associates, fell into the habit of delivering lengthy speeches, and often gave the impression that he was on the verge of a nervous breakdown. When, in 1930, the Ukrainians of Cohoes, New York, allowed one of his instructors to use their community hall free of charge, Avramenko visited the town, described the hall as a "garage," called the Ukrainians of Cohoes a bunch of drunks and cardsharps, and referred to some of the local leaders as ignorant rubes. Not only did this particular dance school fold prematurely, but also the Ukrainian society that had sponsored it unanimously resolved to assign twenty-five dollars from its treasury for a psychiatric examination of Avramenko.[107]

Even Andrii Kist, his closest and most loyal friend, began to express serious concern about Avramenko's behaviour. Kist conceded that Avramenko was sincere and utterly committed but suggested that "it would be better for the cause if sometimes he forgot that he was AVRAMENKO and settled for being a simple, honest Ukrainian patriot." Avramenko, he observed, "is always airborne on the wings of magnificent dreams, but like a little child ... he is incapable of grasping reality. … It is high time he paid more attention to himself and to the people around him. If he really intends to create a Ukrainian ballet, it is time to do so rather than build castles in the air while borrowing pennies for his meals." How could Avramenko preach about liberating Ukraine when he was unable to manage his own life, when he and his closest associates lived on handouts, and when they were reduced to wearing clothes that others had discarded?[108] Kist and Pihuliak urged Avramenko to rein in his ambitions, to limit himself to three dance schools in New York City, to save money that he had been spending on instructors and recitals, and to assemble a troupe that could perform on Broadway. If he focused on choreography, creating a ballet, organizing a skilled troupe, and touring, then he might yet succeed in America. Some of his new American friends offered similar advice and even tried to introduce Avramenko to the impresario Sol Hurok, but to no avail.[109] Avramenko refused to listen and insisted on following his own instincts.

What success he had during these years was largely confined to the Ukrainian community. Since booking major venues was an extremely expensive proposition, almost all of the performances and recitals staged by Avramenko in the United States, and especially in New York City and its environs, took place in Ukrainian National Homes, parish halls, or high school auditoriums. Such performances were not reviewed in the English-language press, and they failed to generate any publicity for the Ukrainian cause. For Avramenko, who had become accustomed to a fair amount of media attention in Canada, this must have been profoundly disappointing and made him even more determined to get back into the spotlight. On the few occasions that he managed to do so, the results were ambiguous at best. As a rule, such performances generated modestly favourable reviews while saddling Avramenko with crushing debts. Consequently, he began to borrow money even more freely and in far larger amounts than he had in the past and to issue appeals for donations that identified his projects with the Ukrainian cause. Moreover, every major financial failure inspired new and more grandiose projects to recoup his losses. Desperate by 1932, Avramenko aggressively solicited donations and loans and increasingly targeted widows, spinsters, the poorly educated, and the gullible to finance his projects.

His first New York City performance, on 19 May 1929 at the Star Casino, 107th Street and Park Avenue, took place in a prestigious and expensive venue. Three weeks earlier, on 26 April, the very popular Paul Whiteman Orchestra and the Rhythm Boys, featuring a young crooner by the name of Bing Crosby, had performed at the Upper East Side venue.[110] At the time, Whiteman was the most successful recording artist in the United States, though that distinction would soon pass to Crosby. Avramenko's performance, featuring 300 student dancers and music by Columbia ethnic recording artist Paul Humeniuk and his orchestra, was meant to introduce the dance master to the American public. It was organized by Kalenik Lissiuk, a recent immigrant from central Ukraine who had succeeded in business and was actively involved in Republican politics.[111] Present at the performance were representatives of the Republican Party, including H. Murray Jacoby, who would represent the United States at the coronation of Ethiopian emperor Haile Selassie in 1930 and who was so impressed by Avramenko that he would invite him to perform at several of his own private receptions in the years to come.[112] The Ukrainian press, including the daily *Svoboda,* also responded favourably and gave Avramenko the kind of ringing endorsement that was sure to fuel his sense of mission. The performance, its reviewer noted, had been no mere dance school recital but "a magnificent tableau of a United Ukraine painted by the artful hand of

Vasile Avramenko, … [whose] goal is to help the Ukrainian dance, like the Ukrainian song, capture first place among the folk arts of all the nations. … Avramenko is not working for himself, he is performing a great national and patriotic labour for the benefit of all Ukrainian people. … We should regard Avramenko's cause as our national cause, as part of the struggle … Ukrainians are presently waging for their liberation, for their statehood." "Thanks to Avramenko," the review concluded, "the Ukrainian dance has become a completely independent branch of the Ukrainian arts."[113]

Unfortunately, the performance did not turn out as Avramenko and his supporters had anticipated. It was not easy to draw a crowd in New York City, and the Star Casino's location and admission prices meant that few Ukrainians were in attendance. To complicate matters, the misfortune that seemed to stalk Avramenko on occasions of this kind struck once again. At 3 p.m., just hours before the performance was scheduled to commence, New York City experienced a sudden and devastating storm. Howling winds and a downpour caused pandemonium everywhere. At Yankee Stadium, where the home team was leading the Boston Red Sox 3-0 on home runs by Babe Ruth and Lou Gehrig, the storm caused a stampede, which left two people dead and sixty-five hospitalized. Within an hour, the temperature had plunged from 80° F to 55° F, and New Yorkers who had not been caught up in the storm decided not to tempt fate and opted for the comfort and safety of their apartments.[114] As a result, the crowd at Avramenko's inaugural performance was sparse, there were no reviews in any of the major newspapers, and Avramenko lost a significant amount of money on the venture.[115] It would take more than a year to pay off the debt.[116]

When Avramenko attempted a second major performance in New York City, he decided to hold it at the Metropolitan Opera House, arguably the most prestigious venue on Broadway. The world's most celebrated conductors, singers, musicians, and dancers had performed at the Met, and Avramenko hoped to bask in their reflected glory. In the years to come, the 25 April 1931 Met performance would become pivotal to the growing Avramenko myth. Held to celebrate the tenth anniversary of his School of Ukrainian Folk Dance and Ballet, the performance was promoted within the Ukrainian community as an act of cultural diplomacy that would draw international attention to the political struggle in Polish-occupied western Ukraine.[117] The performance featured 500 student dancers, a mixed chorus of 100, and a folk orchestra directed by Yuri Kerychenko, all in authentic Ukrainian folk costumes. Young dancers from Avramenko's schools in the northeastern United States were transported to New York City, housed, and fed at their parents' expense. To provide added incentive for parents, the school issued a circular suggesting that the event "would bring to the attention of America the artistic talents of the Ukrainian people and awaken our children to the possibility of attaining success in the world of the American performing arts."[118]

This time the house was packed, and there were a few good reviews. Describing the Ukrainian dance master as "a man of rare personality and superb talents, and possibly a genius," Henry Beckett of the *New York Evening Post* was even more taken with the audience:

> The audience was simply carried away by some of these grand-scale dances. Men shouted and the heartiest applause started halfway through the dance and continued right through to the end. The house was practically filled by men, women and children of Ukrainian birth or descent and the nationalistic spirit was rampant. No wonder Poland got rid of Mr. Avramenko. He makes the Ukrainians proud of being Ukrainians. Of course, this enthusiasm was more than a manifestation of patriotism. It signified the complete absorption of a large audience in what was taking place on the stage. Mentally the audience danced and was part of the festival. It was a fine object-lesson for Anglo-Saxon Americans, now in peril of succumbing to the dread disease of "spectatoritis." … All in all, this performance provided an abundance of melody, harmony, rhythm, color, energy, startling agility and amazing mass effects, both in tableau and in violent motion. It was and is extremely important, beyond almost any other event this season, as a great demonstration of music and dancing of the people, by the people and for the people.[119]

Not surprisingly, this glowing review would be duplicated and distributed by Avramenko for the rest of his career.

However, the Ukrainian American press was not nearly as enthusiastic. Its reviewers expected more from the man who had been promising to create a folk ballet for the glory of Ukraine, and they evaluated the performance as a well-attended artistic failure. Writing in *Svoboda,* the violinist and composer Roman Prydatkevych conceded that the dances and the musical accompaniment were raw, monotonous, and insufficiently refined and that the entire spectacle was too bombastic in its appeal to patriotism. Still, he pleaded with critics to be more indulgent and to consider the many obstacles faced by Avramenko in training his young dancers.[120] The rival *Narodna volia* was much harsher. Many of the dancers, its critic suggested, seemed unsure and unprepared. The entire performance appeared to be "improvised, put together on the run, uncertain, at times pure bedlam." This impression was only "magnified by Avramenko's incongruous presence on the stage," where the dance master constantly directed, exhorted, nudged, pushed, and spurred on his dancers "like a shepherd in an alpine pasture." The finale, in which a figure representing Ukraine, "dressed in priestly vestments and carrying a bishop's scepter," took centre stage, revealed the "utter triviality" of Avramenko's artistic conception. Spectacles of this kind, which reminded the reviewer of plays produced "by amateurs in villages and small towns," were out of place at the Metropolitan Opera House. The review also expressed concern that Avramenko would continue "to swim in shallow water," that he would not make the extra, disciplined, uncompromising effort, free of cheap effects, needed to elevate his work to the level of art.[121]

Regardless, Avramenko's performance at the Met caused hardly a ripple in New York City, much less in the United States. Had it not been for the review in the *New York Evening Post,* it might have gone completely unnoticed. It was, after all, much more difficult to attract media attention in New York City than in Winnipeg or Toronto. The New York press had bigger and better things to write about. On the same weekend, Al Jolson was starring in *The Wonder Bar* at the Bayes Theater, while Noel Coward and Gertrude Lawrence were appearing in *Private Lives* at the Times Square Theater. At the movie palaces, Charlie Chaplin's *City Lights* and *Public Enemy* starring James Cagney and Jean Harlow were big hits. The Metropolitan Opera Company's performance of *Lucia* at the Westchester County Center featured Lily Pons and was attended by the king and queen of Siam and many of New York City's luminaries.[122] Not unexpectedly, then, the *New York Times* arts and entertainment section covered all of these shows and focused on the Library of Congress Chamber Music Festival, which featured performances by soprano Nina Koshetz and Russian pianist and composer Sergei Prokofiev. Coverage of Avramenko's two hours at the Met amounted to one perfunctory paragraph.[123]

The only people who seemed to believe that the Metropolitan Opera House performance had been a grand success that brought the Ukrainian cause to the attention of the American public were Ukrainian politicians in central Europe and Polish-occupied western Ukraine. As a rule, Avramenko's reputation as a "ballet master" and promoter of the Ukrainian cause was greatest among people who were farthest removed from the scenes of his accomplishments. UVO and OUN leader Colonel Yevhen Konovalets wrote to Avramenko from Geneva to express his "heartfelt congratulations and to wish you further success as a propagandist of the Ukrainian arts and of the Ukrainian cause. At this moment, when foreign conquerors on both sides of the Zbruch River are persecuting our people, news of your success far beyond our borders is a singularly luminous moment that encourages our people to persevere and to continue the struggle for the great idea of Ukrainian statehood. May your initiative herald a more animated effort by Ukrainian patriots in America to propagate the Ukrainian name and the Ukrainian cause in the New World!"[124] Another member of the OUN, journalist Mykhailo Seleshko, stationed in Berlin, wrote that all possible methods had to be used to liberate Ukraine and suggested that Avramenko and Koshetz could publicize the Ukrainian cause and do for Ukraine what the celebrated pianist Ignacy Paderewski had done for Poland on the eve of the First World War.[125] The aging western Ukrainian politician Kyrylo Trylovsky even published a lengthy article exhorting Avramenko and Koshetz to take advantage of their fame by delivering fifteen-minute lectures on Ukrainian history and geopolitics, complete with maps and printed information sheets, at all of their concerts, thereby expediting the liberation of Ukraine.[126] These distant admirers seemed to imagine that all of America was talking about Avramenko, Ukrainian folk dancing, and the Ukrainian issue in the aftermath of the Metropolitan Opera House performance. They did not understand that on the North American performing arts scene Avramenko was at best an ephemeral curiosity if not an utter non-entity.

Indeed, by the summer of 1931, Avramenko's stock was beginning to plunge, especially in New York City's Ukrainian community. The ballyhooed performance at the Met had been an artistic failure, and, though well attended, it had failed to resolve his financial obligations. Complaining about the debt notices that he received every day, Avramenko left New York during the summer, hoping to evade his creditors.[127] He planned to recoup at least some of his losses by producing two more extravaganzas, this time at Chicago's Civic Opera House and Cleveland's Public Auditorium in November. By the time he returned to New York City in December 1931, still saddled with debts, Avramenko had devised an even more spectacular project, which he hoped would solve his financial problems once and forever. He would assemble a group of dancers, help Alexander Koshetz organize a new choir, and then tour the United States with Koshetz.[128] Because America was preparing to celebrate in 1932 the bicentennial of George Washington's birth, the tour could be promoted as a Ukrainian tribute to the first president, it would generate much goodwill and publicity for the Ukrainian cause, and, if it attracted sell-out crowds, it just might pave the way for bigger tours of the United States, Central and South America, and even Europe. Once again Avramenko had given his imagination free rein, and he would pay dearly for this lapse.[129]

Although he agreed to tour with Avramenko, Koshetz had few illusions about the venture. He informed one of his European acquaintances that "the notorious Avramenko is trying to drag me into his May performances. It is obvious that he wants to take advantage of me. I would like to take advantage of him, but because he does everything on the run and according to the principle 'we'll manage somehow' I suspect there will be little material advantage in it for me."[130]

If Avramenko's 1927 tours of the prairie provinces had been financial failures, then his much more ambitious 1932 tour of twenty-three cities in the northeastern and midwestern United States, undertaken with a reluctant Koshetz and a hastily assembled Ukrainian chorus, was a complete fiasco.[131] The tour, launched on 1 May with a ceremony beside the Washington Monument and a performance at the Washington Auditorium, was in trouble from the first day. A photo opportunity with the first lady, who was to receive a Ukrainian delegation bearing decorated Easter eggs and highland woodcarvings, had to be cancelled when Mrs. Hoover suddenly had to leave the capital for four days.[132] Because Avramenko had decided to book expensive concert halls, Koshetz observed that ticket prices were much higher than they had been on his first North American tour a decade earlier when the country was not wallowing in the depths of the Depression. As a result, ticket sales were very slow. In Washington, where only 1,500 seats had been sold for the inaugural performance, Ivan Pihuliak was ordered to distribute 2,000 free tickets to local high school and university students in order to save face.[133] Broadcasting the Washington concert on the NBC radio network did not help either. In Wilmington and Baltimore, the performances were given in virtually empty venues.[134] Although attendance picked up somewhat as the tour moved north, it remained very disappointing, and Avramenko's bungling did nothing to help. For the performance in New York City's Carnegie Hall, Avramenko invited the press to the sparsely attended Sunday matinee rather than the well-attended evening show. At post-performance banquets hosted by Ukrainian organizations, his diatribes, aimed at Ukrainian priests and secular community leaders who failed to support the enterprise, provoked boycotts of performances in neighbouring communities.[135]

Although reviews published in the major dailies were on the whole positive, sometimes even flattering, they were brief and frequently stereotyped Ukrainians as a colourful and exotic people, though under the circumstances that was quite understandable. The *New York Evening Post* confided that it was "enthusiastic about Mr. Avramenko because he is so picturesquely and fundamentally Ukrainian. He is teaching the children of Ukrainians to be proud of their inheritance and their beautiful, charming folk ways."[136] The *New York Times* thought it "a trifle naive to perform Ukrainian dances before a backdrop depicting the Capitol in Washington" but conceded that "there is a charming sincerity in the gesture" and concluded that "the whole performance of his ballet reflected great credit upon Mr. Avramenko."[137] According to the *Brooklyn Daily Eagle*, "naiveté and spontaneity were conspicuous virtues of the pageant as a whole; the dances were the dances of the peasants, danced, one imagined, much as the peasants danced them, perhaps still do, in the villages of the Ukraine. ... They danced with the spirit of young people having a good time rather than with the precision of a trained ballet. The element of professionalism was introduced by Mr. Avramenko in a solo Hopak, concluding the first division of the program."[138] The *Boston Globe*, in particular, was struck by the spectacle created by the dancers: "In their vivid, multi-colored costumes and with many strings of bright colored beads around their necks—which, in the whirl, made a curious rattling accompaniment to the instrumental rhythm—the dancers suggested fully the strength and zest of peasant life, and recalled childhood reading about strange lands and people."[139]

Perhaps most disappointing was the fact that reviewers in a number of newspapers—the *Baltimore Sun*, the *Philadelphia Public Ledger*, the *New York World-Telegram*, the *Boston Evening Transcript*, and the *Pittsburgh Sun-Telegraph*—failed to grasp that Koshetz and Avramenko were performing Ukrainian rather than Russian songs and dances and that Ukrainians were not Russians. Reviews in these newspapers referred to Koshetz as "the noted Russian choir director," mentioned the "deep roots dancing has among the Russians," praised Koshetz for his skillful "delineation of Russia in concert form," [140] commented on the choir's "typical Muscovite tone quality,"[141] compared it with "that other Russian organization, the Don Cossacks,"[142] and marvelled at the "curious whirlings and peculiar squatting steps associated with dances of the Russian type."[143] For a tour that proposed to raise the profile of Ukrainians in the United States, this could only be interpreted as a clear and unequivocal failure.

Ultimately, fewer than half of the twenty-four performances attracted more than a handful of spectators, and only three or four showed a profit. Having borrowed a great deal of money to finance the project on the assumption that it would launch tours of North, South, and Central America and Europe with Koshetz, Avramenko was left with a personal debt of more than $14,000.[144] He also managed to turn his idol, Koshetz, into a life-long enemy. The refined and cultivated Koshetz was repelled by Avramenko's vanity, vulgarity, philistinism, lack of discipline, and financial incompetence, and he suspected that Avramenko was trying to use him to save his own floundering career. On 29 May 1932, the day after the tour concluded, Koshetz wrote in his journal that his experience with Avramenko had made him feel "just as if I had spent the entire month drowning in a latrine."[145]

Avramenko spent the summer and fall of 1932 going door-to-door, cap in hand, trying to raise money to pay off his debts. His travels in search of loans and donations took him as far west as St. Louis, Missouri, and everywhere he peppered his appeals with shrill denunciations of Ukrainian newspaper editors and community leaders who had failed to support him and whom he described as idlers who had accomplished nothing.[146] He also launched new projects, convinced that they would be his salvation. In mid-March 1933, he dispatched a small group of dancers and singers, including the soloists Petro Ordynsky and Maria Hrebenetska, on what was billed as the Evening in Ukraine tour. Booked into some fifty to sixty Ukrainian community and parish halls, the tour began to lose money in mid-April, and all the performers were asked to take pay cuts. Thereafter, relations with Avramenko deteriorated rapidly, and the tour fell apart in early May.[147] By this time, however, after a great deal of wrangling, he had negotiated a preliminary agreement with the Ukrainian Chicago World's Fair Exhibit Corporation to produce the Ukrainian Day grandstand show at the 1933 Century of Progress Chicago World's Fair. The terms of the agreement were not attractive, but Avramenko was desperate. He agreed to produce a one-hour program featuring hundreds of singers and dancers and to cover all the costs of production, including rehearsals, costumes, and transportation; in exchange, he would receive 25 percent of the gross gate receipts.[148] The Ukrainian Day festivities, held on 19 August at the Chicago Coliseum, featured the Ukrainian Chorus of Chicago under George Benetzky, a Ukrainian orchestra conducted by Leon Sorochynsky, and a high school band. Most of the program consisted of Avramenko and his dance pupils. He performed a solo dance, while his pupils performed no fewer than twenty-one dances in sets called "Reminiscences from the Carpathian Highlands" and "Glimpses of Ukraine."[149] While the performers acquitted themselves well, attendance was very disappointing because many of Chicago's Ukrainians were unemployed.[150] Because expenses totalled almost $5,000, while receipts were just under $2,500, once again Avramenko was left with a deficit of at least $2,500.[151] This time even the naive optimism that usually sustained him in moments of financial crisis seems to have deserted him, and he confided to friends that he had contemplated suicide … or perhaps he said this only to win their sympathy.[152]

During the fall of 1933, Avramenko found himself at a crossroads. Driven by his obsession with the Ukrainian cause and by his incessant need to prove himself, he had finally run up against a brick wall. It was much more difficult to attract media attention and bring glory to the Ukrainian cause in the United States than in Canada. His erratic behaviour and lack of business sense, not to mention the Depression, which had held America in its grip since the fall of 1929, were combining to pull the rug out from under his dance schools and to subvert all of his major projects. And his hectic schedule and repeated financial failures were taking a toll on his personal life, on the lives of his wife and daughter, and on a growing number of Ukrainian immigrants who had loaned him their hard-earned money.

By the mid-1930s, Avramenko's career as a dance master and impresario was falling apart. In May 1933, over 13 million Americans, including 25 percent of the work force, were unemployed.[153] Among Ukrainian immigrants, the percentage of unemployed was even higher, and it was difficult to persuade parents to spend money on folk dancing lessons and on innumerable dance recitals. Nick Arseny, trying to organize dance schools in Pennsylvania, reported that Avramenko's new sales pitch no longer worked: people simply did not believe that folk dancing would afford their children an opportunity to become "big stars" or keep Ukrainian youth off the streets.[154]

Avramenko's abrasive personality and his overbearing missionary nationalism, which had been alienating friends, colleagues, pupils, and parents since Avramenko had first come to North America, also undermined his career as a dance master. Declaring that "there is only room for Ukrainians in my school," he constantly lectured everyone on how to be a "good Ukrainian," and he berated colleagues who dared to utter so much as one word of English because, in his opinion, such behaviour implied a "betrayal of Ukraine."[155] Ready to sacrifice everything for the Ukrainian cause, he demanded as much from everyone around him. Convinced that his labours on behalf of Ukrainian dancing were a "sacred obligation" that had to be sustained "even if it costs me my life," Avramenko could not understand those who had more mundane priorities.[156] When the selfless Yuri Hassan concluded that it was impossible to make a living as a Ukrainian performer in North America and returned to his studies at the Ontario Agricultural College, Avramenko berated him for wasting his talents on a farm and insisted that Hassan had a duty to "work for the glory and liberation of Ukraine."[157] And when Andrii Kist, skimping on meals and unable to pay the rent, indicated his readiness to work as a harvest labourer or soft drink bottler, Avramenko warned him not to mention the subject again because the Ukrainian cause took precedence.[158] After leaving Canada, Avramenko even expected parents to transport children who were to tour the United States with him from Winnipeg to upper New York State at their own expense. When no one obliged him, he was confounded.[159]

In the United States, Avramenko's incessant jibes and homilies drove away even his closest colleagues. Instructors who chewed gum, smoked, had the occasional drink, played cards, or, heaven forbid, deviated from his instructions concerning teaching methods, dance arrangements, and costumes were sure to feel his wrath. In some instances, Avramenko presumed to dictate whom they could date and when they could marry. Andrii Kist had returned to Czechoslovakia in 1930 and would remain there until 1937. Peter Smook left in 1933, having been berated by Avramenko one time too many.[160] When the recently married Ivan Pihuliak—who probably taught more dancers than Avramenko and certainly earned more money for the school of Ukrainian dance—left penniless and in despair after the Chicago World's Fair, the fate of the dance schools was sealed.[161]

Nor were Avramenko's endless harangues on the decadence of modern music and dance, the evils of gum chewing, the immorality of using lipstick and makeup, and the beauty and superiority of traditional Ukrainian folk attire calculated to attract pupils.[162] Even more than the most ardent nineteenth-century Ukrainophiles, Avramenko was convinced that the Ukrainian folk costume was the primary emblem of Ukrainian identity, and he taught dance classes dressed in boots, an embroidered shirt, baggy pantaloons or *sharavary,* and a knee-length black jacket or *svyta.*[163] He wore this outfit and a lambskin hat at all public appearances, and it took much effort and energy to persuade him to wear a business suit when crossing the Canadian-American border. The mere suggestion that he adopt contemporary Western dress infuriated him. When Kukhta hinted that he should wear a business suit when not on stage, Avramenko retorted that he had no intention of becoming "an internationalist insofar as clothing is concerned." Indeed, he wanted to *compel* Ukrainians "to love their superior native attire."[164] He invited his wedding guests to wear Ukrainian folk costumes, upbraided Ukrainian singers and instrumentalists photographed in frock coats rather than in embroidered shirts, and refused to heed friends who advised him to stop lecturing his pupils and to focus on dance instruction.[165]

By the fall of 1933, Avramenko had only two instructors and a handful of schools in New Jersey and Pennsylvania. Although a few dance courses would be offered during the next few years in Minneapolis, Minnesota; in the remote and isolated Ukrainian colonies around Gorham and Belfield, North Dakota; in Harrah, Oklahoma; and even in Galveston, Texas (where a Ukrainian Orthodox priest acted as the dance instructor), by the spring of 1937 all of Avramenko's American dance schools had folded.[166] Even one of his more inspired publicity stunts failed to revive their fortunes. When pupils from his Baltimore dance school participated in the 1935 White House Easter Egg Roll, Avramenko published postcards with photographs of Eleanor Roosevelt at the event and claimed to have scored a major diplomatic victory for the Ukrainian cause.[167]

His relationship with his wife had been tumultuous since they first met. Born in Canada, educated in Catholic schools, and almost fifteen years his junior, Pauline Garbolinsky had been attracted by his idealism and by all the positive publicity that Avramenko had generated for Ukrainians in Canada. However, it soon became apparent that married life with the fanatical dance master entailed greater demands and offered much less emotional and financial support than she had anticipated. Five weeks after giving birth to their daughter Oksana in March 1929, Pauline was in charge of sewing 300 Ukrainian folk costumes for Avramenko's New York City début at the Star Casino.[168] On those occasions when Avramenko returned to Canada to apply for readmission into the United States, Pauline would remain in New York City with her infant daughter, cleaning, mending, packing, and hauling to the post office costumes and props that had to be sent to dance instructors in all parts of Canada and the United States. She also resented the fact that Avramenko, who usually left her and the child penniless, told everyone that she was "as helpless as a child" and threw temper tantrums when she accepted invitations to stay with friends in his absence.[169] And Avramenko was frequently absent during these years, lecturing, establishing new schools, teaching, recruiting dance instructors, commuting from one city to another, preparing performances, attending rehearsals, and trying to hustle loans and donations for his many projects. In December 1931, just before Christmas, Avramenko informed Pauline that he would spend the holidays and all of January in Cleveland, Pittsburgh, and Chicago making preparations for his tour with Koshetz. This would be "one of the great achievements of the School of Ukrainian Dance," and, after telling Pauline that she could spend Christmas wherever she pleased, he cautioned her "not to torment anyone with your petty concerns or stand in the way of the great Ukrainian cause."[170] By 1933, after the Chicago World's Fair fiasco, which had been financed in part with a $1,000 loan from her father, Fred Garbolinsky, Pauline and little Oksana found themselves in dire straits. While Avramenko travelled as far west as California, seeking new opportunities and trying to raise money, there were days when Pauline and Oksana had nothing to eat.[171] His wife and child's predicament was "unpleasant," Avramenko conceded, but "the cause could not suffer."[172] A year later Avramenko, who still owed Fred Garbolinsky more than $700, begged him to send more money because his daughter and granddaughter would soon be homeless.[173]

Pauline was greatly embarrassed by Avramenko's efforts to borrow money from her father and tried to resolve the financial crisis by taking a job, a step that deeply offended her husband.[174] Like a true peasant patriarch, Avramenko expected his wife to take care of domestic chores, look after their daughter, and help with his dance schools and public performances, preferably in some inconspicuous manner lest his own status as breadwinner be brought into question. He also shared the peasant patriarch's belief that women's behaviour and sexuality had to be regulated by a strict moral code and kept under constant surveillance. Thus, Avramenko was adamantly opposed to his wife's use of lipstick and makeup. When he had to leave New York City in the summer of 1929, he instructed friends to visit Pauline and verify whether she was still "painting herself."[175] In the years that followed, as they drifted apart because of his prolonged absences, he continued to harangue Pauline, forbidding her "to paint herself, to play cards, to smoke, to attend foolish balls in revealing gowns,"[176] and to socialize with other men—especially educated and successful ones who were not disinclined to criticize Avramenko. Maintaining that decent women did not wear lipstick, he urged her to submit to "the great Ukrainian cause, for which one should not only abandon evening gowns and makeup but for which it is worth giving one's life."[177] By the spring of 1935, Pauline and Avramenko were living apart, and, when he learned that she had been seen in the company of another man, the marriage finally came to an end in March 1936.[178]

Most disturbing for Avramenko were the many letters that he had been receiving since the fall of 1933 from simple Ukrainian immigrants who had believed that he would do great things for the Ukrainian cause and entrusted him with their money. Now they were begging, asking, and demanding that he return their loans. Some, like the widow Olena Kulchytska of Cleveland, who had loaned Avramenko $1,200 in 1931, lamented that they were cold, hungry, and obliged to borrow money to stave off eviction from their apartments.[179] Others reported that they needed the money because they had lost their jobs, had medical bills to pay, or were unable to send their children to school.[180]

And so, with his dance schools collapsing and his inability to pay back his debts, Avramenko had no alternative but to reinvent himself. Even in the depths of the Depression, between 45 and 55 million Americans continued to attend movies every week, and musicals featuring dance numbers were an especially popular form of diversion. Having already dabbled with film by making movies of dance recitals and Ukrainian community events, Avramenko now decided to become a motion picture producer. By producing motion picture versions of popular Ukrainian operettas, he could showcase all of the Ukrainian folk arts—song, dance, music, and costumes—at once, and by subtitling or dubbing the films into English their appeal would extend beyond the Ukrainian immigrant community. One successful motion picture could recoup all of his financial losses, help to settle his debts, and restore his reputation. All that remained to be done was to persuade his countrymen that what they really needed was a "Ukrainian Hollywood."

MOTION PICTURE PRODUCER

CHAPTER 3

After spending the summer recording songs and dubbing films in Paris, vacationing on the Riviera, and spurning emissaries sent to lure her back to Nazi Germany, Marlene Dietrich left Europe on 20 September 1933 and returned to her new home in the United States. By the second week of October, she was at Paramount Studios in Hollywood, where Joseph von Sternberg was putting the finishing touches on the screenplay of *The Scarlet Empress.*[1] A nightmarish vision of how Catherine the Great of Russia lost her innocence, *The Scarlet Empress* would be the sixth of seven von Sternberg features starring Dietrich. With sets inspired by German expressionism and scenes of pillage, rape, torture, and sadomasochism, the film would be described as a "relentless excursion into style" by von Sternberg[2] and as "self-indulgent nonsense" by reviewers in the popular press.[3] When finally released in September 1934, *The Scarlet Empress* was a failure at the box office, though recently film critics and historians have elevated it to the status of a masterpiece, "one of the cinema's most dazzling achievements."[4]

Also in Hollywood in October 1933 was Vasile Avramenko, on the run after the fiasco at the Chicago World's Fair. Obtaining loans and donations from Ukrainian immigrants in far-flung rural colonies, he had made his way to Hollywood, where he hoped to break into motion pictures. On 6 October the first issue of the *Ukrainian Weekly* informed its readers that "our well known master of the Ukrainian folk-dance, Vasile Avramenko, is at present in Hollywood, the centre of the moving picture industry, where, it is reported, he may take part in several productions which may feature Ukrainian dancers. It is hoped that Avramenko will be able to give Hollywood a clearer conception of the Ukrainian people than it has had to date."[5] In later years, Avramenko would maintain that, while in Hollywood in the fall of 1933, he had been offered a lucrative contract to dance in a film about Catherine the Great.

According to his account, negotiations broke down when the film company insisted that the dances that Avramenko was to perform in the film had to be presented and billed as "Russian" dances.[6] Although the story might be apocryphal, it is certainly not difficult to imagine a head-on collision over this issue involving the uncompromising Ukrainian dancer and the American-born, German-educated, Jewish director (or more likely one of his minions), who always insisted on absolute control over even the most minute details in his films.

A Fascination with Film

By the mid-1930s, Avramenko was no stranger to films and filmmaking. He had seen his first motion picture, a comedy starring Max Linder, in 1910 at the Illusion Theatre in Vladivostok.[7] In 1921, an American crew sent by the YMCA had filmed Avramenko and his dancers at the Kalisz internment camp, but despite promises to return with a finished product no one had ever seen that film.[8] Several years later, in 1924, Paul Crath had shot a performance by Avramenko's dance pupils in Prague and proceeded to screen the footage in North America.[9] Although he was not paid for either film, Avramenko understood that it would be much easier to conduct research and teach folk dancing if he could film and screen the dances.

In the United States and Canada, where motion pictures became the major form of entertainment for a majority of the population during the 1920s, Avramenko realized just how powerful the medium was and how many lucrative opportunities it offered. During the winter and spring of 1927, Alexander Koshetz and the remnants of the Ukrainian National Chorus had ended their career with a sixteen-week engagement at Grauman's Egyptian Theater in Hollywood. For $2,000 a week, the chorus performed in the "prologue"—a stage show preceding the feature film—to the blockbuster *Old Ironsides,* a story about Barbary pirates in the eighteenth-century Mediterranean starring Wallace Beery.[10] After the engagement, several chorus members, who had befriended Avramenko in Europe and continued to correspond with him, found work singing in movietone and vitaphone shorts that were especially popular during the late 1920s, when synchronized music and speech were being introduced into motion pictures.[11]

Only days after Avramenko decamped in New York City with his wife Pauline and Andrii Kist in December 1928, he received a letter from Koshetz alumnus Dmitri Yakubenko in Hollywood. Yakubenko urged his old friend to send publicity photos to Warner Brothers and Fox Studios because both were producing vitaphone and movietone shorts featuring vaudevillians whose talents were vastly inferior to Avramenko's. He also offered to assemble a few vocalists and assured Avramenko that together they "could earn good money with little effort."[12] Because his obligations made a trip to Hollywood impossible, Avramenko was advised to have himself filmed performing one of his solo dances in New York City. A good English-speaking manager could then bring his talents and abilities to the attention of Hollywood scouts and agents.[13]

In January 1929, Avramenko learned that a recently constructed film studio in Kyiv wanted to produce several popular films based on Ukrainian folklore and was looking for someone to supervise the dance scenes and run a studio dance school. Apparently, the studio had considered Avramenko but concluded that he would not return to Soviet Ukraine because he was too great a nationalist. Instead, the studio had offered the position to Avramenko's assistant, Ivan Pihuliak. Indignant at having been passed over and clearly envious of the invitation extended to his colleague, Avramenko told Pihuliak to go to Soviet Ukraine "if you wish to become a slave and a Muscovite underling!"[14] Although Pihuliak decided to remain in North America, Avramenko began to think more seriously about making films. Even if he did not land a Hollywood contract, footage of his performances could be screened in Ukrainian communities in North America, central Europe, and Polish-occupied western Ukraine, it would promote his dance schools and recitals, and it might even generate some badly needed revenue.[15]

The rapid evolution and success of the Soviet Ukrainian cinema between 1922 and 1930 must have made a strong impression on Avramenko and his circle of friends. The Ukrainian film industry traced its origins to the first decade of the twentieth century.[16] The "golden age" of Ukrainian cinema was launched in 1922 when Soviet authorities placed film production in the republic under the jurisdiction of the All-Ukrainian Photo-Cinema Administration (VUFKU), a branch of the People's Commissariat of Education. New studios were built in Kharkiv and Kyiv, technical staff increased from fewer than fifty to more than 1,000, and film production grew from four films in 1923 to sixteen in 1924, twenty in 1927, thirty-six in 1928, and thirty-one in 1929. The number of movie theatres in Ukraine increased from 265 in 1914 to 5,394 in 1928.[17]

During the 1920s, VUFKU extended invitations to experienced filmmakers and gave those who had fallen from grace in Moscow an opportunity to make films. Piotr Chardynin, the first Russian director to adapt literary classics to the screen, served as VUFKU's chief director in the mid-1920s. He produced big spectacles such as *Ukrazia* (1926) and several Ukrainian historical dramas. Most significantly, when his aversion to planning and writing scenarios cost the Jewish-Russian documentarian Dziga Vertov (Denis Kaufman) his job in Moscow, VUFKU offered him employment. He proceeded to produce three films, including his masterpiece *Man with a Movie Camera* (1929), an investigation of the filmmaking process and an avant-garde portrait of "a day in the life" of several Soviet cities.[18] In 1927–28, VUFKU also produced four Yiddish films based on stories and screenplays by Isaac Babel and Sholom Aleichem, though the project was discontinued after Communist Party officials criticized the films for being "backward looking" rather than "progressive."[19]

Above all, VUFKU produced many films on Ukrainian themes during the 1920s. The best included Chardynin's *Taras Shevchenko* (1926), about the Ukrainian poet; *Taras Triasylo* (1927), about a seventeenth-century Cossack uprising; *The Shoes* (1928), based on a story by Gogol; *Boryslav Is Laughing* (1927), after Ivan Franko's novel about western Ukrainian oil workers; *Mykola Dzheria* (1927), an adaptation of Nechui-Levytsky's novel about a fugitive serf; *Two Days* (1927), a film set during the civil war; and *The Downpour* (1929), a film about an eighteenth-century jacquerie, directed by Ivan Kavaleridze, a sculptor who had studied under Auguste Rodin in Paris alongside Alexander Archipenko. Popular, critically acclaimed, and occasionally screened in Ukrainian Labour Temples in Canada and the United States, most of these films were ultimately censured by Communist Party officials for their alleged nationalism and formalism and banned in the 1930s.

Alexander Dovzhenko was the most prominent Soviet Ukrainian director of the era. Rejecting the stridency and aggressive didacticism of ideologically driven Soviet directors, Dovzhenko subordinated plot to imagery and metaphor. *Zvenyhora* (1927), his first major film, encapsulated more than 1,000 years of Ukrainian history and legend in a story of buried treasure recounted by an old man to his two grandsons, the elder a committed Bolshevik revolutionary, the younger a doomed counterrevolutionary nationalist. While the film repudiated Ukrainian émigré nationalists and looked forward to a modernized Soviet Ukraine, it also celebrated the Ukrainian countryside, revelled in ancient folklore, and had nothing to say about Ukraine's mutual destiny with Russia. *Arsenal* (1929), about the repression of a Ukrainian workers' strike in the Kyiv munitions factory by UNR forces, was also a powerful anti-war statement and a mythical representation of workers' victory in defeat. The plot of *Zemlya* (Earth; 1930), Dovzhenko's masterpiece and one of the most critically acclaimed films in cinema history, concerned the murder of a young peasant who had persuaded poor villagers to purchase a tractor and turn to collective farming. Above and beyond this, the film was a lyrical look at the natural cycle of life, death, and rebirth and a celebration of the beauty of the Ukrainian countryside. Conceived and filmed before the horrors of Stalinist collectivization, the film optimistically anticipated the triumph of a new social order in the Ukrainian village. Because its lyricism overshadowed the didactic storyline, the film was condemned by Communist Party critics. Dovzhenko's last important film and first talkie, *Ivan* (1932), used the construction of a massive hydro dam as its storyline but was primarily about the disruption of natural rural rhythms of life by industrialization.[20] By that point, VUFKU had been disbanded, the production of Ukrainian films was drastically curtailed, and both Pihuliak and Avramenko were glad that they were still in New York City.

The 1928 release of *The Cossacks,* one of the last big budget MGM silent feature films, also provided impetus for Avramenko's reflections on the production of motion pictures. In Winnipeg, theatre owners promoted the film, which starred John Gilbert and Renée Adorée, by booking Meros Lechow, one of Avramenko's very young male dancers, to perform Ukrainian folk dances between screenings of the feature.[21] Although the film was based on a novella by Leo Tolstoy and set among early-nineteenth-century Russian Terek Cossacks who inhabited the northeastern slopes of the Caucasus Mountains, Avramenko and his entourage regarded the film as a misrepresentation of the lifestyle of *Ukrainian* (Dnieper) Cossacks. Andrii Kist complained that the film had "Russianized" the Cossacks and declared that it was an insult to the history and legacy of Ukrainians. He insisted that Ukrainians in Europe and North America had to produce their own feature films about Ukraine. Such films, he maintained, would constitute a greater achievement than all of Mykola Sadovsky's drama troupes and tours combined.[22] When he returned to Europe, where he spent the years between 1930 and 1937 teaching school in the Subcarpathian region of Czechoslovakia, Kist continued to write to Avramenko about the importance of film and plunged into the motion picture industry. In 1934, he had one of the lead roles in the Czech film *Marijka Nevernice* (Faithless Marika), based on a story of revenge by the writer Ivan Olbracht and directed by avant-garde writer and filmmaker Vladislav Vancura. The film focused on the interaction of poor Subcarpathian Ruthenian (Ukrainian) peasants with their Hassidic Jewish neighbours and addressed the issues of class conflict, exploitation, and emigration of Jewish youth to Palestine. Although not a commercial success, the film enjoyed a run in Prague and was apparently screened on two separate occasions for Czech president Thomas Masaryk.[23]

When Kist left the United States in the summer of 1930, Avramenko was already making plans to film a dance performance even though he did not have the money or opportunity to do so until the next spring. On 25 April 1931, several weeks after obtaining a $4,500 loan to stage the dance recital at the Metropolitan Opera House from New York City window washer Ivan Redchuk,[24] Avramenko produced his first "motion picture": a twenty-five-minute recording of the dress rehearsal prior to the big recital. Another seven or eight months passed before he finally unveiled the picture to a Ukrainian-American public that did not quite know what to make of a silent, black-and-white film celebrating what had been billed as a festival of music and colour.[25] Undeterred, Avramenko announced his intention to purchase land near New York City and build a Ukrainian cultural centre where short films such as *Ukrainske vesillia* (Ukrainian Wedding), celebrating all of the Ukrainian folk arts, could be made in collaboration with artists, including Alexander Koshetz and Mykhailo Haivoronsky.[26]

In the spring of 1932, Avramenko hired several young men to tour with his film of the performance at the Met, several travelogues and newsreels produced in western Ukraine, and a very bad silent version of *Taras Bulba,* made in Europe shortly after the First World War. During the next year, dance instructors and others employed by Avramenko's School of Ukrainian Ballet toured the northeastern and midwestern United States screening these films, promoting the school, and raising funds for projects such as the Chicago World's Fair performance.[27] In 1933, footage of the Chicago World's Fair, old Charlie Chaplin two-reelers made during the First World War, and a silent version of *The Life of Christ,* a feature film guaranteed to make a profit in Catholic and Orthodox communities during Lent, were added to the repertoire of Avramenko's itinerant projectionists.[28] Finally, in 1934, the circuit expanded into Canada when several Ukrainian Orthodox priests and community organizations were persuaded to invite Avramenko's projectionists to deliver "educational lectures." As long as the Canadian screenings were not advertised and admission prices remained below a thirty-cent ceiling that required payment of an entertainment tax, the deception could be maintained and the payment of customs duties evaded.[29]

It is within the context of these road shows that Avramenko's first trip to Hollywood took place in the fall of 1933. Avramenko travelled with two associates from Chicago to Hollywood via Milwaukee, Minneapolis-St. Paul, North Dakota, and San Francisco, screening his films, delivering lectures, soliciting loans and donations, and writing ahead to friends in Hollywood, asking them to contact people in the film industry on his behalf and instructing them to emphasize that he was a "creative force" rather than a mere dancer.[30] Although it is not inconceivable that he was offered a contract to dance in *The Scarlet Empress* and then rejected it, the correspondence that survives in his archive reveals that Avramenko spent much of his time prior to and during his stay in Tinseltown writing to affluent and supportive acquaintances all over North America in a desperate effort to raise money that would allow him to produce a short film showcasing his dancing talents.[31] Unable to raise the money, by mid-November Avramenko was on his way back to New York City empty-handed. His most lucrative port of call in the fall of 1933 turned out to be North Dakota, where the inhabitants of several isolated Ukrainian rural communities donated almost $3,000 after he lectured on his plans to establish a Ukrainian film industry.[32]

When he returned to New York City in December 1933, Avramenko decided to focus on filmmaking, leaving his few surviving dance schools in the hands of instructors such as Roman Fenchynsky and Nick Arseny. While the Depression had made it very difficult to earn a living as a Ukrainian folk dancing instructor or to attract spectators to dance recitals, attendance at motion pictures continued to expand even during the hard times of the 1930s. Weekly attendance in the United States grew from 40 million in 1929, to 45 million in 1932, to almost 60 million in 1940, leading many contemporaries to conclude that the film industry was enjoying a "golden age."[33] Little wonder that Avramenko used the $3,000 that he had raised in North Dakota to purchase a new and better movie camera and then opened a small film studio on 7th Street with money obtained from two widows, Anna Strilbycka and Anna Kohut.[34]

Avramenko spent much of 1934, the year that his marriage began to fall apart, producing several short (two- to four-reel) films about Ukrainian-American communities and institutions. Shot and edited by his young associates Michael T. Lawryk and John Podlesny, these first productions were little more than homemade newsreels about Ukrainian life in North Dakota; the "Providence" Ukrainian Catholic Fraternal Association; the Ukrainian Orthodox community in Northampton, Massachusetts; the Ukrainian National Association; the Ukrainian Self-Help Society in Pittsburgh; and the Organization for the Rebirth of Ukraine (ODVU), the American arm of the underground Organization of Ukrainian Nationalists.[35] It appears that the content of many of these films was interchangeable, spliced together to fit the occasion and to maximize the novice motion picture producer's income. In May 1934, for example, Avramenko informed the central executive of the Ukrainian National Association that he was shooting a film provisionally titled "History of Ukrainian Emigration." However, if the UNA donated $1,000 and permitted Avramenko's cameramen to film its headquarters and the *Svoboda* presses in action, then the film could be screened as "History of the Ukrainian National Association."[36] Most of these films were premiered in New York City at the Ukrainian National Home, 217–219 East 6th Street, between January and March 1935, and were then sent on the road.[37] Some were so bad that critics immediately turned on Avramenko, accusing him of trying to fool the public and of playing at being a filmmaker.[38]

Avramenko was not discouraged. He was already making plans to produce a feature film based on the oldest and most popular Ukrainian operetta, *Natalka Poltavka,* absolutely convinced that the film would "bring fame and glory" to the "Ukrainian cause." In February 1935, while his newsreels on Ukrainian American life were being received with little if any enthusiasm in Ukrainian community halls and church basements, Avramenko wrote to the stunningly beautiful, Kyiv-born, Hollywood actress Anna Sten (Anna Stenska-Sudakevych).[39] The daughter of a Swedish mother and a Ukrainian father, Sten had starred in Soviet and German films before Samuel Goldwyn brought her to Hollywood, spent millions on publicity, and cast her in three films—*Nana, We Live Again,* and *The Wedding Night.* Directed by Dorothy Arzner, Rouben Mamoulian, and King Vidor, and starring Lionel Atwill, Fredric March, and Gary Cooper alongside Sten, all three films failed at the box office.[40] Although Sten did not reply to Avramenko's inquiries, Avramenko refused to give up. He pressed ahead with his plans to make feature films and to create what he now began to refer to as a "Ukrainian Hollywood."

Audacious as these plans might appear, they were certainly not unprecedented. After the triumph of the Hollywood studio system during the 1920s, minorities, especially African Americans and eastern European immigrants who wanted to see themselves represented on the silver screen as multidimensional human beings rather than caricatures, had to produce their own movies. The many low-budget "race" and "ethnic" films made during the interwar years suggest that there was a demand for motion pictures of this kind.

The earliest race films were made shortly before the First World War. The release of D.W. Griffith's *The Birth of a Nation* (1915), a great film vitiated by its racism and uncritical celebration of the Ku Klux Klan, galvanized African Americans to produce films that challenged Griffith's racial stereotypes and his historical revisionism. Dramas such as *The Scapegoat* (1917) and documentaries such as *The Birth of a Race* (1918) celebrated the accomplishments of African Americans. The first ethnic films, aimed at Jewish immigrants, were produced by Sidney Goldin, who had emigrated from Ukraine. They told stories of immigration, documented the work of Jewish community organizations, and indicted anti-Semitism in the Tsarist Empire. *The Oath of the Sword* (1915) and *The Dragon Painter* (1919), produced by Sessue Hayakawa, the first Asian Hollywood star, were aimed at Japanese Americans, while James

Leong's *Lotus Blossom* (1921), a film based on an ancient Chinese legend, was produced for the Chinese-American market.

During the 1920s, race films emerged as an independent industry. On the eve of the Depression, there were 700 theatres in the United States patronized primarily by African Americans. They screened short slapstick comedies starring black vaudeville performers, "race westerns," and newsreels created for an African-American audience. The most successful African American film company was established by Oscar Micheaux, whose most memorable film, *Within Our Gates* (1920), examined lynching from an African-American perspective.[41]

The Yiddish cinema also became a phenomenon during the interwar years. With 10 million Yiddish speakers worldwide, more than 100 Yiddish-language feature films, as well as countless shorts and documentaries, were produced in Europe and North America between 1911 and 1941. A major turning point occurred in 1921 when Sidney Goldin returned to Europe to make films. *East and West* (1923), made in Austria and starring Molly Picon, was a success on both sides of the Atlantic. *Remembrance* (1924), filmed in Poland, featured Ukrainian-born Maurice Schwartz, director of New York City's Yiddish Art Theater. Schwartz in turn made the first Yiddish feature film in the United States, *Broken Hearts* (1926), a romantic melodrama about immigrant life in New York City. The advent of the talkies provided the American Yiddish film industry with added impetus because many Jewish immigrants did not understand English. The most successful feature-length American-made Yiddish talkie—*Uncle Moses* (1932)—starred Schwartz, was directed by Goldin, and was produced by Joseph Seiden's Judea Pictures. Between 1930 and 1936, at least nineteen Yiddish shorts and sixteen Yiddish feature films were produced in the United States alone.

The most productive period of Yiddish filmmaking in the United States was launched with the Polish-made musical comedy *Yidl with a Fiddle* (1936), about a young woman who wanders with a troupe of klezmer musicians, disguised as a boy. Featuring New York City–born Molly Picon and produced by Joseph Green, the film became an international hit. Green, an actor who came to the United States from Poland with a Yiddish drama troupe in 1924 and had bit parts in Hollywood, wanted to produce authentic, high-quality, Yiddish feature films. By the mid-1930s, he spent half of the year making films in Poland, which he screened in Europe and North America, including *The Dybbuk* (1937), a stylish, expressionistic film based on Anski's play about mysticism, evil spirits, and unfulfilled love.[42]

The success of *Yidl with a Fiddle* sparked another outburst of Yiddish filmmaking in the United States that produced twenty feature films between 1937 and 1941, including Maurice Schwartz's celebrated adaptation of Sholom Aleichem's *Tevye the Milkman* (1939), which Hollywood would remake as *Fiddler on the Roof* in 1971. That last prewar spurt of activity would be spearheaded by Roman Rebush, a New York City film distributor who decided to produce quality movies based on Yiddish stage classics after he visited the set of Avramenko's first feature film in the summer of 1936.[43]

Natalka Poltavka

The first steps toward the creation of a "Ukrainian Hollywood" were taken in the summer of 1935. His reputation briefly restored by publicity generated at the White House Easter Egg Roll in April, Avramenko seems to have been able to raise some money during the summer. Buoyed by this success, he engaged Michael J. Gann, an Odessa University–educated Russian Jew who ran a small art gallery and entertainment agency and dabbled in the production of short art films, as his manager.[44] By October, the Avramenko Ballet and Film Studio and Gann's Art Gallery and Continental Entertainment Bureau were located at 747 Broadway (near 8th Street) in lower Manhattan. A grand opening ceremony, emceed by Gann and featuring performances by young opera singers, violinists, pianists (none of them Ukrainian), and a few of Avramenko's dancers, took place on 12 January 1936.[45] Then, no longer encumbered by his wife, Pauline, and angling to free himself of all child support payments,[46] Avramenko threw himself into the production of *Natalka Poltavka* with his characteristic fervour.

Early in 1936, Avramenko's supporters, including Anna Strilbycka and Anna Kohut, the two generous widows who had already made substantial contributions to his film projects, formed a Committee for the Production of the First Ukrainian Talking Film. Composed primarily of rank-and-file members of the nationalist Organization for the Rebirth of Ukraine (ODVU), the committee was chaired by Maksym Boychuk. In April, it dispatched its deputy chairman, Vasyl Droboty, on a fundraising tour of Ukrainian communities in the United States. Simultaneously, the committee published the first and only issue of *Promin* (The Ray) to publicize the production of *Natalka Poltavka*—which was ignored by most Ukrainian American newspapers, including *Narodna volia* and the daily *Svoboda*, because their editors were no longer willing to lend any credence to projects promoted by Avramenko.[47]

Harping on the fact that Ukrainians had to have an independent film industry to propagate their culture, language, and idea of Ukrainian liberation, the articles in *Promin* played on Ukrainian immigrants' insecurities and desires for recognition. One of the articles stated that "you say there are about a million Ukrainians in America" and then inquired, "what have these people ever done to deserve notice or praise? … Did you not in many instances feel ashamed of your national identity because you were a member of an unknown, divided and scoffed-at race?" Having summoned these anxieties, the article reassured readers that "there is in the making one of the greatest institutions ever built and conducted by Ukrainians in America. This institution is the Ukrainian Film Studio, established by our famous ballet-master, Vasile Avramenko." If allowed to develop, this institution would "produce more tangible and beneficial work for the Ukrainians than the complete conglomeration of all the past efforts of the Ukrainians of this country." It would become the greatest source of propaganda for Ukraine on the face of the Earth, unify the Ukrainian people, and win international recognition for "Ukrainian drama, literature, song, music and dance." Above all, the production of *Natalka Poltavka* and the success of the Avramenko film studios would be a boon to Ukrainian-American youth. It would enable them to learn about Ukrainian customs, traditions, and life in a pleasant and entertaining manner and allow them to explain, in a "simple and delightful" way, who they were and where their parents came from by taking their non-Ukrainian friends to the movies. And, if confronted by scepticism about Ukrainian culture, they would be able to point to Ukrainian films with satisfaction and declare, "well, we Ukrainians do have something to be proud of." The Avramenko film studio might even help young Ukrainian Americans to make a living in some of the trades and professions connected to the film industry.[48]

Apparently, few people took Avramenko's bombastic appeal to heart. In May 1936, after it became clear that the committee was having trouble raising money by way of private loans and donations, Avramenko Film Production Incorporated, a shareholder-controlled company with capital of $25,000, was established in New York City. Its board of directors was almost identical to the committee, and almost all of the shareholders were rank-and-file members of the ODVU. The largest shareholders, Ivan Petrovsky (who became chairman of the board) and Ivan Stadnyk, each purchased $5,000 worth of shares. Avramenko received a contract granting him artistic control of the film, a weekly salary of twenty-five dollars, and 50 percent of net profits.[49]

Having raised enough money to begin production, Avramenko and Gann turned their attention to recruiting creative personnel. The original play, written for the stage by Ivan Kotliarevsky in 1818, had to be adapted for the screen and new scenes added to vary the pace and inject more humour. Although Avramenko claimed and received credit for the screenplay, it appears that Dr. Lonhyn Cehelsky, an émigré politician and newspaper editor, also had a hand in the writing.[50] Because neither man had any experience with motion pictures, the screenplay was subsequently rewritten on the set before being made into a movie. Recruiting a musical director also presented a problem. Alexander Koshetz and Leon Sorochynsky, the first two choices, refused to work on the film because of previous experiences with Avramenko. Koshetz expressed doubt that Avramenko could finance the project and demanded money up front if he was to participate.[51] Sorochynsky, who also doubted Avramenko's ability to pay, was even more concerned that Avramenko would try to run the music department. "You have become accustomed to command and, regrettably, to insult people," he wrote to Avramenko. "I prefer to work on the basis of a sincere understanding, and I simply hate and refuse to tolerate insults, especially when they are undeserved." Moreover, Sorochynsky gleefully admitted that he had recently started to chew gum when his nerves were on edge and that this would make work with Avramenko absolutely impossible because everyone knew how intolerant he was of gum chewers.[52] At the last moment, Professor Constantine Shvedoff, a Russian who had taught at the Imperial Conservatory in Moscow and worked with the Moscow Opera and Moscow Art Theatre, was hired as the film's musical director.[53] He successfully adapted and augmented the musical score, originally arranged by Mykola Lysenko in the 1880s.

Casting the lead roles went more smoothly, and Avramenko and Gann assembled as fine a group of singers and actors as was possible under the circumstances, especially if one considers that Ukrainians lacked an organization as professional as the Yiddish theatre in their community. Thalia Sabanieva, a Metropolitan Opera soprano of Greek origin who had been born in the Crimea and performed in various Russian and Ukrainian venues, was chosen to play the young lovelorn blonde heroine. An excellent singer, Madame Sabanieva—short, plump, and well into her forties—was physically unsuited for the role, though such casting was not unusual in operatic productions. The other lead singer-actors were well chosen. They included Michael Shvetz, an excellent comedian with a deep bass voice who had performed with opera companies in Odessa, Petrograd, Moscow, and Kyiv; Dmitri Creona, a tenor of Greek origin born in the Crimea who had performed with opera companies in Odessa and Athens; Olena Dibrova, who had been a soloist with the Ukrainian National Chorus; Mathew Vodiany, a veteran character actor and a mainstay of the Ukrainian theatre; Vladimir Zelitsky, another character actor who had apprenticed with Stanislavsky's Moscow Art Theatre; Theodore Swystun, a popular Ukrainian recording artist with a rich baritone voice who also happened to be ODVU's chief American organizer and the brother of prominent Ukrainian-Canadian lawyer and activist Wasyl Swystun; Mykhailo

Skorobohach, who had directed many plays staged by ODVU; and Maria Bodrug-Berezovska, the Canadian-born daughter of Reverend Ivan Bodrug of Toronto, a coloratura soprano and an aspiring opera singer.[54]

Ultimately, the fate of the film rested on the shoulders of the director, and Avramenko and Gann's first choice proved to be inauspicious. Leo Bulgakov, a Russian native of the Don region and a graduate of Moscow University, had worked as an actor and stage director with Stanislavsky and the Moscow Art Theatre before coming to the United States with that group. Although he had directed three B movies for Columbia Pictures, Bulgakov was a Broadway stage director who knew little about set design and camera work.[55] In July, before the actual filming commenced, he rehearsed the principal actors and worked with them on character development and mimicry. On the set, however, the Russian director seemed to be out of his element, and as filming approached he indicated that he needed some help. Help came in the shape of Edgar Georg Ulmer, a young, well-travelled, and experienced filmmaker whose promising Hollywood career had been derailed a year or two earlier by Universal Studios founder and owner Carl Laemmle Sr.[56]

Even in Hollywood, there was no one quite like Ulmer, who worked on some of the most celebrated films in the history of the medium with a veritable "who's who" of German, Austrian, and American producers, directors, writers, and cinematographers before his twenty-fifth birthday, but had to settle for a career as the "King of Ethnic and B Movies." He was born on 17 September 1904 in Olomouc (then Olmütz), a town in the Austro-Hungarian province of Moravia (now in the Czech Republic). The son of a Jewish wine merchant and his Viennese wife, Ulmer remained unaware of his Jewish heritage until he was admitted as a special student into a Jesuit school, where he developed a life-long appreciation of classical music, German and French literature, and Jesuit morality plays that would leave a mark on some of his best films. Sent to a home for orphans in Uppsala, Sweden, after his father died at the front during the Great War, Ulmer returned to Vienna around 1920 and apparently enrolled as an art director trainee in producer Max Reinhardt's theatrical academy. Working primarily on set construction in theatre and in the new film industry, Ulmer participated in the making of silent film classics such as Paul Wegener's *The Golem* (1920), Robert Wiene's *The Cabinet of Dr. Caligari* (1920), and Fritz Lang's *Die Nibelungen* (1924), though his uncredited contributions amounted to little more than being "hunkered in the wings with a claw hammer, helping build the sets," as film historian David Kalat has suggested.[57]

In 1924, probably with the assistance of Viennese actor and acquaintance Joseph Schildkraut, who had already made a name for himself in films such as D.W. Griffith's *Orphans of the Storm* (1921), Ulmer made his first trip to the United States. Before returning to Europe, he visited New York City's Yiddish Art Theatre, founded in 1918 by future filmmaker Maurice Schwartz. For the remainder of the decade, Ulmer commuted between Germany and the United States, working mostly as an uncredited set designer, assistant art director, or writer on a number of films that would become classics. In Germany, he worked for the legendary F.W. Murnau on *The Last Laugh* (1924) and *Faust* (1926). He might also have worked on Fritz Lang's *Metropolis* (1926) and *The Spies* (1928), though Lang always insisted that he had no recollection of Ulmer. In the United States, Ulmer worked on low-budget westerns such as *The Border Sheriff* (1926) for Universal Studios; on Ernst Lubitsch's *The Student Prince in Old Heidelberg* (1927) for MGM; and on Murnau's first Hollywood classic, *Sunrise* (1927), as well as on his *Four Devils* (1928) and *City Girl* (1929) at Fox Films. His final German film project, for which he received credit as co-director and writer, was the feature-length docudrama *People on Sunday* (1930), on which Ulmer collaborated with future Oscar winners Robert and Curt Siodmak, Billy Wilder, Fred Zinnemann, and Eugene Schufftan. The portrait of "a day in the life" of Berlin, the film was loosely inspired by Dziga Vertov's *Man with a Movie Camera* produced by VUFKU in Kyiv. In 1931, Ulmer also served as an uncredited writer, supervising editor, and production manager on Murnau's and legendary documentarian Robert J. Flaherty's *Tabu: A Story of the South Seas*, an exotic docudrama about an ill-starred Tahitian couple that was filmed on location and portrayed the island's culture with respect and insight.

By 1933, with the Nazis firmly in control of Germany, Ulmer had settled down in the United States. His first American directorial project was *Damaged Lives*, a cautionary melodrama about the dangers of venereal disease, based on a work by French playwright Eugene Brieux. *Damaged Lives* was released by Columbia Pictures through a subsidiary and did very well at the box office after being condemned by the Legion of Decency. Then, after working as set designer on Frank Borzage's *Little Man, What Now?*, Ulmer was asked to direct Universal's *The Black Cat* (1934), a horror film that teamed Boris Karloff and Bela Lugosi, stars of Universal's 1931 screen blockbusters *Frankenstein* and *Dracula*, for the first time.[58] The film's story revolved around American newlyweds on a honeymoon trip in the Carpathian Mountains. Brought to a secluded modernist mansion by a fellow traveller after an automobile accident, the young couple find themselves caught in a deadly struggle between their travelling companion, who was betrayed and lost his family during the Great War, and their host, a brilliant but evil architect, who bedded and murdered their new friend's wife and daughter and now sacrifices virgins in Satanic rituals.

1. Mykola Sadovsky.

2. Vasyl (Kostiv) Verkhovynets and Alexander Koshetz.

3. Alexander Koshetz and the Ukrainian National Chorus, Mexico City, 31 December 1922.

4. Vasile Avramenko, “Gonta” solo dance, publicity photo.

5. Vasile Avramenko, “Woe of Israel” solo dance, publicity photo.

6. Vasile Avramenko, “Chumak” solo dance, publicity photo.

7. Vasile Avramenko, “Dovbush” solo dance, publicity photo.

8. Vasile Avramenko, Volodymyr Kukhta, Yuri Hassan and Alexander Koshetz, Winnipeg, November 1926.

9. Victor Moisiuk, Volodymyr Kukhta, Vasile Avramenko and Ivan Pihuliak, Winnipeg, 1927.

10. Vasile Avramenko, Winnipeg, 1928.

11. Pauline Garbolinsky, Winnipeg, 1928.

12. Vasile Avramenko, Leon Sorochynsky and Andrii Kist (top row, centre-right), publicity photo for tour of the Prairie provinces, Winnipeg, 1927.

13. Vasile Avramenko (top left), Pauline Garbolinsky (middle centre) and Andrii Kist (top right) with junior dance class, Winnipeg, 1928.

14. Vasile Avramenko with dance pupils, probably in New York City, c. 1930.

15. Julian Stechishin, 1928.

16. Alexander Koshetz with chorus and dancers, Washington Bicentennial tour, May 1932.

17. Vozny (Mathew Vodiany) flirts with Natalka (Thalia Sabanieva) in *Natalka Poltavka* (1936).

18. Vyborny (Michael Shvetz) offers matrimonial advice to Vozny (Mathew Vodiany) in *Natalka Poltavka* (1936).

19. Petro (Dmitri Creona) pines for Natalka while working as an agrarian labourer in *Natalka Poltavka* (1936).

20. Vozny (Mathew Vodiany) and Palamar (Vladimir Zelisky) inebriated and belligerent in *Natalka Poltavka* (1936).

21. Vyborny (Michael Shvetz) and Vozny (Mathew Vodiany) flanked by wedding guests in *Natalka Poltavka* (1936).

22. Edgar G. Ulmer, c. 1940.

23. Vasile Avramenko (standing) with Antin Rudnytsky, 1938.

24. Odarka (Maria Sokil) and Ivan Karas (Michael Shvetz) ponder their uncertain future in *Cossacks in Exile* (1938).

In the denouement, the Satanist and the avenger are consumed in a fiery explosion after the villain has been chained to a rack and skinned alive (off screen).

A commercial success and Universal's biggest money-maker in 1934, *The Black Cat* should have launched Ulmer's career as a mainstream Hollywood director. Instead, within a year, Ulmer was unemployed. On the set, Ulmer, who had recently divorced his first wife, met and fell in love with nineteen-year-old apprentice script supervisor Shirley Kassler Alexander. As fate would have it, she was married to Max Alexander, the favourite nephew of Carl Laemmle Sr., founder and president of Universal Studios. When Kassler divorced Alexander and married Ulmer, the couple were barred from Universal, and Laemmle blacklisted Ulmer, who would not find work in Hollywood for almost a decade. After directing four low-budget westerns, including *Thunder over Texas* (1934), under the pseudonym John Warner, Ulmer moved to the east coast to find work. In 1935, he directed *From Nine to Nine,* a "quota quickie" thriller, produced in Canada for the British market.[59] The film was shot in Montreal in nine days, and the Ulmers' meagre earnings were exhausted after Shirley had to have an appendectomy. At this low point, according to Kassler's obituary, salvation came in the shape of "a crazy Ukrainian, Vasile Avramenko, who wanted to make a Ukrainian musical, and hired Ulmer, with a $50 advance to direct *Natalka Poltavka.*"[60]

Tipped off by a technician friend, Ulmer went to New York City and began his career as an ethnic filmmaker. On the set of *Natalka Poltavka,* the Ulmers met film distributor and aspiring producer Roman Rebush, who wanted to make Yiddish films. Although he did not speak the language, Ulmer would direct four Yiddish features during the next four years: *Green Fields* (1937), *The Singing Blacksmith* (1938), *The Light Ahead* (1939), and *American Matchmaker* (1940). The first two were big commercial hits in Europe and North America, and *Green Fields* won a Best Foreign Picture Award in Paris in 1938. Before returning to Hollywood in 1942, Ulmer would also direct *Cossacks in Exile* (1938) for Avramenko and *Moon over Harlem* (1939), an African American crime melodrama with musical numbers by jazz clarinetist Sidney Bechet, and he would make instructional films for the auto industry, the army, and the National Tuberculosis Association.

Once he was on the set of *Natalka Poltavka,* Ulmer put together a film crew, helped Avramenko and his staff to rewrite the screenplay, and designed the village set with Fedor Braznyk (Braznick), an Orthodox Church painter and a proprietor of a costume rental agency who was one of Avramenko's closest friends. The set itself was located on a farm northwest of Trenton, New Jersey, roughly halfway between Lambertville and Flemington. Free of telephone poles and blessed with gorgeous landscapes, the farm and several buildings had been rented for sixty dollars a week from Tymofei and Evfrozyna Jaremenko, who also sold fresh food and milk to the performers and crew.[61] When it came time to construct the set, a small army of carpenters and one old man who knew how to cut traditional Ukrainian thatched roofs appeared at the site and completed the necessary work in several days. Then, to make the set more realistic, every Ukrainian who owned a farm in the vicinity contributed a few animals free of charge. "It was all for the effort," an incredulous Ulmer remarked, decades later, in an interview with Peter Bogdanovich.[62]

Most of the location filming and all of the musical recording took place in September. The musical score, consisting of thirty-three choral and eight dance numbers, was recorded on 2 September at Reeves Sound Studio in New York City. "It was something I thought I'd never live through," Ulmer recalled. "The mainstays of the Ukrainian clubs had to be there, we couldn't do anything without an audience, because they had to put up the money. The two hundred sponsors were there who arrived with kit and kaboodle.... When a number was played, these people went into ecstasy. It took me hours to get them still again.... They now felt that a miracle was happening. Their art was back. I have never been in such a group—never, not in Germany, not in Italy, France—never." Nor did the location shooting get under way smoothly. According to Ulmer, Bulgakov behaved as if he was Cecil B. DeMille, Frank Capra, and Gregory La Cava rolled into one, and this angered the crew and the Ukrainian investors. When the rushes of the first two days of shooting failed to meet expectations, Avramenko and company asked Ulmer to take over as the film's director. Bulgakov was fired, and he was not mentioned in the final credits. When Ulmer's rushes were screened after the fourth day of shooting, 100 spectators "went into absolute delirium.... I couldn't get out of the projection room because everyone was kissing me and carrying on." Even if we allow for Ulmer's tendency to embellish, there is no doubt that Avramenko and his associates were very pleased with the new director.

Working with the Ukrainians also turned out to be a memorable experience for Ulmer, who spoke German and English but no Ukrainian or Russian. His recollections about the film's big dance scenes indicate that this was a job unlike any other. All week he had been worried that it would be impossible to stage and film the dance scenes:

> Then on Sunday night when I came back to the farm, there were cars with license plates from all over America and Canada. ... It was one of those things I couldn't believe. Visualize—I went on the set and there were 200 boys and girls in the most magnificent costumes and this

> guy, Avramenko, stood with a whip. … That was the way he gave them the rhythm. We had magnificent results with all these crazy things. Of course, I had to cut the picture myself. When they saw the first reel cut together they were screaming "Bravo!" Unbelievable. ... The picture had one thing which I could never recapture again—the enthusiasm of that mad bunch. It showed on the screen.

Nor would Ulmer forget Avramenko: "Nothing was impossible for Avramenko. … The man was so enthusiastic. I couldn't say no to him. … He was the spark of everything."[63]

Filming wrapped up on 3 October 1936, and for the next two months the film was edited and the musical score synchronized with the action sequences. Without any financial records, it is not clear just how much it cost to produce the final product. Ulmer seemed to think that *Natalka Poltavka* had been produced on a budget of $18,000. By December, Avramenko was issuing press releases stating that *Natalka Poltavka* had cost $30,000 to produce, and he was writing to friends and acquaintances that he now had debts totalling $40,000. However, he was still convinced that the film would gross at least $100,000 at the box office, thereby providing the shareholders with a return on their investments and helping him to settle his debts. Everything would depend on the reviews and distribution.[64]

Natalka Poltavka had its world premiere in New York City on 25 December 1936 at the Venezia Theater on 7th Avenue. Although there was trouble with the projector and the sound system failed, the special screenings on that day were attended by Ukrainian Orthodox Church dignitaries and overflow crowds. Indeed, as many as 7,000 spectators, many of them non-Ukrainians, might have attended the film during its one-day premiere.[65]

Like all operettas, *Natalka Poltavka* (also released as *The Girl from Poltava*) had a threadbare plot. Natalka, the young heroine, and her sweetheart Petro, a poor orphan raised by her parents, vow to remain faithful to each other after Natalka's father, who disapproves of the match, orders Petro to leave the village. During the next two years, while Petro wanders from village to village looking for work as an agrarian labourer, Natalka and her mother move to another village to stave off poverty after the father's death. When Petro, who still loves Natalka, spurns the amorous advances of a wealthy landowner's daughter and finds himself out of work once again, he decides to return home. In the meantime, moved by pity for her poor, aging mother, Natalka reluctantly accepts a marriage proposal from Vozny, an aging and corrupt but wealthy county clerk. On the day of Natalka's betrothal, Petro and his new friend Mykola meet Vozny and his best man, Vyborny, an inebriated village councillor. From the ensuing conversation, Petro concludes that Vozny's betrothed is none other than his Natalka. On the day of the wedding, Mykola mixes with the wedding guests and manages to inform Natalka that Petro is in the village. Convinced that Natalka still loves Petro, Mykola runs to give his friend the good news. Just as her mother is about to bless Natalka's marriage to Vozny, Petro begins to sing in the distance, and Natalka rushes out to meet him. When the guests learn why Natalka has fled, a mob led by the jilted groom pursues the fleeing lovers. Apprehended in each other's arms, Petro is threatened by the mob while Vozny vows to have Natalka imprisoned for breach of promise. But her determination to marry no one but Petro, and his readiness to sacrifice his own happiness and all of his earnings for her safety, ultimately persuade Vozny to give Natalka her freedom. As the film ends, the new happy couple and a cheering crowd return to the village, where Natalka and Petro are married.[66]

Only days before Avramenko's film premiered a Soviet Ukrainian version of *Natalka Poltavka,* directed by Ivan Kavaleridze and produced in Kyiv, was rushed to the United States by Amkino, the American distributor of Soviet films, and booked for an extended run at the Roosevelt Theater. The first Ukrainian operetta to be filmed in the Soviet Union, it had been produced to dispel the impression that Ukrainian immigrants in the United States could make the kind of film that the Soviet film industry had failed to produce. Although the film featured superb male and female soloists, its musical score was pedestrian, it lacked action, and having been shot in a studio it failed to take advantage of the beautiful countryside around Poltava.[67] Nevertheless, its presence in the United States confused potential customers, complicated efforts to screen and distribute the film produced by Avramenko, and did nothing to encourage people who saw it to take another chance on a Ukrainian operetta.

When Avramenko's *Natalka Poltavka* finally opened for an extended run at the Belmont Theater, 125 West 48th Street, on 13 February 1937, the reviews in *Variety* and the *New York Times* were quite encouraging. They declared the American-made version, directed by Ulmer, superior on all counts to the Soviet version directed by Kavaleridze. According to *Variety,*

> this is the second version of "Natalka Poltavka" … to reach New York. … The [first] was billed as an Amkino production and Russian-made [sic].… The latter version, which is American-made … and listed as an Avramenko Film Production, is head and shoulders above the other feature.… This American-produced picture has even tempo, a nice mixture of humour with the more serious moments, and above

> all—action. And it boasts marvellous voices. Besides all this, it has been given nice backgrounding. [The] scripting team … performed a bang-up job of sustaining interest without deviating too much from the central idea. … Avramenko, Gann and E.G. Ulmer were responsible for the swift directorial pace maintained. With some skilful editing … this production may find a following in arty houses, and is certain in the foreign languages.[68]

The *New York Times* reported that *Natalka Poltavka* "is a sure fire success on the operatic stage wherever there live enough Ukrainians to make an audience. And it must be noted that in the case of the amusing and entertaining near operetta now at the Belmont Theatre, the made-in-America product is more enjoyable than the imported [Soviet] article. This is due to the fact that it contains more funny incidents and is photographed much better than the 'Natalka Poltavka' shown at the Roosevelt Theatre."[69] Reviewers also commended the film for its "simple and engaging melodies," its "considerable pastoral scenery," and its comedic sequences. Negative criticism was confined to observations that "Thalia Sabanieeva sings, rather than looks the role of Natalka," as the *New York American* politely observed, and to "the exaggerated gestures and emotions" that characterized stage actors who had never performed in front of a camera.[70]

In the following months, as *Natalka Poltavka* premiered in a number of North American cities, reviews continued to be encouraging, and the film generated considerable public interest. Mrs. Bracken, wife of Manitoba premier John Bracken, attended the film's Canadian premiere at Winnipeg's Orpheum Theatre on 4 March 1937. The province's first lady participated in the opening ceremonies and commented briefly on the contributions made by Ukrainian immigrants to farming and culture in Canada. During the next three days, 8,000 to 10,000 people saw the film even though admission prices, which ranged from twenty-five to seventy-five cents, were higher than for most first-run feature films.[71] The *Winnipeg Free Press* remarked that "nostalgia … gripped at the throats of many as this simple little operetta of peasant life unfolded against an authentic background of humble thatched farm homes, rolling hills and waving fields of grain." All of the lead actors "were in splendid voice and their singing left nothing to be desired. … For the rest, 'The Girl From Poltava' is enriched by sweet and stirring songs of the Ukraine. The story is slow and strained at times, but the music lacks for nothing. Sweet, rich voices, blended in full chorus, offer a variety of sad songs, of happy ones, of stirring Cossack ballads that interpret more effectively than mere dialogue, the nature and philosophy of the race."[72]

After a successful two-week run at Chicago's Sonotone Theater in mid-March, the film moved to Toronto on 29 March 1937 for a one-week run at the Madison Theatre on Bloor and Bathurst. There the city controller, William Wadsworth, and Nancy Pyper, director of the Hart House Theatre, attended the premiere. Augustus Bridle, *Toronto Daily Star* arts critic, described *Natalka Poltavka* as a "splendid music-fest" and concluded that "musically this was one of the best film productions of the year. The choruses have the brilliance, depth and sonority of the best Russian choirs heard here. The orchestral support is never overdone. Sabanieva of the 'Met' is ... a lovely clear-toned soprano who knows how to act. Vodiany ... plays Vozny, as side-splitting comedy."[73] The *Toronto Evening Telegram* published four stills from the film and a much lengthier review. The film, its reviewer insisted, was "a brilliant example of what may be done with comparatively limited resources when inspired artists with one great purpose to draw them together join forces under an indomitable leader." Not only was the singing magnificent, but the film also succeeded on all levels: "Comic episodes are freely interspersed throughout the piece. Quite apart from the melodious music, which includes the playing of the ancient leerna, by an old ballad singer, the graceful vivacity of the dancing, the lively series of incidents, the picture has authentic charm. The photography is most artistic and the scenes of village and pastoral life are especially lovely."[74]

Only in Los Angeles, where the film opened on 28 May 1937, did it receive a chilly reception, though once again the musical score, singing, and exotic costumes assuaged critics. The *Los Angeles Daily News* commented that

> it was very pleasant to close one's eyes, forget about Natalka, and simply listen to the rich voices and fine recording. The direction is very slow. Too much time is spent building up the old Ukrainian atmosphere. ... Consequently the effect is that of a series of lovely photographs rather than cinematic cohesion. ... Close adherence to detail in costume, background and peasant types gives the picture interest which it cannot, or does not, obtain from the story. If less importance had been attached to keeping the script as like the original as possible, better screen results could have been achieved. But the music makes up for everything, as do isolated bits of native dances and ceremonies.[75]

Reviews of *Natalka Poltavka* in the Ukrainian press on both sides of the border were also good. The mere fact that Avramenko had managed to produce a Ukrainian motion picture with a fine musical score and excellent voices was enough to satisfy most reviewers. The film's positive reception in the

English-language press was a bonus and a source of pride for many Ukrainians in the United States and Canada. Nevertheless, the film did not meet with universal approval. Immediately after its release, the American daily *Svoboda* published several letters and articles critical of the innovations introduced into the screenplay, especially tavern scenes and peasant drunkenness.[76] Anatol Demo-Dovhopilsky repeated similar criticism on the pages of the American *Natsionalist* and the Canadian *Novyi shliakh*. Rather than presenting Ukrainian men as easily manipulated drunkards and Ukrainian women as submissive victims, the producers should have "read between the lines" of Kotliarevsky's play and drawn attention to the enserfment of the Ukrainian peasantry and the destruction of Ukrainian political liberties by the Russians. Dovhopilsky also maintained that the ensemble dances were poorly choreographed, Avramenko's solo dances were monotonous, the acting of Sabanieva and Creona was stiff and unnatural, and the otherwise fine cinematography had been vitiated by shots of bovine udders while Natalka sang one of her sorrowful laments. Ukrainians, Dovhopilsky concluded, should be ashamed that an uneducated, uncultivated, and ignorant man such as Avramenko had been allowed to misrepresent them and their culture. In the future, his energy would have to be channelled by men of culture, intellect, and discernment.[77]

The longest and most devastating critique of the film, penned by Alexander Koshetz, was published in *Svoboda* in mid-April. Although Koshetz realized that the original stage version of *Natalka Poltavka* moved too slowly and was rather monotonous by the standards of modern motion pictures, he argued that the screen adaptation was seriously flawed. Instead of adapting the stage version to the cinema, the film's screenwriters and producers had mutilated it, cutting several scenes and much of the original dialogue and replacing them with characters, dialogue, and scenes of their own invention. Particularly offensive and tasteless, in Koshetz's opinion, was the transformation of a serious dramatic work, which blended social commentary with subtle humour, into a slapstick comedy, a burlesque of Ukrainian peasant life. Many of the central characters had been transformed into vulgar, filthy, unkempt, often drunken buffoons, simply to get cheap laughs. As a result, the final product was not the deeply humanistic work created by Kotliarevsky but a vulgar, anachronistic parody of the Ukrainian village. Koshetz was especially offended by a lengthy tavern scene, which featured an out-of-place American-style bar and cabaret songs, and by the Chaplinesque chase sequences. The film, he maintained, had resurrected all of the stereotypes popularized by "Little Russian" playwrights who made a career out of mocking Ukrainians. Similarly, though he had high praise for Constantine Shvedoff's musical score,

Koshetz maintained that it lacked an authentic Ukrainian flavour. In particular, orchestra conductor Joshua Fishberg did not understand the national nuances in many of the melodies. Koshetz took further exception to the use of a melody traditionally associated with the mighty Dnieper River as background for scenes set on the shallow Vorskla River; he thought it inappropriate that the dance scenes featured symphonic arrangements of folk music; and he insisted that some of the songs added to the score and performed by Natalka were absolutely contrary to the psyche of a Ukrainian peasant girl. Careless set decoration likewise infuriated Koshetz. The village church had an inappropriate Russian-style onion dome; miniature windmills were out of place in Poltava province; Natalka's peasant house was tiny in outside shots but large enough to hold fifty wedding guests and a performing dance ensemble in interior shots! The costuming, too, was inappropriate. Peasant girls such as Natalka did not wear corsets, elaborately embroidered white blouses, or lacquered shoes that looked as if they had been purchased on 5th Avenue; farm labourers and vagabonds such as Petro and Mykola did not wander about the countryside in spotless white shirts; and women did not work in the fields in their Sunday skirts. Accusing the film's screenwriters and directors of arrogance and illiteracy, Koshetz concluded that this was not the way to introduce foreigners to Ukrainian culture or attract American-born Ukrainian youth back into the community. Young people would not acquire respect for their heritage if exposed to movies such as *Natalka Poltavka*—they would avoid the Ukrainian community altogether.[78]

It was no coincidence that the review appeared in *Svoboda*. By 1937, the most influential Ukrainian daily in North America and its editor, Dr. Luka Myshuga, had been feuding with Avramenko for almost four years. While Avramenko had routinely accused the paper of torpedoing his initiatives and killing "great Ukrainian projects," Myshuga had brought Avramenko's financial and public relations indiscretions to the attention of his wife, Pauline.[79] Already convinced that Myshuga and his associates at *Svoboda* had contributed to the failure of his marriage, Avramenko reacted to the Koshetz review in a manner that shocked even those who were accustomed to his erratic behaviour. First he fired off a letter accusing *Svoboda* of publishing "dishonest reviews" and stating that neither the daily nor its parent body, the Ukrainian National Association, had any right to criticize his film because they had not invested a single penny in its production and had refused to publish positive reviews. Then he took aim at Koshetz in a letter that amounted to little more than a personal attack on his critic. Koshetz, who had refused to participate in the film unless he was paid up front and who knew nothing about filmmaking, was not a credible critic, according to Avramenko. What right had a man such as Koshetz—whom Avramenko accused of subscribing to Russian monarchist newspapers, using Russian in his own home, and even scratching the Ukrainian trident off photographs—to criticize the film for its "Russian" and "Little Russian" qualities? If there were shortcomings in the film, then they were because Koshetz, who placed money above everything, had refused to work with Avramenko, who had sacrificed everything for the Ukrainian cause. Why, Avramenko wanted to know, had Koshetz failed to publish a critique of the "Bolshevik" *Natalka Poltavka*? He concluded by challenging Koshetz and his educated advisors to produce a film of their own: "Then I will acknowledge that you are a hero, Ukrainian history will record your name in golden letters, and I will bow my head before you!" While Myshuga opposed publication of the letter, Koshetz insisted that it be reproduced as received because "it reflects Avramenko's personality so faithfully and so exceptionally well." Koshetz even announced that the original would be deposited at the Ukrainian Museum in Prague, where documents chronicling his career were on display.[80]

Koshetz's review and Avramenko's rebuttal generated a flurry of correspondence in the Ukrainian press and among Ukrainian community activists. While representatives of Avramenko Film Production Incorporated accused Koshetz of trying to destroy a corporation that had made great sacrifices to produce a Ukrainian film, Koshetz tried to explain that criticism was a vital function in every civilized society, absolutely necessary if the arts were to survive and thrive. One need not fear negative criticism, he insisted; rather, one had to fear the triumph of a climate of opinion in which criticism was not tolerated.[81] Only one article generated by the controversy addressed the criticisms made by Koshetz. In a letter published by the Detroit weekly *Ukrainska zoria* (Ukrainian Star) in mid-May, Michael J. Gann reminded Koshetz that the sentimental *Natalka Poltavka* had to be enlivened with a few realistic and comedic scenes. For that reason, scenes featuring Natalka's father, a tavern, and a mob pursuing Petro were introduced. Gann also pointed out that the movie was not a morality play for school children. It was a movie for adults, and they knew that peasant life was full of taverns, drunks, pigs, chickens, fights, and even bloody *samosudy* (vigilante justice) in the course of which peasant mobs brutally executed those who had violated village norms. The film set, Gann added, had been based on pictures and photographs of Ukrainian villages published in a variety of books. And the film's musical director had been given the freedom to use melodies as he saw fit: the melody traditionally associated with the Dnieper River had been used as background music for evening scenes on the Vorskla River because it had been composed as a nocturne. Finally, contrary to suggestions that Fishberg's work as orchestra conductor had been insensitive to national nuances, Gann revealed that the orchestra had been conducted by Shvedoff.[82]

Significantly, no other Ukrainian newspaper in North America printed Gann's open letter to Koshetz. Ukrainian nationalist mythology venerated the Ukrainian peasant as the embodiment of moral and national virtue, and any discussion of his vices was out of the question. Editors might also have been intimidated by the fact that Koshetz did not conceal his anger at a Ukrainian newspaper that allowed a Russian Jew such as Gann to instruct him on Ukrainian art and the proper depiction of Ukrainian peasants in motion pictures. The undercurrent of anti-Semitism revealed in this episode would continue to have repercussions for the reception of *Natalka Poltavka* and Avramenko's next feature film.[83]

From the outset, the major problem faced by *Natalka Poltavka* and the reason that it failed to make money for its producers and investors was distribution rather than bad reviews. By the 1930s, the Hollywood studio system was firmly in place, and distributing an independently produced motion picture was a daunting proposition. The Big Five (Paramount, Fox, MGM, Warner Brothers, RKO) and the Little Three (Universal, Columbia, United Artists) studios produced 500 feature films annually and released at least 400 prints of each simultaneously. Moreover, the Big Five had their own film exchanges and theatre chains that did not accept motion pictures produced by anyone outside the eight major studios. Although the studios controlled only 15 percent of the theatres, they were the finest downtown venues with over 30 percent of all theatre seats and from 50 to 75 percent of total box office revenues.[84]

Independent film producers such as Avramenko Film Production Incorporated had only two options when it came to distribution. They could sell exclusive rights to distribute a film (in a given territory during a specified time period) for a flat fee or a fee and a percentage of the gross gate. If an individual buyer or a film exchange could be found, this was the most economical method of distribution. Or they could take the film on the road, renting it to theatre owners on a percentage basis or renting theatres for a specified number of days at a flat fee and then keeping all of the box office revenues.[85] Although Roman Rebush, the Jewish-American film distributor who had helped to organize Amkino in 1926 before striking out on his own as the proprietor of Kinotrade in 1932, was briefly involved in the distribution of *Natalka Poltavka,*[86] it appears that Avramenko and his associates relied predominantly on the second method, travelling from city to city and trying to cut deals with individual theatre owners. Since flat theatre rental fees were often prohibitively expensive in the United States and Canadian urban centres such as Toronto and Montreal, Avramenko tried to find theatre owners prepared to screen the film on a percentage basis. There were few of them, and when they could be found their theatres were usually located in the seediest part of town. In Montreal, Avramenko's associate Mykola Novak managed to book a theatre for only two midnight screenings.[87] In Winnipeg, on the other hand, he was able to rent the downtown Orpheum Theatre for three days for a mere $300, reaping a net profit of almost $3,000.[88] It appears that Avramenko's focus on urban theatres that could screen 35 mm prints of *Natalka Poltavka* also cost Avramenko dearly. Had he dispatched a few associates with 16 mm prints to all the small towns with Ukrainian church halls and National Homes, he could have increased revenues substantially.[89]

Ultimately, there were too few Ukrainians in North America, and they were so widely dispersed, that it was impossible to make a profit with any Ukrainian feature film, much less sustain a motion picture industry. In the mid-1930s, there were about 300,000 people of Ukrainian origin in Canada and up to 1 million in the United States. While Ukrainians in the United States were concentrated in the urbanized Northeast, they tended to be more assimilated and less fluent in the Ukrainian language than their Canadian counterparts. Ukrainians in Canada lived in relatively remote and inaccessible rural prairie districts, and a minority were scattered right across the country. Taking a Ukrainian film on the road could be a very expensive proposition, especially in Canada or the American Midwest, where great distances threatened to swallow all of the box office receipts. In sharp contrast, the Yiddish film industry had a solid base in America. By the 1930s, there were almost 5 million Jews in the United States, over 80 percent had emigrated from eastern Europe, and almost 60 percent, or about 2.5 million, were concentrated in New York City and its environs. *Yidl with a Fiddle,* which had its North American premiere in New York City on 31 December 1936, exactly six days after *Natalka Poltavka,* enjoyed a six-week exclusive engagement at the Ambassador Theater in the heart of the Broadway theatre district. It was then screened simultaneously in three New York City neighbourhood theatres and in other major urban centres throughout the spring of 1937. Several months later *Green Fields,* produced by Rebush and directed by Ulmer on the same farm as *Natalka Poltavka,* had an eight-week run at the Squire Theater west of Times Square. At its conclusion, it was picked up by the Loews-MGM chain and distributed as the B feature on a bill with *Second Honeymoon,* a screwball comedy starring Tyrone Power and Loretta Young.[90] Exposure and distribution on this scale were simply inconceivable for a Ukrainian-language film, which could hope at best to attract a few thousand spectators in a handful of North American urban centres and small audiences in widely dispersed Canadian rural and frontier communities.

When it became apparent that *Natalka Poltavka* would not make enough money to reimburse its investors and creditors, Avramenko Film Production Incorporated began to implode. Several weeks before Koshetz published his controversial review, an Avramenko Film Production board meeting in New York City had degenerated into a wild melee when the auditing committee refused to accept Avramenko's receipts for advertisements on Jewish radio programs and meals with individuals who had helped to arrange screenings.[91] Although Avramenko and the board appear to have resolved or at least buried their differences after the review was published, by the summer they were at each other's throats once again. Apparently, Avramenko had failed to make any payments for the exclusive rights to screen *Natalka Poltavka* in thirty-six American states that had been sold to him for $10,000 earlier that year.[92] And, after signing a declaration stating that he would raise money for the corporation, he told people that the corporation would soon be bankrupt and discouraged further donations.[93] By this point, Avramenko had decided to break with the corporation and to produce his next feature film, *Cossacks in Exile,* in Canada, where his credibility was still relatively unscathed and where support for *Natalka Poltavka* had been most encouraging.

Cossacks in Exile

On 22 September 1937, almost ten years to the day after he launched his ambitious if ill-fated tour of the prairie provinces, Avramenko returned to Winnipeg. The city's Ukrainians had turned out in droves to see *Natalka Poltavka,* local weeklies had published rebuttals to Dovhopilsky's critique of the film, and members of the Ukrainian Orthodox youth organization SUMK in nearby Tyndall had staged a demonstration condemning such criticism as "the work of Judas" and proclaiming their pride in Avramenko's legacy.[94] In Gimli, sixty miles north of Winnipeg, a SUMK branch organized by Hryhorii Tyzhuk several years earlier, had even named Avramenko its patron.[95] Surely he would find support and encouragement here in his hour of need.

Displaying the energy and determination that set him apart from all of his contemporaries, Avramenko immediately visited every Ukrainian parish and community organization in the city delivering lectures on the significance of the Ukrainian film industry and the film that he now proposed to produce. At all of these public appearances, he exercised that elemental and frightening "demonic power over the common people" noted by a perceptive observer years earlier.[96] The Ukrainian film industry, Avramenko assured his audiences, was vital for the national salvation of the younger generation, and it would serve as a powerful weapon for the propagation of Ukrainian culture before the nations of the world. Ukrainians in North America had to produce several films every year to prevent Soviet filmmakers from demoralizing the population and earning a great deal of money in the bargain. Ukrainian Americans had done their bit by financing *Natalka Poltavka,* and now it was time for Ukrainian Canadians to finance *Cossacks in Exile.* If the public came to his aid with loans and donations totalling $100,000, then a second Ukrainian motion picture could be ready for distribution by the summer of 1938.[97] Simultaneously, in order to drum up more publicity and stimulate some cash flow, Avramenko called meetings of all former dance pupils and their parents and announced plans to launch courses taught by his handpicked instructors.

Within ten days, after private meetings with prominent and influential Ukrainian community leaders, the formation of a Supporters' Committee of Avramenko Film Production was announced.[98] At this point, the committee, which included several municipal politicians, two dentists, a notary public, and a journalist, hoped to finance the film by soliciting donations and loans, though it was intimated that a company with a dominion charter and the right to sell shares might also be established. By year's end, at least twenty-seven Supporters' Committees had been established all across western Canada, from Kenora, Ontario, to Lulu Island, British Columbia, though most of them were in Manitoba. Formation of the committee in Kenora on 11 October provided a major impetus for fundraising when Ukrainian residents of the small town, led by local merchants Peter Ratuski and Sam Hancharyk, who had attended Avramenko's dance classes eleven years earlier, donated and pledged $3,300.[99] A week later, at a special tea reception to drum up support for the project in Winnipeg, Avramenko introduced Ratuski and Hancharyk and then browbeat those in attendance into pledging $2,000.[100] When yet another reception honouring Avramenko and promoting the film was held at the Canadian Ukrainian Institute Prosvita hall on 28 October, J.W. Wilton, a local publisher, and J.T. Thorson, a prominent Canadian jurist and a member of Parliament for Selkirk, whose brother Charles ("Cartoon Charlie") worked as an animator for Disney and Warner Brothers, were seated at the head table.[101] Soon farmers such as Nykola Pasiechko of Domain, Manitoba, and widows such as Sofia Greshchuk of Saskatoon were pledging, loaning, and donating large sums for the production of *Cossacks in Exile.*[102]

Just as all the pieces seemed to be falling into place, Avramenko's plans went awry. In New York City, the directors of Avramenko Film Production

Incorporated announced the creation of the Ukrainian Film Corporation after concluding that Avramenko would never live up to his agreements and that he was actively working against the first corporation's interests. Ukrafilm, as the new corporation came to be called, retained the rights to *Natalka Poltavka,* announced that it had no ties with Avramenko, and revealed plans to produce *Marusia,* a feature film based on yet another nineteenth-century Ukrainian operetta. Leo Bulgakov would direct the film from a screenplay by Vladimir Kedrovsky and Andrii Kist, and the orchestral and choral music would be arranged and conducted by Roman Prydatkevych and Alexander Koshetz.[103] Winnipeg's Ukrainian community leaders, who had been unaware of just how acute the financial crisis and internal conflicts within Avramenko's first film company had been, were dismayed by these developments, and their discomfiture increased as details of Avramenko's business practices began to leak out of New York City. By mid-November, they had abandoned his sinking ship. *Ukrainskyi holos* and *Kanadyiskyi farmer,* two of the largest and most influential Ukrainian weeklies in Canada, expressed grave concerns about Avramenko's plans to raise $100,000 by means of personal loans and donations and then announced that they would not publish any appeals, advertisements, articles, or reports about efforts to finance and produce *Cossacks in Exile.* It was their policy, they insisted, not to publish such materials when they related to personal profit-making ventures.[104] The city's influential Ukrainian National Home Association also adopted a resolution declaring that it could not support Avramenko's efforts to finance the film with unsecured personal loans.[105] By this point, most prominent members of the city's Supporters' Committee had also resigned.

But Avramenko's luck had not run out. A fortuitous turn of events in New York City and popular enthusiasm at the grassroots level in Canada prolonged his career as a motion picture producer for at least another year. Inadvertently, Ukrafilm provided Avramenko with a great deal of free publicity when, immediately after its formation, the corporation finally sold rights to screen *Natalka Poltavka* in Ontario and the three prairie provinces. In countless mining centres, railway towns, and rural hamlets all across Canada, Ukrainian farmers and labourers had an opportunity to see a Ukrainian motion picture, often for the first time in their lives, and the man prominently identified in the credits as its "general production director" was none other than Vasile Avramenko. No less significantly, when Ukrafilm approached Alexander Koshetz to work on *Marusia,* he demanded that Michael Gann publish an apology in the Ukrainian press for having challenged the conductor's critique of *Natalka Poltavka* the previous spring.[106] Although Gann reluctantly complied, he realized that his days at Ukrafilm were numbered because the company was playing the nationalist card and promoting itself as more Ukrainian than Avrafilm, as the new entity came to be called. By late November, Gann had left Ukrafilm and agreed to work with Avramenko and his Canadian backers.[107] In the months that followed, Gann not only ran Avramenko's New York City office and helped to recruit talent for the production of *Cossacks in Exile* but also ensured that a crew of skilled cameramen, technicians, and makeup artists were available for the film through his contacts with Roman Rebush, Edgar G. Ulmer, and the newly formed Collective Film Producers Company.[108]

Meanwhile, in an effort to deflect criticism of Avramenko's fundraising methods and in the forlorn hope of imposing financial accountability on the entire project, the Avramenko Film Company Limited was formed in Winnipeg on 9 December 1937 by the remnants of the local Supporters' Committee. The company's board of directors consisted of Vasile Avramenko, president; Peter Ratuski, vice-president; Dr. Mykyta Mandryka, secretary-treasurer; Ladislaus Biberovich, manager; and Sam Hancharyk, director. Company offices were located in Mandryka's Winnipeg insurance agency at 502 Confederation Life Building, 457 Main Street. On 25 December 1937, at a special reception in the Ukrainian Reading Association Prosvita hall, J.T. Thorson, MP, who had agreed to act as the company's solicitor, presented Avramenko and the other directors with the company's dominion charter. According to that charter, the company could issue and sell 4,000 preferred shares at a nominal value of twenty-five dollars per share and 10,000 common shares without a nominal value. Holders of preferred shares would be entitled to an annual 5 percent dividend on their investments, and they would receive one common share for each two preferred shares purchased. Beyond that, preferred shares would not entitle holders to participate in company meetings or share in its profits. Holders of common shares, on the other hand, would not be entitled to an annual dividend, but they received the right to participate in company meetings and share in its profits (provided there were any). The charter also stipulated that Avramenko was to receive $4,500 in six equal monthly instalments "for moneys spent and obligations incurred by him" to that point, as well as up to 8,000 common shares as payment for the screenplay that he had written and the "experience and knowledge of the production of moving pictures" that he brought to the company. Mandryka and Biberovich were to receive 500 common shares each, and Ratuski and Hancharyk 100 each, as remuneration for their work on behalf of the company.[109] Thus, while Avramenko managed to secure control of the company and was in a position to reap most of its profits, he and his fellow directors would have nothing to show for their efforts if the film was not a success at the box office.

In the months that followed, Mandryka and Biberovich assumed most of the administrative burden, and Mandryka in particular became the responsible and reassuring public face of Avrafilm. A lawyer by training, Mandryka had been elected to the Ukrainian Central Rada in 1917 as a member of the Ukrainian Socialist Revolutionary Party. After serving with the UNR's diplomatic corps and lecturing at the Ukrainian Free University in Prague, he had immigrated to Winnipeg, where his efforts to rally liberal and democratic elements met with little enthusiasm among established groups of all political hues. Biberovich, the son of western Ukrainian stage actors, was a secondary school German-language instructor who had also immigrated to Canada in the 1920s and failed to find a permanent niche. By 1937, Mandryka was working as a notary public and insurance salesman, while Biberovich, who had worked briefly as a steamship agent, was trying to make a living as a Ukrainian journalist.[110] The incessant wrangling that characterized Ukrainian-Canadian public life had jaded both, and each was eager to participate in a project that would have some tangible and lasting results. This perspective prevented them from abandoning Avramenko and the people who had already invested in the project and encouraged them to make a stab at harnessing, controlling, and channelling the creative energies of the volatile dance master-turned-motion picture producer. To no one's surprise, both would come to regret their decision.

Fundraising, which included the sale of preferred shares, the negotiation of loans and donations, and efforts to sell provincial screening rights, began in earnest in January 1938. While Mandryka manned the fort in Winnipeg and Gann took care of business in New York City, Avramenko and Biberovich were sent out into the field to raise money. At first, their efforts bore little fruit because Avramenko was anxious to get back to New York City, and Biberovich wasted several weeks in futile pursuit of the wealthy Ukrainian-American philanthropist Jacob Makohin.[111] Mandryka, in turn, had trouble selling shares in Winnipeg because the CNR and CPR, which employed many Ukrainian men, began laying off workers.[112] Six itinerant agitators and salesmen were also engaged to sell shares in western Canada, but it seems that their travel expenses consumed most if not all of the funds that they managed to raise. Paul Yavorsky, the young SUMK organizer who had been hired during the winter, drove Mandryka to distraction with his antics. Having raised a grand total of $165 in Winnipeg, The Pas, and Edmonton, Yavorsky announced his intention to travel to Vancouver and Hollywood. Mandryka vetoed these plans, complaining that Yavorsky simply did not have the qualities required for fundraising. He proposed to use Yavorsky as a dance instructor in Winnipeg, northern Ontario, or Montreal, but his suggestion was ignored, and Yavorsky continued to travel all over Canada with meagre results until the fall, when, after a brief interlude in the New York City office and as an extra on the set, he was finally assigned to teach dancing in Edmonton.[113] His colleagues were not much more successful. Bazaars and raffles, as well as dance courses in Winnipeg and its environs, generated some publicity but, as a rule, little money. Avrafilm's *Vistnyk* (Herald), a twenty-four-page bulletin published in 5,000 copies in January, April, and August because most Ukrainian weeklies refused to publish the company's publicity articles and advertisements, also showed large deficits.[114]

Efforts to sell provincial screening rights proved to be more difficult than anticipated because Ukrafilm agents consistently offered lower prices for the rights to *Marusia* and incessantly agitated against Avrafilm. The rights to screen *Cossacks in Exile* in Manitoba were sold for $6,000 in January to a consortium consisting of two carpenters, a shoemaker, a labourer, and a farmer.[115] As competition between Ukrafilm and Avrafilm became more intense during the ensuing months, the Alberta rights were sold in July for a mere $3,500, while the British Columbia and Saskatchewan rights were sold in November for $800 and $4,000 respectively.[116] In the meantime, directors Ratuski and Hancharyk borrowed $6,000 and advanced the sum to the company on the condition that they would be reimbursed once the Ontario screening rights were sold.[117] Avrafilm also tried to sell the Canadian rights to an English-language version of the film to be dubbed after release of the Ukrainian print. In May, a Vegreville, Alberta, theatre owner expressed interest in purchasing these rights for $75,000, including $25,000 down, but local lawyers advised him to wait until the film was ready and he had obtained guarantees that it would be dubbed into English. A three-man delegation, led by Peter Ratuski, was dispatched to Alberta to negotiate with the theatre owner but returned home only with large expense claims.[118]

It was therefore up to Avramenko to generate the cash flow required by the company. Appealing unabashedly to patriotic Ukrainian sentiment, denouncing communism, pandering to popular prejudices, enticing prospective investors with pipe dreams, and resorting to outright intimidation, he got the job done. In leaflets, bulletins, and above all speeches, some of them three or four hours long, Avramenko announced that the production of *Cossacks in Exile* was a "great Ukrainian cause," a "miracle" that would bring glory to the Ukrainian people. It would help to build a Ukrainian studio in Hollywood where Ukrainian actors, directors, cinematographers, and technicians could be trained, thereby laying the foundations for a national film industry when Ukraine gained independence. Every sincere Ukrainian, Avramenko declared, was obliged to support the project morally and financially. If appeals to nationalism proved to be insufficient, Avramenko did not shrink from invoking baser instincts. Speaking before a group of militant émigré war veterans in Kenora, at a time when a minority in the Ukrainian community still harboured illusions about an alliance with Fascist Italy and Nazi Germany, Avramenko praised Mussolini and Hitler and encouraged the crowd to emulate their iron will and determination. An awe-struck veteran wrote to his superiors that after Avramenko's speech it was at last possible to talk about these "great men" and their achievements at Ukrainian public meetings in Kenora without being hissed off the podium.[119] Several days later, in Montreal, Avramenko told his listeners that Hollywood child singer Bobby Breen, star of several RKO musicals who earned thousands each week, was a Ukrainian boy from Regina discovered by Jewish talent agents who paid off his parents, spirited him off to Hollywood, and changed his name.[120] Although *Kanadyiskyi farmer* immediately exposed the story as an old canard—Bobby (Borsuk) Breen was a native of Toronto, the nephew of a rabbi, and had been discovered by Eddie Cantor—it is doubtful that the simple souls who fell for Avramenko's deception, and persuaded themselves that their children might become millionaires if there was a Ukrainian film industry to give them a leg up on the competition, were dissuaded from showering Avramenko with money. At the same time, he promised generous donors and investors that he would give them or their children parts as extras in the film, a ruse also exploited to encourage enrolment in dance courses offered in Winnipeg, Fort William, and Montreal in 1938.[121] By June, Avramenko had raised $21,000, of which almost half had gone to cover pre-production expenditures.[122]

Not surprisingly, his fundraising efforts generated controversy. After his whirlwind tour of Ontario in February 1938, there were reports that Avramenko was making too many personal attacks on Alexander Koshetz; questions were raised about the Supporters' Committees that never published their financial accounts; rumours circulated that money raised in Canada for *Cossacks in Exile* was being used to pay off old debts in the United States; and there were complaints that Avramenko shouted and screamed at anyone and everyone who challenged him.[123] Several months later a man who had failed to honour a pledge because he had fallen ill and lost his job complained that threats to publish his name in the press revealed a fundamental kinship between Avramenko and the Bolsheviks: both treated individual human beings and their needs with contempt and subordinated everything to the realization of grand utopian projects.[124] J.T. Thorson and Mandryka also questioned Avramenko's fundraising methods, though their concerns were practical rather than philosophical. Thorson was shocked to learn that Avramenko was focusing on loans and donations in Ontario and that the company was issuing contracts and trying to sell screening rights before the requisite number of shares had been sold. He likewise expressed unease about the company's unbalanced books on more than one occasion.[125]

Only Mandryka, at the centre of the company's activities, appreciated the full extent of Avramenko's machinations. When he wrote to Avramenko on 26 February 1938, he was beginning to grasp the problems that lay ahead:

> I received your agitated letter today. We really do not understand each other, and this is why: you think it is necessary, above all, to start producing the film with or without money, and you believe things will somehow turn out well. You live on high hopes and faith in an imminent miracle. That is how you made *Natalka*. However, not all dreams come true, and miracles rarely happen. You did manage to make *Natalka*—and that was certainly a miracle—but your hope that this miracle would make money and that you would be able to pay back your creditors did not materialize. And that is a terrible thing! That money belongs to the people. The same fate awaits *Cossacks in Exile* if financial matters are not managed correctly from the outset. You say that you have lost faith or confidence in me, but I have told you, and I am telling you again, quite frankly, that I did not have, do not have, and will never have any confidence in your business skills (and no one else has any confidence in them either). I only believe in your artistic talent and patriotism. But that is not enough to handle people's money wisely.

Mandryka, Biberovich, Ratuski, Hancharyk, and the others, he continued, would not allow Avramenko to borrow money and fail to return it. They wanted to put the project on a sound business footing. That was why a strong company had been established, and that meant raising money by selling shares. Mandryka also told Avramenko that "we are not working to vanquish our 'enemies,' we are working to accomplish our objective. The results of our work will give us victory over the enemy." If Avramenko found this unacceptable, then he was requested to dismiss Mandryka immediately.[126] Mandryka was retained, but Avramenko did not change his fundraising methods or fiscal proclivities. He neglected to submit financial reports, and he used money obtained for *Cossacks in Exile* to pay child support, settle debts with his father-in-law, and make loans to the Ukrainian Orthodox congregation in

Montreal. In May, he even used over $1,000 to purchase the South American and Far Eastern screening rights to *Natalka Poltavka* from rival Ukrafilm.[127]

When production of *Cossacks in Exile* finally got under way during the first week of May 1938, much of the preliminary work had already been completed. Avramenko had prepared a screenplay that was being revised and edited by Biberovich, now ensconced in the company's New York City office; Edgar G. Ulmer had been hired to direct the film and was scouting locations; and Antin Rudnytsky and Maria Sokil, two genuine Ukrainian stars, had signed contracts with Avrafilm. A pianist, conductor, and composer, Rudnytsky had studied at the Berlin Academy of Music with Arthur Schnabel and Franz Schreker, taught at the Conservatories of Music in Kharkiv and Kyiv, and worked as a conductor and musical director with the National Opera in Kyiv and the Lviv Municipal Opera before his thirty-second birthday. His wife, Maria Sokil, a lyric soprano, had been *prima donna* with opera companies in Kharkiv, Kyiv, and Lviv; performed as a guest artist in Moscow, Leningrad, Warsaw, Vienna, Prague, and Berlin; and emerged as the most popular singer on Ukrainian radio.[128] Almost immediately after the couple had arrived for a tour of North America in December 1937, Avramenko and Gann had contacted and invited them to participate in the film. By February 1938, Rudnytsky had come aboard as the film's musical director, and Sokil, who at thirty-six was considered too old for the lead role in *Marusia,* had agreed to sing and act the middle-aged female lead in *Cossacks in Exile.*[129] In late April, a week before auditions and rehearsals were scheduled to begin, Rudnytsky submitted the musical score, which he had arranged in railway wagons and hotel rooms between performances.[130]

While Sokil's and Rudnytsky's participation added to the film's prestige, generated publicity, and ultimately attracted spectators, it also imposed restrictions on the production process. Because both had European engagements in the late summer and fall and were initially scheduled to leave North America in late June, the film's production schedule had to accommodate their needs. In practical terms, this meant that Rudnytsky's musical score needed to be recorded prior to filming and that Sokil's scenes had to be shot first. This would not have been a problem on most sets, but *Cossacks in Exile* was a film produced by Avramenko, notoriously incapable of working according to a plan or timetable.

Rudnytsky and the film's directors conducted vocal auditions for *Cossacks in Exile* during the first week of May at the Steinway Piano Company hall in New York City. Almost 200 singers, including many veterans of the Ukrainian National Chorus, competed for lead roles and places in the chorus. When more than thirty women, including several matrons well past fifty, vied for the supporting role of Oksana, the film's young romantic heroine, rumours that all of the singers would be old men and women began to circulate and were gleefully fanned by rival Ukrafilm.[131] Ultimately, very capable singers with acting experience filled the major roles. Michael Shvetz, the veteran opera singer and actor who had one of the comic supporting roles in *Natalka Poltavka,* was selected to play the male lead opposite Maria Sokil. He was joined by Dmitri Creona and Vladimir Zelitsky, who likewise had appeared in *Natalka Poltavka;* Alexis Tcherkassky, a classically trained Russian singer (identified as a Ukrainian for publicity purposes) who had sung opposite Lily Pons; and Nicholas Karlash, a veteran of the Ukrainian National Chorus who had experience performing with a number of opera companies. The young romantic female supporting role that had provoked so much competition went to American teenager Helen Orlenko, primarily on the strength of her poster girl good looks and despite having long manicured fingernails that infuriated Avramenko.[132] Many of the small non-singing supporting roles, on the other hand, went to people, often Ukrainian Canadians, with absolutely no acting experience. They included General Vladimir Sikevitch, an aging veteran of the UNR army who looked but overacted the part of the Cossack commander Kalnyshevsky, and Avrafilm directors Mandryka and Hancharyk, who played a Russian military envoy and a mounted Cossack respectively.[133]

During the next few weeks, while Rudnytsky rehearsed with the soloists and choir for five to six hours every day, Dmitri Kornienko, a Kyiv-born NBC studio musician and leader of New York's popular Oriental Orchestra, assembled the musicians. Then, from 6 to 9 June, the singers and a twenty-three-man orchestra under Rudnytsky's direction recorded the film's vocal and orchestral soundtrack at the Film-Art Studios in the Bronx. Fifty-three vocal and orchestral numbers totalling more than ninety minutes were recorded at a cost of just over $3,000.[134] While all concerned were extremely pleased with the results, Avramenko and Rudnytsky found themselves in the middle of a bitter political controversy the moment they stepped out of the studio. Ukrainian newspapers in the United States and Canada had published an open letter from several Ukrainian musicians accusing Avramenko and Rudnytsky of favouring Russian and German musicians at the expense of Ukrainians. Few people realized that the letter had been written by Roman Prydatkevych, an employee of the rival Ukrafilm Corporation and the man who had arranged and conducted *Marusia*'s orchestral soundtrack.[135] Although Rudnytsky explained that there were very few classically trained professional Ukrainian musicians in New York, that four Ukrainians had played in his orchestra, and that musicians who knew Russian, German, or French had been requested because he spoke those languages, a month passed before the rebuttal was published.[136] In the meantime, the notion promoted by its rival, that Avrafilm was not a Ukrainian enterprise, received wide circulation, casting a cloud over the production just as it got started.

No doubt Avrafilm's close collaboration with Rebush, Ulmer, and Collective Film Producers fed rumours that the company and the motion picture that it was producing were not quite as "Ukrainian" as they should be. Ulmer had spent much of May scouring the countryside around New York City trying to find a secluded location where *The Singing Blacksmith,* a Yiddish feature, and *Cossacks in Exile* could be shot. When suitable spots were found in Westchester County, the local residents made it clear that they did not want Yiddish and Ukrainian pictures produced on their property. Just days before the recording sessions in the Bronx, Ulmer and his staff of two adolescents and four elderly Jews finally found an excellent setting with rolling terrain, patches of forest, grassland, wild flowers, and a small lake near Newton, New Jersey, about sixty miles northwest of New York City. The site belonged to the Little Flower Monastery run by German Catholic Benedictine monks who were more than happy to oblige the Yiddish and Ukrainian filmmakers. Overjoyed, Avrafilm and Collective Film Producers resolved to rent 800 acres and split the costs.[137] As New York newspapers, which published stories about Newton's "miniature" Hollywood, subsequently discovered, a nudist camp and property belonging to the pro-Nazi German-American Bund flanked the monastery. "There's Freedom in the Newton Hills—for Jewish and Ukrainian Actors, Monks, Nudists and Nazis," the *New York Mirror* would declare.[138]

Avrafilm's publicity releases and its bulletin made absolutely no mention of its close collaboration with a Jewish film company, a Jewish film workers' union, Jewish cameramen, and Jewish suppliers such as Ira Greene, who rented equipment to the Ukrainian company. Indeed, when the company published photographs of all the principals involved in the film and then distributed them to the Ukrainian press, Ulmer's photo was missing. As Biberovich explained, "for the moment we should not distribute Ulmer's [photograph] because his facial features are decidedly 'Semitic,' and this would only give rise to new attacks [on Avrafilm] and even more gossip."[139]

By early July, Biberovich had edited the screenplay, and Shirley Kassler-Ulmer was preparing a shooting script.[140] The set had been designed, and a Ukrainian village with thatched peasant homes, a domed church, a reading hall, windmills, wells, and storks' nests was being erected. A menagerie of domestic and barnyard animals had been obtained to add realism to the set, and costumes, wigs, and a variety of props were being readied. Young extras, mostly Ukrainian Canadians who had paid their own way to perform in the film, were also beginning to congregate in New York City. The largest contingent came from Winnipeg, where their departure had been chronicled in Ukrainian newspapers and in the *Winnipeg Free Press.*[141] Led by Ivan Tokaryk, who had been teaching dance classes in the city since the fall of 1937, the contingent included dance soloist William Yacyna, four male and eight female dancers, a chaperone, and a few others who had come along for the ride. After arriving aboard a Greyhound bus on 9 July, they were given a tour of New York City that included a visit to Radio City.[142]

Filming commenced on location at the Little Flower Monastery on 18 July 1938. During the ensuing nine days, all of the scenes featuring Maria Sokil, whose departure had already been postponed several times, were filmed. The entire cast and crew consisted of about 100 people and included twenty cameramen, technicians, wardrobe and makeup specialists, and about forty young dancers and extras from Canada. All were accommodated in Newton's two hotels and in several private homes. While the lead singers and actors had to be on the set at 6:30 a.m. for makeup, the actual filming took place between 9:00 a.m. and 5:30 p.m. Lunch, prepared by a small army of Ukrainian female volunteers, was served at noon in a common dining room, where teenaged dancers and extras from Canada sat next to and mingled with actors, cinematographers, directors, and producers. The weather was terrible during these nine days—incessant downpours and a storm that caused extensive damage in many parts of New Jersey—but there was nothing to do but shoot because Sokil and Rudnytsky had to board an ocean liner for Europe on 27 July.[143] In the end, some of the sets had to be reconstructed under a giant tent that had been erected as a precautionary measure, and several scenes were shot with the aid of artificial light. Thanks to the technical skill of Ulmer and his cameramen and electricians, when the rushes were screened it was impossible to tell that the scenes had not been shot outdoors in natural sunlight.

On the second day of filming, pandemonium broke out among members of the Winnipeg contingent when one of the female dancers from that city was awarded a walk-on speaking role by Avramenko and featured in several close-ups. The chaperone who had accompanied the dancers caused a scene and threatened to pack up and leave with her youthful charges. Within hours, Avrafilm's Winnipeg office was also expressing grave concern about Avramenko's decision. It appears that the young lady at the centre of the controversy had a reputation for her free and easy lifestyle. The film's backers were anxious that news of her prominence in the film might cause a scandal, discourage loans, and hurt box office returns when the film was screened in Winnipeg. When they urged Biberovich to reason with Avramenko, he replied that with Avramenko "sex appeal is stronger than reason."[144] When they subsequently told Avramenko that the scenes would have to be reshot or cut out of the film in Winnipeg, he shot back that he would "cut off something" from the anatomy of anyone who dared tamper with the film.[145] This resolved the issue, albeit not to everyone's satisfaction.

By 27 July, about half of the film, including all scenes featuring Maria Sokil and Michael Shvetz, had been shot. Because Avrafilm's cash reserves had been depleted by this point, filming was interrupted, and Avramenko was sent out on the road with the rushes to raise an additional $10,000. Proceeding directly from New York to Montreal, he managed to borrow $5,000 there during the first week of August.[146] He then travelled across northern Ontario to Winnipeg, making brief stops in Fort William, Sioux Lookout, and Kenora. When he tried to get another $3,000 out of Ratuski and Hancharyk, an infuriated Mandryka accused him of having the morals of a Hottentot and compared his behaviour around the two small-town merchants to that of a bear around honey.[147] After giving interviews to the Ukrainian press in Winnipeg, Avramenko made his way back to New York City via southern Ontario. Unable to raise any money in Sudbury and Sault Ste. Marie, he had about $8,000 by the time he reached Hamilton, where he raised another $2,000.[148] In Toronto, he negotiated with the prosperous proprietor of a bakery, though it appears that he had already earmarked these funds for future projects.[149] On 2 September, Avramenko was back in New York City with the $10,000 needed to complete shooting.

While he was away, wardrobe expert Fedor Braznyk had designed new costumes, actors whose scenes were yet to be filmed had gone into rehearsal, arrangements had been made to rent horses for military scenes, and construction of the Cossack Sich or stockade had been completed. Ulmer spent the hiatus working on *The Singing Blacksmith* while principal cameraman William Miller was under contract to Paramount during the last two weeks of August.[150] And the rumour mill continued to spin. On 6 August, Ukrafilm announced that the filming of *Marusia* had been completed and maliciously insinuated that *Cossacks in Exile* had collapsed as a result of Sokil's departure.[151] The rival company also suggested that, if the Avrafilm picture was ever released, it would be screened as a thirty-minute short.[152] Potential donors and investors gave credence to these rumours, causing great unease in Avrafilm offices in Winnipeg and New York City.

When shooting resumed on 12 September, Mandryka and Hancharyk—accompanied by their wives and several Avrafilm employees from

Winnipeg—were on the set. Also present was a second contingent of dancers and extras from Canada and the American east coast. The dancers included eight prominent members of SUMK as well as a large group from Passaic, New Jersey, led by Avramenko's associate Nick Arseny.[153] Once again the weather intervened, parts of the set were destroyed in a storm, and shooting dragged on. Interrupted for a week on 20 September, it resumed on 27 September and finally came to an end two days later. Because the dancers had been sent home on 21 September, ten Benedictine novices were recruited to fill in as extras. This time all of the scenes with dialogue were filmed, and only the burning of the Cossack stockade and images of the local countryside remained to be captured on celluloid.[154] The production unit now turned its attention to these details and to the preparation of English subtitles. The conflagration was finally filmed on 31 October, and Biberovich reported that the footage was excellent, though it would have been even better had not the Jewish cameramen retreated prematurely from the advancing flames.[155] Ulmer, Gann, and Biberovich also tried but failed to persuade Mandryka that some stock footage of landscapes and storms should be purchased and several "miniatures" built. Constructing and filming miniature sets of palaces and war fleets, Ulmer maintained, would provide the film with transitional sequences between scenes that appeared to be unconnected. Mandryka, beginning to panic because total expenditures had already exceeded the $50,000 mark, refused and suggested that these improvements could be made when and if an English-language version of the film was released.[156]

On 1 November 1938, Ulmer's *The Singing Blacksmith* opened to rave reviews at the Continental Theater on Broadway, where it continued to pack the house for four weeks before moving to neighbourhood theatres for another two or three months. Free to focus exclusively on cutting, editing, and synchronizing the final version of *Cossacks in Exile,* Ulmer, Gann, and film editor Jack Kemp worked feverishly to complete the job, often staying in the laboratories well past midnight. When the work was finally done on 27 November, Ulmer indicated that he was very happy with the final product, though he regretted that there had not been enough money to build and film the miniatures.[157] His cheerful mood faded when he saw the window cards that had been printed to advertise the movie and the libretto that would be distributed to all spectators. Twice during the fortnight after the movie's completion an agitated Ulmer stormed into Avrafilm's New York City office demanding that all of the window cards and librettos be taken down or destroyed because they violated his contract by identifying Avramenko as the "director" or "general production director" of *Cossacks in Exile.* "This will cost the company plenty of money," Ulmer threatened the last time he walked out on 9 December.[158] Clearly, he had failed to appreciate the size of Avramenko's ego or foresee the film's fate at the box office.

While Ulmer and his assistants prepared the film for release, Avramenko had gone out on the road once again to raise money, stage dance performances, and drum up pre-release publicity for the picture. Publicity was urgently needed because two other feature films were competing for Ukrainian audiences in North America. In July, Amkino had released Ivan Kavaleridze's *Zaporozhets za Dunaiem,* the Soviet Ukrainian version of the operetta on which *Cossacks in Exile* was based. Although reviews of the film were not good, the Soviet picture attracted substantial audiences in several rural communities.[159] More significantly, Ukrafilm's *Marusia* had premiered in Winnipeg on 29 October after a month-long marketing blitz that included radio advertisements, posters and placards on city buses, and the release of phonograph records featuring songs from the musical score. Several of the film's lead actors were Ukrainian Canadian, the dance soloist was Avramenko alumnus Meros Lechow of Winnipeg, and the Canadian premiere at the Orpheum had been attended by Premier John Bracken, Mayor John Queen, and Mrs. Tupper, wife of the lieutenant governor.[160] Fearing that audiences might not flock to a third Ukrainian feature film, Avramenko hit the road again in late October, travelling back and forth between Montreal, Edmonton, and Calgary at least twice during the next month. While he managed to stage several dance recitals that promoted the film's imminent release, he was unable to raise any money because people were unwilling to make loans or donations now that the film had been completed.[161] And his travel and hotel expenses ate up substantial sums of money at a time when the company had to deal with large film laboratory and equipment rental bills. "My God, my God, just think how many urgent debts we could settle with all the money he has wasted on travel recently," lamented a frustrated Biberovich in mid-November.[162]

Finally, on 1 December, after a two-day train journey from New York City, a relatively composed Biberovich arrived in Winnipeg clutching a 35 mm print of the film. Two days later *Cossacks in Exile* had its world premiere at Winnipeg's Orpheum Theatre on Fort Street before a sell-out crowd that included Lieutenant Governor W.J. Tupper, J.T. Thorson MP, Ukrainian Catholic bishop Basil Ladyka, and many other dignitaries. During the first day, almost 4,000 people saw the film.[163]

Cossacks in Exile was based on *Zaporozhets za Dunaiem,* an operetta by Semen Hulak-Artemovsky first staged in 1863. The story begins in 1775 amid rumours that the Russian empress Catherine II has decided to destroy the

Zaporozhian Sich, a stronghold on the Dnieper River and the last bastion of the freedom-loving Ukrainian Cossacks. The Cossack commander Kalnyshevsky orders his men to prepare for war with the Russians and sends a delegation to the empress in a last-ditch effort to prevent bloodshed. Meanwhile, in a village near the Sich, Oksana, the beautiful adopted daughter of the jovial and hen-pecked Ivan Karas and his wife, Odarka, is being pursued by Prokip, an older suitor, though her heart belongs to Andriy, a young Cossack. One day, as the villagers sing and perform a festive Easter dance, Andriy rushes in, announces that the Russian armies are invading, bids Oksana farewell, and leaves to defend the Sich. At the Sich, Kalnyshevsky and his officers receive the Russian empress's emissary, General Tekely. When the Cossacks refuse to surrender their liberties and join the Russian Army, Tekely orders his units, which have been waiting in ambush, to burn the Sich. Kalnyshevsky, the last Cossack commander, is seized and banished to a monastery on the Solovetsky Islands in the White Sea northwest of Arkhangelsk. As he leaves Ukraine, he recites a prayer for the freedom of his land and people. Their fortress destroyed, the Cossacks disperse. A large contingent, including Ivan, Odarka, Oksana, and Prokip, sail down the Dnieper, across the Black Sea, and into the Danube River delta. There they settle under the protection of the Turkish sultan, build villages just like those in their homeland, and resume their traditional way of life: Ivan carouses, Odarka quarrels and makes up with her husband, and both worry about Oksana, who pines for the missing Andriy and refuses Prokip's overtures. One day the sultan visits the Cossack villages, eager to see for himself how his former allies are adapting to life in his domains. Pretending to be a Turkish noble, he approaches Ivan's home, befriends the gregarious Ukrainian, and then sends a servant to escort him to his palace. At the palace, Ivan is dressed in the finery of a Turkish noble, taken on a tour of the harem, and questioned by his host. As they talk, Ivan tells his new friend that he would like an audience with the sultan to ask if the Cossacks might return to their native Ukraine. Still unaware of his new friend's identity, Ivan returns home at dawn and when confronted by Odarka teases her that he has become a Turk and is no longer a Cossack. In the meantime, the long-lost Andriy finally arrives, but his reunion with Oksana is brief. When the jealous Prokip sees the young lovers embracing, he tells the Turks that they are spies. After a struggle in which a Turk is killed, Andriy and Oksana are seized and taken to the scaffold for execution. Fortunately, as befits an operetta, the sultan and his guards arrive on horseback in the nick of time. Revealing that Oksana's father saved his life in battle years ago, the sultan pardons Oksana and Andriy and allows the homesick Cossacks to return to Ukraine. A brief celebration ensues, and then the Cossacks sail down the Danube toward the Black Sea and their native land.[164]

Like *Natalka Poltavka, Cossacks in Exile* received encouraging and generally positive reviews. In Winnipeg, where civic pride played a role, the critics were openly enthusiastic. "Compliments may sincerely be extended to the Avramenko Film Company … for the excellent production, *Cossacks in Exile*," declared the *Winnipeg Free Press*.

> It is a Ukrainian opera, filmed artistically with very attractive settings and with sound re-production which does full justice … to the voices of principals and chorus. … Romance is there, too, but this is subordinated to the general trend of the story, and comedy is so cleverly introduced that it forms one of the most pleasing features of the bright and entertaining narrative. This comedy is chiefly brought out by Maria Sokil, soprano, and M. Shvetz, playing opposite each other. … His magnificent voice sounds with remarkable clarity from the silver sheet and the singing of Maria Sokil is what one might expect from a vocalist who has come to be known as one of Europe's leading prima donnas.[165]

The *Winnipeg Evening Tribune* added that "the picture brims with good humour and good music, striking at times almost a Gilbert and Sullivan vein. Hollywood experts were wisely employed to handle the technical end. As a result, the photography is outstanding. … This is not the first Ukrainian film produced on this side of the Atlantic but the third. But this so sprightly, interesting and well-executed, shows finally that Ukrainian-language films as a means of cultural expression of the race [sic] have definitely 'arrived.'"[166]

During the next two months, the film was screened at least fifty times in more than forty prairie communities, though an extremely cold winter, particularly in Alberta, forced cancellations in many venues.[167] More than 2,700 saw the film in Saskatoon at the Daylight Theatre on 10 December.[168] Two members of the provincial cabinet attended the Edmonton premiere before a capacity crowd at the Dreamland Theatre on 22 December.[169] After the Edmonton screenings, USRL and SUMK activist Ivan Danylchuk wrote to Avramenko that the movie was magnificent, the actors performed like real professionals, the singing was enchanting, the scenes were moving, and as a result tears of sorrow and tears of joy swelled up in the eyes of all the spectators.[170] His colleague, lawyer Peter Lazarowich, who had discouraged several Albertans from purchasing the film's screening rights the previous summer, was even more fulsome: "My God, what beauty, what an artistic achievement, what a manifestation of the immortal and glorious past of our people. ... On more than one occasion tears flooded my eyes, and let me tell you, they were not only tears of sorrow, they were tears of joy and tears of pride. You have immortalized the beauty of our music, of our folk songs, of our culture. Anyone who walks out of the theatre without a sense of pride in his Ukrainian heritage must have a stone where his heart should be."[171] Although Rudnytsky and Ulmer should have been at the receiving end of such compliments, there is no denying that the film would not have been produced but for the will, energy, and dogged determination that Avramenko brought to the project.[172]

When the picture came to Toronto for four screenings in the Eaton's Auditorium at the corner of College and Yonge on 11–12 January 1939, it was well received, but attendance did not match expectations. Recent concerts by Mykhailo Holynsky and Maria Sokil, screenings of the rival *Marusia,* and Ukrainian Christmas celebrations had diverted the attention of an already exhausted Ukrainian community.[173] Nevertheless, the reviews were favourable. Augustus Bridle of the *Toronto Daily Star* observed that the film had been a "patriotic thrill" for 2,500 Ukrainians who packed the auditorium for two screenings on the first evening. "The film adaptation is historical in realism and comic in most of the dramatic development. Its leading actors are all extremely flexible in technique. ... Shvetz, in the leading masculine role, is a splendid comedian. ... The comedy is well sustained. The whole production is at a high level of natural drama with much of the spontaneous quality seen in the best Russian [sic] films."[174] The populist *Toronto Evening Telegram* published a much lengthier review extolling the vocal talents of the cast, the dexterity of the dancers, and the acting skills of that "ineffable comedian" Michael Shvetz. "The film, not to slight its various excellencies, is chiefly distinguished for the beautiful singing of Mme Sokil, permeated often-times with an exquisite nostalgia and, when occasion requires, gay and sparkling as a racing brook in summer sunshine. ... The production moves with spirit, is simpler in form than the earlier Soviet film version and the photography, accomplished in New Jersey, is in the main very good, if with occasional lapses from clarity."[175]

Cossacks in Exile premiered in New York City on 27 January 1939 at the Belmont Theater, 123 West 48th Street, and ran until 9 February. The theatre, just off Broadway, was selected because management agreed to screen the film for a percentage of the gate receipts rather than a flat rental fee. Avramenko, not permitted to speak at the opening ceremonies, described the Belmont as a "pig-sty" and the premiere as a "funeral."[176] However, once again the reviews were positive. The *New York Times,* which had not noticed that the film was a Canadian production, described it as "highly agreeable both to the eye and the ear." After summarizing the plot, the review concluded: "While the tragedy of the sons of the steppes is indicated, most of the incidents are humorous, as befits an operetta. Burly Michael Shvetz is very amusing. ... His adventures with the Sultan ... are genuinely funny. Fine voices are displayed by the principals, including the aged bard who sings of the Ukraine's glory and sorrow. The chorus work is good and so are the dance numbers. The photography is clear as is the sound reproduction."[177] The *New York Daily News* observed that "there is a sweetly-sad nostalgic quality to the music of the Ukrainian operetta *Cossacks in Exile*. ... Its music is the most attractive feature of the film. ... Except for the music, however, and some of the native dancing, the picture moves at a pedestrian pace. ... There are touches of comedy here and there in the picture and one spectacular sequence that shows the burning of the village. The fire scenes are an outstanding part of the film because the flames are realistically produced in color."[178] The film, which also received good reviews in the *New York Herald Tribune* and the *Brooklyn Eagle*, was subsequently screened in several theatres in New Jersey during the last half of February and then on Manhattan's Lower East Side, in Brooklyn, and in the Bronx in early March.[179] After its Chicago debut at the Sonotone Theater, the Russian-language *Novoe russkoe slovo* (The New Russian Word) commended American Ukrainians for producing three feature films in two years and preserving their cultural heritage so successfully in a foreign land. The reviewer praised the singing and acting of Sokil, Shvetz, and Tcherkassky but noted the film's low production values and gently chided Rudnytsky for excessive "Italianization" of Ukrainian folk melodies.[180]

Although Alexander Koshetz, who had arranged all of the choral music for *Marusia*, did not publish any reviews of Avramenko's second feature film, he expressed his not unbiased opinion in private letters exchanged with colleagues. Koshetz thought that the rival film fell far short of pre-release publicity. Its mediocrity and historical illiteracy "produced a strong Little Russian stench," according to the prickly conductor. The Russian actors, in particular, were wooden, lifeless mannequins, and the film's language was "Little Russian" rather than literary Ukrainian. Koshetz maintained that Ukrafilm's *Marusia* and Kavaleridze's *Zaporozhets za Dunaiem* were better films than *Cossacks in Exile*. He also expressed regret that participation in the rival *Marusia* denied him the opportunity to publish a review because, if he had, "all of Avramenko's Jews and Russians would lose their trousers."[181]

As the new year dawned, everyone involved in the production of *Cossacks in Exile* realized that the fate of the picture and of Avrafilm itself would hinge on the box office receipts. The company's expenditures between 9 December

1937 and 31 December 1938 had totalled almost $61,000. Although not insignificant, they were certainly not excessive, even by the standards of independently produced B movies. Legal costs and pre-incorporation expenses had totalled just over $5,000, while the cost of running the New York City office came in at less than $10,000, even when office manager Biberovich's ($700) and assistant producer Gann's ($1,850) salaries were included. Of the remaining $46,000, only $21,000 had been spent on salaries and production costs. The salaries of the cast and directors were the smallest expenditures: Antin Rudnytsky had earned $1,600, Edgar G. Ulmer $1,260, Maria Sokil $750, Michael Shvetz $325, Alexis Tcherkassky $250, Nicholas Karlash $200, Dmitri Creona $150, and Helen Orlenko (whose singing voice had been dubbed) $40. Film editor Jack Kemp and costume maker Fedor Braznyk had earned $440 and $790 respectively. Much greater sums had been spent to rent recording studios, film laboratories, and filmmaking equipment and to pay for the services of unionized cameramen, makeup artists, and other technicians. The costs of feeding and accommodating up to 100 people on the set for at least four weeks must have also been significant. It is not clear how the remaining $25,000 had been spent, though one can surmise that travel, hotel accommodation, advertising, and various expenses claimed by the company's employees in and around New York City consumed the lion's share.[182]

Ultimately, problems with distribution rather than excessive production costs doomed the picture and sealed the fate of Avrafilm. In the summer of 1938, Roman Rebush had offered to distribute the film in the United States and abroad, but Avramenko had refused to pay him a 10 percent commission, while Avrafilm's directors had voiced concerns about his pro-Soviet past and doubts about the range of his contacts.[183] Biberovich tried to find European distributors and corresponded with a variety of Ukrainian acquaintances, including the publicist Pavlo Lysiak in Lviv[184] and the Kyiv-born avant-garde émigré Parisian filmmaker Eugene Deslaw (Yevhen Slabchenko), who had worked with Abel Gance and other cinematic luminaries.[185] However, prospects for European screenings remained bleak. Rudnytsky warned that, even if the Polish government permitted screening of the film in the western Ukrainian provinces that it occupied, Polish ultranationalist hooligans would be sure to vandalize theatres and harass audiences and exhibitors.[186] Deslaw expressed the opinion that there would be little if any interest in another film as mediocre as *Natalka Poltavka* among sophisticated European moviegoers.[187] Gann, in turn, tried to sell *Cossacks in Exile* to Indian distributors in Bombay, who turned down the Ukrainian film while purchasing a short called *Gypsy Melody*.[188] In fact, when *Cossacks in Exile* was released in December

1938, it had no American or international distributors, there was no money to advertise or book screenings in the United States, and in Canada distribution was in the hands of inexperienced small-town merchants, craftsmen, labourers, and farmers who had purchased provincial screening rights. By February 1939, the Alberta and Saskatchewan distributors had declared bankruptcy and were unable to pay the money that they owed Avrafilm.[189]

Rarely booked into theatres for more than one or two days and often limited to special screenings, the film's box office receipts were usually in the red. Nor did expensive mailing campaigns and ads in English-language dailies increase attendance, especially among non-Ukrainians. Two weeks after the Winnipeg premiere, Mandryka had to take $200 out of his own pocket to balance the books.[190] In Montreal, where the lone screening on 16 December 1938 grossed $1,500, the net profit amounted to a mere forty-one cents because it had cost over $1,000 to rent the theatre and Avramenko had distributed 300 complimentary tickets to supporters.[191] When the film was screened once again at Montreal's downscale Arcade Theatre on 3–4 February 1939, it yielded a four-dollar deficit.[192] In Hamilton, it was only possible to book two screenings at the Playhouse Theatre, one at midnight and one in the afternoon. The film was also screened in Windsor and Ottawa in January before moving to Sudbury and Fort William, where it actually made modest profits of $300 to $500.[193] In Calgary and Nelson, screenings were cancelled because of meagre attendance. When it was finally booked into several second-run Winnipeg neighbourhood theatres for a week in the summer of 1939, the ten- and fifteen-cent admission prices guaranteed negligible returns. By that point, with war approaching, provinces such as Ontario were making it increasingly difficult to screen foreign films. Soon the only screenings that took place in Canada were confined to church basements and community halls.

The greatest problems were encountered in the United States. Hard pressed to settle large debts for the use of camera equipment and film laboratories, and faced with theatre rental fees of $825 to $1,500 up front, the film's American premiere had been postponed for almost two months.[194] Poor attendance during the two-week run at the Belmont, which had been expected to generate substantial revenues and interest among distributors, and a series of deficits after screenings in New Jersey, New York City neighbourhood theatres, Detroit, and Cleveland (where only 160 spectators turned out), inevitably sealed the fate of Avrafilm.[195] The rights to distribute *Cossacks in Exile* outside the United States and Canada were finally sold for $1,500 down and 25 percent of the gate receipts to Variety Film Distributors in February 1939, but the political climate in Europe inhibited demand for the film, and with the outbreak of war in September the market collapsed entirely.[196]

25. Extras dressed as eighteenth century Ukrainian Cossacks on the set of *Cossacks in Exile* (1938).

26. Young people dance while elders look on in *Cossacks in Exile* (1938).

27. Oksana (Helen Orlenko), Odarka and Ivan's teenaged ward in *Cossacks in Exile* (1938).

28. The sultan (Nicholas Karlash) and Ivan (Michael Shvetz) visit the harem in *Cossacks in Exile* (1938).

29. Vasile Avramenko in his New York City office, c. 1940.

30. Souvenir program of "Glory to Canada" pageant, Winnipeg, 1946.

31. Cast of "Glory to Canada" pageant, unidentified city, 1946.

32. Vasile Avramenko, Hollywood actor John Hodiak, and Michael J. Gann, New York City, 1954.

33. Paul Yuzyk, Fr. Stefan Semczuk, Mayor Steve Juba, Vasile Avramenko, Metropolitan Ilarion (Prof. Ivan Ohienko), Michael Hryhorczuk MLA Manitoba Attorney General, and unidentified man, Winnipeg, 1957.

34. Vasile Avramenko and Paul Yuzyk, London, 1960.

35. Vasile Avramenko presented with flowers and a special certificate at the Ukrainian Free University, Munich, West Germany, 1970.

36. Bishop Isidore Borecky, Vasile Avramenko, Metropolitan Maxim Hermaniuk, Bishop Ivan Bukatko and filmmaker Yaroslav Kulynych, Vatican City, c. 1964–65.

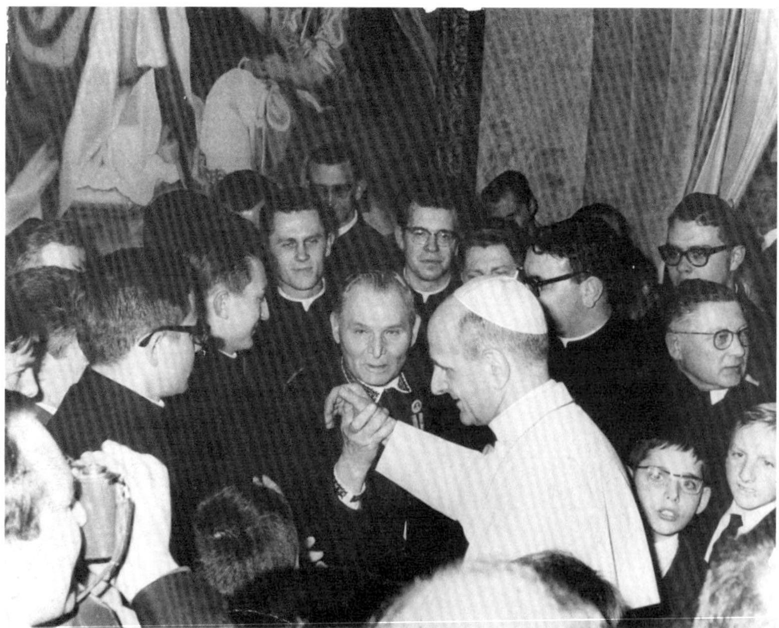

37. Vasile Avramenko kisses the ring of Pope Paul VI, Vatican City, 25 February 1965.

38. Vasile Avramenko, holding miniature Ukrainian, American and Israeli flags, with unidentified man, c. 1970.

39. Vasile Avramenko with Israeli teenagers in Ukrainian costumes, Jerusalem, 1971.

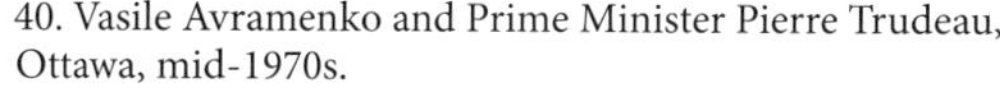

40. Vasile Avramenko and Prime Minister Pierre Trudeau, Ottawa, mid-1970s.

41. Vasile Avramenko, inveterate traveller, mid-1970s.

STUDIO
Tel. 388-3800

24 HOUR EXCHANGE
Tel. 384-4466

VASILE AVRAMENKO
Ukrainian Ballet-Master and Film Producer

Avramenko Ukrainian Dance Academy
Film Studio

1706 SUNSET BLVD. HOLLYWOOD, L.A. 26, CALIF.

42. Vasile Avramenko's card, c. 1972.

Needless to say, failure at the box office generated dissension within Avrafilm and produced an endless round of accusations and recriminations. Biberovich and others in the New York City office attributed the small audiences to the apparently widespread perception that Avrafilm had "given away" Ukrainian money to Jews, who had been involved at all levels of production.[197] Gann, put in charge of American distribution by Mandryka and the Winnipeg office in March, rejected this interpretation. He maintained that it was virtually impossible to book a Ukrainian film into theatres in the aftermath of the recent Carpatho-Ukrainian crisis because articles in some Ukrainian American papers, subsequently translated and published in major American dailies, had argued that Hitler and his expansionist policies might yet benefit Ukraine. Coming as it did shortly after Kristallnacht, such speculation in the Ukrainian press repelled theatre owners, many of them Jews.[198]

By this point, all hell had broken loose. When major creditors realized that box office receipts in Canada, and particularly those in New York City, were well below expectations, they started clamouring for their money. At one point, at least four lawsuits were being contemplated in Winnipeg alone, though several of the claimants settled out of court.[199] In New York, Mecca Film Laboratories and the company that had rented electrical equipment to Avrafilm demanded payment and threatened to impound and auction the film.[200] At its March 1939 shareholders' meeting, Avrafilm announced that it had cost $61,415 to produce *Cossacks in Exile* and that the company still had debts totalling almost $47,000 due to pre-release delays and poor attendance in cold winter weather. Creditors and shareholders were asked to give the company another six months to return loans and pay dividends.[201] While Biberovich had left the company by this point, Mandryka soldiered on as distribution manager.[202] Embarrassed, and perhaps slightly guilt-ridden for having allowed himself to become so deeply involved in one of Avramenko's schemes, Mandryka was committed to settling the company's debts and helping Ratuski, Hancharyk, and others recover the money that they had loaned and invested. He would look after the remnants of Avrafilm well into the 1940s.

The End of a Career

Avramenko remained in Canada until the fall of 1939. His solution to the financial crisis that now afflicted Avrafilm was consistent with behaviour that he had displayed since arriving in North America. When one project failed, he launched a second one and used money raised for that endeavour to settle debts incurred by the first. This time Avramenko announced not one new project but a dizzying variety of film projects, some of which he had started promoting even before the completion of *Cossacks in Exile.*

The first of these undertakings, one that never left the drawing board and had been eliminated from serious consideration by the winter of 1939, involved the production of more Ukrainian feature films. *Cossacks in Exile,* it was bandied about, could be dubbed with English-language dialogue, or a completely new English-language remake could be shot in Hollywood starring Deanna Durbin and Jeanette MacDonald.[203] More realistically, plans to make a film about Dovbush, starring Maria Sokil and Mykhailo Holynsky, with a musical score by Antin Rudnytsky, were revealed, and films about Mazepa and Taras Bulba were contemplated.[204] Ultimately, no attempt was made to raise money for these endeavours, and after the failure of *Cossacks in Exile* in New York City they were laid to rest.

Avramenko's second project involved the production of several low-budget educational films, including *Skarby Ukrainy* (Treasures of Ukraine), a concert film featuring performances by prominent Ukrainian vocal artists, choral groups, instrumentalists, and dance ensembles,[205] and *Talanty Ukrainy* (Talents of Ukraine), a documentary about the life of Ukrainian-Canadian teachers and their pupils. The latter, to be realized in collaboration with SUMK, the Ukrainian Orthodox youth association, actually got off the ground and obtained some funding before being abandoned the instant a better alternative presented itself. Formation of the Avramenko SUMK Film Studio, with headquarters in Montreal, was announced in November 1938. Paul Yavorsky, appointed the studio's deputy head and administrator, was sent out to organize rural supporters' committees and raise funds. The studio listed several prominent USRL activists, including Julian Stechishin's wife, Savella, as "artistic consultants," and it mailed circular letters on very impressive (and expensive) stationery to 1,500 Ukrainian-Canadian teachers and community activists.[206] Yavorsky, at the same time teaching dance courses and booking screenings for *Cossacks in Exile,* provided Avramenko with leads concerning potential investors.[207] By February 1939, several thousand dollars had been raised, but the poor showing of *Cossacks in Exile* at the box office, the spate of financial claims against Avrafilm, and opposition from USRL leaders in Montreal, Edmonton, and Winnipeg put the venture's prospects in question.[208]

It was at this point that a third and timely project presented itself, and Avramenko decided to seize the opportunity. In May 1939, Kalenik Lissiuk, the New York City businessman who had helped to arrange Avramenko's performances at the Star Casino and the Metropolitan Opera House, returned from Europe with film footage chronicling recent events in the Subcarpathian region of Czechoslovakia. There, in the aftermath of the Munich Agreement, Prague had granted autonomy to the region, renamed Carpatho-Ukraine, which many Ukrainians saw as the nucleus of an independent Ukrainian state. These dreams had collapsed in March 1939 when Nazi Germany annexed the Czech lands and Hungary invaded and annexed Carpatho-Ukraine. Nevertheless, a symbolic declaration of independence and a brief armed struggle between Ukrainian militiamen and Hungarian regulars had inflamed Ukrainian nationalist ardour and caught the attention of the international media.[209] Avramenko did not have to be persuaded that Lissiuk's footage could be edited into a documentary that would attract Ukrainian and non-Ukrainian moviegoers interested in recent events in central Europe. In June, with several thousand dollars obtained from a handful of investors in Toronto and Minneapolis, the Kobzar Film Corporation, Vasile Avramenko, president, was incorporated in New York City.[210] During the next few months, the corporation purchased almost $10,000 worth of film footage shot by Lissiuk (and his son Petro, killed during the fighting) as well as one print of Vancura's *Marijka Nevernice* (Faithless Marika) that Lissiuk had managed to obtain.[211] Michael Gann, Andrii Kist, Ladislaus Biberovich, Jack Kemp, and several others were hired to write, direct, and edit a documentary on *The Tragedy of Carpatho-Ukraine* and to re-edit Vancura's film. In the meantime, Avramenko returned to Canada to raise money. This time he concentrated his efforts on remote frontier mining towns, where details of his financial shenanigans were not yet known. Typically, he borrowed money at between 4 percent and 15 percent and promised to return the loans within a year.[212] By November 1939, Avramenko was back in New York City, working on several films simultaneously and travelling to raise more money.

Premiered on 25 March 1940 at the Theater in the Clouds on the fiftieth floor of the Chanin Building, 122 East 42nd Avenue, in New York City, *The Tragedy of Carpatho-Ukraine* was promoted as a documentary that condemned aggression and invasion. It opened with an account of Ukrainian history from the medieval principality of Kyivan Rus' to the emergence of autonomous Carpatho-Ukraine. The narrator's observations on Ukrainian history, folk customs, religious life, and culture were illustrated with still photos, animated maps, and footage of contemporary Ukrainian villagers and townsmen. A soundtrack credited to Antin Rudnytsky included Ukrainian choral songs and instrumental numbers and provided the background music. The narrator informed viewers that the film hoped to promote "Ukrainian aspirations for national independence and emancipation" and stressed that the contemporary Ukrainian independence movement was "neither pro-German, nor anti-American, nor anti-British." Scenes of the government of autonomous Carpatho-Ukraine meeting in the city of Khust to discuss relations with neighbouring states ensued and were followed by shots of young men enlisting in the local volunteer militia, training without arms, and developing into disciplined units. After a sequence depicting the enthusiastic reaction of Ukrainian Americans at fundraising rallies for Carpatho-Ukraine, the film shifted back to developments overseas. Reacting to Hungarian aggression, the Carpatho-Ukrainian parliament in Khust was shown issuing a declaration of independence. Laws were passed, Reverend Dr. Avhustyn Voloshyn was elected president, and the Ukrainian national anthem was sung. After the president's acceptance speech, the parliament issued decrees on language and national symbols. The film concluded with another presidential speech vowing that enemies and aggressors would be confronted and vanquished.[213] While much of the film consisted of authentic documentary footage, it appears that some parts, including scenes of executions carried out by the Hungarian invaders and Carpatho-Ukrainian popular resistance, were "staged" or "re-created," though apparently based on actual events.[214]

The documentary had little chance of succeeding at the box office. It lacked the music, singing, dancing, and humour, not to mention the direction and cinematography, that had drawn attention to and earned the two feature films moderate praise. After a brief run at the Sunshine Theater in lower Manhattan, screening rights were sold to Kalenik Lissiuk and Mykola Novak, who now made a living exhibiting Ukrainian, ethnic, and religious films. They took the film on the road and might have made some money in New Jersey and Pennsylvania by screening *Natalka Poltavka, Marusia,* or *Cossacks in Exile* on the same program, booking only church basements and community halls, and skimping on advertising.[215] Efforts to screen and distribute the film in Canada were more problematic. Although presentations were made in several cities, the film received little exposure because it was not economically feasible to tour the prairie provinces with it. In Montreal, where Avramenko was now held in contempt because many local people had lost money on his feature films, it was very difficult to arrange a screening.[216] Toronto finally saw the film in January 1941 after lawyer Theodore Humeniuk obtained permission to hold two showings, but there, as elsewhere in Canada, no one was interested in purchasing screening rights.[217] In December 1940, Avramenko indicated that he still owed $8,000 for production costs. The print of *Marijka Nevernice,* renamed *Forgotten Native Land—The Struggle for Survival* (Zabutyi ridnyi krai—Borotba za zhyttia), was apparently also ready for North American distribution, but Avramenko had mortgaged it to pay for the editing and could not screen the film until he obtained $6,000.[218]

By the winter of 1940–41, his career as a motion picture producer had come to an end. After fifteen years as a dance instructor, concert impresario, and filmmaker, Avramenko owed tens of thousands of dollars to hundreds of people. Every week reminders of these debts, which he was rarely able to settle, arrived in the mail from every corner of the United States and Canada.[219] No longer welcome on the American east coast or in the midwest, and with his reputation in Canada seriously damaged after the financial failure of *Cossacks in Exile,* Avramenko resolved to evade critics and creditors alike by moving to California. Still harbouring illusions of fame and glory and eager to make a name for himself in Hollywood, he was losing his grasp on reality and becoming increasingly marginalized in the North American Ukrainian immigrant community. His creative years were behind him, and Vasile Avramenko would spend the rest of his life trying to cash in on the good memories and run away from the bad ones.

FUGITIVE

CHAPTER 4

On 25 May 1943, Aimee Semple McPherson, the pioneer radio evangelist and faith healer, who had weathered a series of sexual and financial scandals while transforming revivalism into show business with her Hollywood-inspired sermons, received a letter.[1] Mailed to her office on the second floor of the 5,300-seat, $1.5 million Angelus Temple in the Echo Park district of Los Angeles, the letter began thus: "Forgive me please, that I write you without knowing you personally, but I have had the honor many times to attend your Services in your Temple, where Jezus [sic] Christ, who suffered for all mankind, has led me." After expressing his admiration for Sister Aimee's majestic services, "especially your Prayers for America, and for Washington, the Father of our country," the correspondent solemnly declared that "I, also, have walked out of your Church as a new person, with great hope in this vital hour for our country." His Christian credentials and admiration for Sister Aimee thus established, the correspondent proceeded to the matter at hand. "I am a director and producer of big festivals, also creator of various motion pictures. My last large show was staged in Washington, D.C., attended by Mrs. Roosevelt and other high personalities, whom I met there, and who had supported me morally. I also staged these great patriotic American-Slavic Festivals in New York, Chicago and other cities. With all my heart, I feel that your glorious Church is the place where I can frame with my new show, 'Prayer for America,' your unique and Divine personality." After indicating that a review was enclosed and asking for an appointment with the flamboyant preacher and her advisors, the writer concluded his missive: "With great respect and admiration, Sincerely yours, Vasile Avramenko."[2] Perhaps only Avramenko would have had the audacity to offer his services as a producer to a woman described as the "Barnum of religion," the "Mary Pickford of revivalism," and the creator of "the most perennially successful show in the United States."[3]

Sister Aimee, who was ill and preferred to turn to Charlie Chaplin and others in the film industry for advice on the production of her spectacles, did not take the time to reply to this desperate plea for employment from an unknown self-proclaimed director, producer, and filmmaker. Nonetheless, it appears that the charismatic preacher, whose efforts to bring the gospel to Broadway and popularize it with motion pictures must have struck Avramenko as the work of a kindred spirit, left a lasting impression on him. During the next thirty years, as debts, scandals, and a series of stage fiascos forced the aging dance master and film producer to take to the road and transformed him into something of a fugitive, many of his spectacles would bear the patriotic and quasi-religious stamp of Sister Aimee's pageants. Avramenko increasingly fantasized about and tried to produce massive patriotic pageants under the banner "Prayer for America," "Glory to Canada," or a variation on these themes. On the few occasions that he managed to stage such spectacles, he failed ignominiously, further undermining what remained of his tarnished reputation.

The Hollywood Years

Vasile Avramenko moved to Hollywood in December 1940, taking up permanent residence in April 1941 immediately after another financial fiasco. In the winter of 1940–41, no longer able to obtain funding from Ukrainians, Avramenko had approached Madame Margarita Agreneva-Slaviansky and her Russian chorus.[4] Flattering the aging diva by paying tribute to the "immortal soul" of her father, a famous singer and choir director who had popularized the song "Volga Boatmen," Avramenko proclaimed his commitment to the unification of all the Slavic peoples and proposed a Slavic American Music and Dance Festival.[5] Organized with the aid of a committee of Czechs, Slovaks, Slovenes, Poles, Serbs, Russians, and Ukrainians, and staged at Chicago's Civic Opera House on 16 March 1941, the festival was a resounding financial failure because of Avramenko's reckless spending.[6] Instead of realizing its objective of "Pan-Slavic and Slavic-American unity through cultural activity," the festival, financed with loans obtained from non-Ukrainians, bred animosity toward Avramenko's countrymen, tarred by his fiscal irresponsibility.

Several weeks after the festival, Slavka Vesela, a Czech committee member who had urged friends and relatives to invest in the enterprise and worked without pay on the project for six months, expressed her frustration with Avramenko's sudden disappearance and the cynical manner in which Avramenko referred his creditors to her office. Friends who had made short-term loans, she informed him, were being threatened with foreclosure on their homes, her mother had lost all of her savings, and she could not pay for her own child's medical care.

> Now I know the reason why everyone distrusts and looks down upon the Ukrainian people, it takes only a few such as you … to put a blotch upon the fair name of any nation. … A man who lives on the money he begs out of trusting women, nothing more or less than a panderer, that's what you are. In fact I have a list of over a hundred people here in Chicago alone to whom you owe money, and to some of them you owe the money for over ten years and they have not seen a penny yet. … You pretend to be honest and you are the biggest blackguard, thief and liar the world has ever seen or known.[7]

When major investors also began to complain, Avramenko gave them several prints of *Cossacks in Exile* as collateral for his debts without consulting Avrafilm's board of directors. He would resort to this expedient frequently during the next thirty years until there were no prints of either of his feature films to give away.[8]

Avramenko spent the next four years in Hollywood trying unsuccessfully to evade angry creditors. He rented a storefront at 5444 Hollywood Boulevard and announced the opening of the Avramenko Ballet-Film Studio. There he tried to screen his feature films and offer Ukrainian folk dancing classes, two enterprises doomed to failure because there were few Ukrainians in Los Angeles and even fewer willing to associate with him.[9] Isolated from and ostracized by his own countrymen, Avramenko attempted to cultivate the larger and more affluent Russian émigré community. He visited Russian newspaper editors, tried to promote a "grand all-Slavic performance" in California, and even told the Russian press that he was not a Ukrainian "separatist," prompting Winnipeg's *Ukrainskyi holos* to declare that Avramenko had thereby burned all bridges with the Ukrainian people.[10] He also wrote to Serge Jaroff, founder and conductor of the Don Cossack Chorus, expressing a desire to work for the "Russian-Slavic Idea,"[11] and he informed the Russian philanthropist V.B. Sergievsky that he yearned to tell the world that "the great and glorious Slavic nation" was still alive.[12] All the while he continued to correspond with Madame Agreneva-Slaviansky, obsequiously referring to her as a "saint."[13] Above all, Avramenko participated in the social life of the Russian community. He attended Russian New Year celebrations hosted by Nina Koshetz, was present at the opening of Mary Bran's Russian Theater Bureau, and hobnobbed with Leo Bulgakov at the Russo-American Club.[14] Yet, for all his efforts, these contacts failed to revive his career. The Russian-American Art Club held the occasional meeting in his studio, and in the winter of 1942–43 Avramenko staged one or two "ballet" performances featuring the "Prayer for America" motif at San Francisco's Russian Center, but no one was prepared to invest money in any of his grand festival and film schemes.[15] By the summer of 1942, the Avramenko Ballet-Film Studio had closed its doors.

Irrepressible as always, Avramenko was not prepared to give up. In the summer of 1942, buoyed by news that J.T. Thorson, the MP for Selkirk and formerly Avrafilm's solicitor, was now the minister of national war services, Avramenko wrote to him to pitch a film called *Victory Parade.* Because the new department was responsible for wartime morale and national unity, Avramenko naively calculated that Thorson would fund a film showing Ukrainian Canadians supporting the war effort at home, in the workplace, and on the battlefront. He failed to consider the terrible impression that his fundraising methods had made on Thorson in 1938, and he did not realize that the government now had the National Film Board at its disposal.[16]

Stymied in Ottawa, Avramenko turned to acquaintances in Hollywood. He managed to locate Edgar G. Ulmer and communicated his readiness to collaborate on new projects with the director, whom he professed to respect for his skill and talent. Ulmer's parting memories of Avramenko were not necessarily conducive to further collaboration, and by 1942 his prospects had improved considerably. His "ethnic" and "race" films, especially those made for the Yiddish market, had demonstrated that Ulmer could make good motion pictures quickly on tight budgets. The Hollywood studios were aware of this. At 20th Century Fox, Darryl F. Zanuck wanted Ulmer to direct pictures starring Shirley Temple, while Paramount considered hiring him to direct a remake of *The Blue Angel* with Veronica Lake. Ulmer declined the first offer, and nothing came of the second project. Nevertheless, in 1942, he found steady work with Producers' Releasing Corporation (PRC), the poorest of Hollywood's poverty row B studios. PRC paid Ulmer a mere $250 a week, but the job offered security and gave him a great deal of artistic freedom. During the next four years, Ulmer would be the star director and unofficial head of production at PRC. He directed fourteen films, many of them in six days of shooting on budgets as low as $20,000. Some were terrible, others, such as *Girls in Chains* (1943), were memorable only because of their titles. However, a few of his movies stood out as examples of his virtuosity. They included the horror classic *Bluebeard* (1944), starring John Carradine; *Strange Illusion* (1945), a film noir adaptation of *Hamlet,* starring Warren William; *Detour* (1946), a film noir classic about a hitchhiker who accepts a fateful ride from a manipulative floozy; and *The Wife of Monte Cristo* (1946), a swashbuckler. These were some of the best B movies of the 1940s.[17] Consequently, when Avramenko tried to pitch a short "Russian musical featurette" to Ulmer and PRC, there was no reply.[18]

The indefatigable Avramenko also tried to contact Ukrainians who had managed to break into the motion picture industry, though at the time few of them were household names or wielded great influence. He did not approach Bill Tytla, who had joined Walt Disney in 1934 and played a prominent role in designing and animating *Snow White and the Seven Dwarfs* (1937), *Pinocchio* (1940), *Fantasia* (1940), and *Dumbo* (1941), because the cartoonist from Yonkers was not in the public eye. Avramenko had heard of George Montgomery (Letz), whose parents had emigrated from the German colonies around Mykolaiv in southern Ukraine. The handsome actor had been promoted to supporting and co-starring roles alongside Gene Tierney, Betty Grable, Ginger Rogers, and jazz musician Glenn Miller after making countless appearances in Gene Autry and Roy Rogers westerns. Avramenko dined with his older siblings shortly after Montgomery married singer Dinah Shore.[19] He also knew John Hodiak, who had appeared in MGM's *Song of Russia* (1943), a wartime celebration of Russian-American friendship, and then got his big break when 20th Century Fox chose him to play John Kovac, a leftist stoker, in Alfred Hitchcock's *Lifeboat* (1944), a psychological thriller about nine people stranded in a lifeboat in the middle of the Atlantic. Avramenko wrote to Hodiak's parents to remind them that they had been neighbours on Grayling Street in the Detroit suburb of Hamtramck in 1928. He inquired whether John had studied dancing with him, praised the young actor for retaining his Ukrainian surname, and announced plans to cast him as Dovbush, Mazepa, and Taras Bulba in three motion pictures that he planned to produce.[20] He also wrote letters to Edward Dmytryk's parents just as the Canadian-born director was completing his masterpiece *Murder My Sweet* (1944), a film noir classic and perhaps the finest adaptation of a Raymond Chandler novel. Dmytryk and his relatives were praised for their "love of Ukraine" and invited to attend exclusive screenings of *Cossacks in Exile* at which only directors would be present.[21] Mike Mazurki (Mykhailo Mazurkevych), who had played the dull-witted, soft-hearted thug Moose Malloy in Dmytryk's *Murder My Sweet*, was not importuned at this point, though he and Jack Palance would cross paths with Avramenko during the 1960s. When none of the stars answered his letters, Avramenko flew into a rage and declared that they could all go to hell. Writing to one of his few remaining friends, he insisted that they lacked "Ukrainian pride" and dismissed the whole lot as "slaves and miserable toadies"—apparently blind to the irony that his own behaviour in the presence of wealthy Russian émigrés merited the same characterization.[22]

In May 1943, more than two years after moving to Hollywood, Avramenko finally capitulated and took a factory job. For the next two years, he worked as a presser at the Allied Record Manufacturing Company, a branch of Columbia Records. For fifty-five dollars, he was on the job from 7 a.m. to 4 p.m. five days a week plus another half day on Saturdays.[23] Still unable to communicate fluently in English, Avramenko did not get along well with the other workers. In the course of one scuffle, he was thrown against a hot plate and sustained a large burn on his right forearm and another burn on the right side of his chest.[24] On another occasion, someone stole his wallet containing eighty-five dollars.[25] It is clear that Avramenko hated the job and was ready to do anything to free himself from the routine. The letter to Aimee Semple McPherson was written several weeks after he started working at the factory. Within a month, he also wrote to his former wife, Pauline (Garbolinsky) Avramenko, inviting her and their daughter Oksana to join him in Hollywood on the pretext that Oksana could continue her education while earning a good living as a film extra.[26] Pauline, who had not received child support payments from him for almost two years, refused,[27] probably suspicious, as she had been in 1936, that he would try to exploit their teenaged daughter for his own ends. Shortly thereafter, correspondence among Avramenko, Pauline, and Oksana came to an end.

The final year of the war was especially difficult for Avramenko. In August 1944, he declared personal bankruptcy because creditors in Chicago were having his wages garnisheed.[28] Several days before Christmas, he was struck by a car while crossing the street, though he did not sustain serious injuries.[29] At this time, Avramenko lived in fleabag hotels that charged five dollars a week. Finally, in January 1945, his application for American citizenship was rejected. Although he had passed the written exam, during the interview that followed he was grilled about his involvement with the Organization for the Rebirth of Ukraine (ODVU) and the Hetmanite movement. In particular, he was asked to explain allegations made in the book *Sabotage! The Secret War against America*, co-authored by Michael Sayers and Albert E. Kahn, two communist fellow travellers.[30] A strange mixture of half truths, hyperbole, and outright fabrication, the book not only placed the two Ukrainian organizations, whose leaders had been openly sympathetic to Germany prior to 1941, at the centre of a "Nazi espionage-sabotage machine in the United States" but also identified Avramenko as a leading ODVU operative (though the nationalist organization consistently criticized him after the release of *Natalka Poltavka* and his break with Ukrafilm in 1937).[31] He would have to wait until November 1961 to become an American citizen.[32]

A Fresh Start

The end of the Second World War brought Avramenko's career, which had been in a long decline, a much-needed boost that provided a twenty-year reprieve from obscurity. After the war, more than 200,000 Ukrainian refugees in central Europe had managed to avoid voluntary or involuntary repatriation to the Soviet Union. Between 1947 and the mid-1950s, about 80,000 of these displaced persons or DPs were resettled in the United States, 35,000 in Canada, 20,000 in Australia and Great Britain, 10,000 in Belgium and France, and about 15,000 in South America, primarily Brazil and Argentina. Another 15,000–20,000 remained in Germany and Austria, where the DP camps had been located.[33] The arrival of so many displaced Ukrainians, virtually all of them deeply committed to the "Ukrainian cause," and many of them homesick, distressed, and at least momentarily alienated from their new surroundings, was a windfall for Avramenko. He could cater to their nostalgia for the homeland and appeal to their patriotic generosity, all the while secure in the knowledge that they were unfamiliar with the details of his checkered past and likely to dismiss any unpleasant revelations as unjustified attempts to blacken the reputation of a man who had sacrificed everything for the national cause. And when the newcomers who settled in Canada and the United States realized just who Avramenko really was, there would still be Ukrainian communities in South America, Europe, and Australia that could be tapped in support of new grandiose schemes.

In the summer of 1945, Avramenko left Hollywood for New York to determine whether he could attract dance pupils and financial backers in the city that had been his home for almost a decade.[34] Apparently, he could not, and by October he had relocated to Canada, living in inexpensive hotels or the homes of acquaintances and moving from one city to the next.[35] Unlike the United States, Canada provided a more hospitable environment for Avramenko. There his financial diversions had been confined to a two-year period just prior to the war, and there had been fewer victims than south of the border. Because a number of prominent community leaders had endorsed his projects in the past, and even helped Avramenko to solicit funds in good faith, there were influential people in Canada with a vested interest in humouring him and putting the best face possible on his accomplishments, past and present. While the Ukrainian Self-Reliance League (USRL) and its youth affiliate now distanced themselves from Avramenko, having been burned just prior to the war, other Ukrainian-Canadian organizations were ready to embrace the dance master. The Ukrainian National Federation (UNF), established in 1932 to provide moral and financial support for the militant Organization of Ukrainian Nationalists and its underground, had been trying with some success to reinvent itself as a cultural-educational organization since 1939. Between 1941 and 1944, it had invited Alexander Koshetz to run choral workshops at its Winnipeg Ukrainian summer school for high school and university students. After Koshetz's death, the UNF's youth affiliate, which included Avramenko alumni such as Paul Yuzyk among its activists, became a leading promoter of Ukrainian folk dancing and was prepared to work with Avramenko.[36] Perhaps most significantly, several of his pupils or their siblings had attained a degree of influence outside the Ukrainian-Canadian community. Yuzyk, for example, was a university instructor and active enough in the Progressive Conservative Party to be rewarded with a seat in the Canadian Senate in 1963. Other alumni included members of large urban municipal councils, provincial legislatures, and Parliament. All of them were savvy enough to realize that Avramenko and Ukrainian folk dancers could provide photo opportunities that would be especially useful at election time.

During his first postwar sojourn in Canada, between 1945 and 1947, Avramenko offered Ukrainian folk dancing courses in Ottawa, Toronto, Winnipeg, and Fort William, aided by former associates Victor Moshuk, Ivan Tokaryk, and John Ewanchuk. At the conclusion of each course, a "Glory to Canada!" pageant was staged, though the production consisted of little more than the traditional dance recital. At some point during the performance, a dozen young women, dressed in robes and wearing crowns on their heads, marched on stage. Each represented one of Canada's provinces, Great Britain, the United States, or Ukraine, and each paid tribute to the Allied victory with some patriotic rhetoric. The pageants were typically mounted in high school auditoriums and featured the dancing of talented young soloists such as ten-year-old Natalie Pook, who charmed crowds in Ottawa and Toronto.[37]

In Winnipeg, William Kurelek, a shy and awkward nineteen-year-old at the time, attended Avramenko's classes and "practiced fanatically at home in the garage" because girls dreaded dancing with him and one of the instructors treated him "like a dumb animal." The young painter persevered because the "intense fire" of the driven dance master, who "seemed to be burning himself out with ambitious projects in the cause of Ukrainian Nationalism," captivated him.[38] While Avramenko's *Gonta* solo was the highlight of the evening, the Winnipeg dance performance and pageant, staged at the Playhouse Theatre in conjunction with a Ukrainian National Youth Federation congress organized by Paul Yuzyk, received scathing reviews. According to the *Winnipeg Tribune,* "almost every dance was repetitious in routine and far too long.... The whole performance ... lacked cohesion and needed many more rehearsals to qualify [for] more than amateur status. The general direction between orchestra and dance routine was almost entirely overlooked. Entrances and exits were tentative in effect and lacked all sense of unity." As for the "Glory to Canada!" pageant, it was "far too ambitious an undertaking to carry out successfully without further rehearsals. Everyone participating wore a solemn expression and the elocutionary efforts of leading characters were in a similar vein, despite the glory of conflict and victory over a common foe. Long pauses between interludes and static action on stage also marred the performance."[39] But the three performances in Winnipeg, including one called *The Ukrainian Refugee's Reply to Stalin,* raised over $1,000 for Ukrainian refugee relief, and for once Avramenko was able to leave a city without a deficit.[40]

When he returned to Canada for another extended sojourn in 1950, it was to celebrate the twenty-fifth anniversary of Ukrainian folk dancing in the country. Although the twenty-fifth anniversary of Avramenko's first dance school in Kalisz and the twentieth anniversary of Ukrainian folk dancing in Canada had already been observed in Winnipeg in December 1946, the celebrations in Toronto, which included several performances culminating with an extravaganza at Massey Hall in December 1951, signalled a new departure in his career.[41] As it became increasingly difficult to attract dance pupils, Avramenko began to focus on the celebration of his past achievements. During the next fifteen years, he lobbied and cajoled enough people to stage a series of jubilee celebrations in Winnipeg, Toronto, and Montreal in honour of the twenty-fifth, thirtieth, and fortieth anniversaries of Ukrainian folk dancing in Canada, the fortieth anniversary of his arrival in North America, the forty-fifth anniversary of his career as a performing artist, the forty-fifth anniversary of his first dance school in Kalisz, as well as his sixtieth and seventieth birthdays.[42] As a former associate wrote, "people have organized many jubilees for you, and you have organized even more for yourself, so every time I read about you it concerns another jubilee."[43] On at least two occasions, in 1954 and 1966, national fundraising campaigns were mounted to present Avramenko with "jubilee gifts" that would enable him to work on his projects.[44] Such celebrations were usually attended by a wide array of Ukrainian politicians, including Mayor Steve Juba of Winnipeg, whose sister had attended dance classes in 1927, Manitoba attorney general Michael Hryhorczuk, and Vegreville MP Ambrose Holowach, both former pupils, and Paul Yuzyk, who emceed more than one concert and banquet.[45] In the process, myths of "Avramenko the ballet master," who had brought the Ukrainian performing arts to Broadway, "Avramenko the Hollywood director," who had made the first two Ukrainian talkies, and "Avramenko the Ukrainian patriot," who had saved a generation of Ukrainian youth from assimilation, were purveyed to the public.

The celebration of past accomplishments also drew Avramenko back into motion picture production. In 1954, while preparing a "Glory to Canada!" pageant in Montreal, he began to put together a retrospective about his career pretentiously titled *Triumph of the Ukrainian Dance.* Produced at a cost of about $15,000, more than half the sum borrowed from a jubilee committee formed in Montreal, the film consisted primarily of excerpts from documentaries and feature films produced by Avramenko during the 1930s.[46] By the time the film premiered in high school auditoriums and parish basements in December, Avramenko was no longer on speaking terms with most of his benefactors.[47] Several acquaintances, including Dr. Stephan Rosocha, who had held a cabinet post in the ill-fated Carpatho-Ukrainian government of 1939, were hired to tour Canada with the film during the winter of 1954–55.[48] After each performance, donations for the first of Avramenko's many jubilee gifts were solicited from the public.[49] While gate receipts failed to cover the costs of exhibiting the film, much less its production, Avramenko found a willing ally in Rosocha, who would organize jubilee celebrations for the aging dance master and publicize his projects on the pages of *Vilne slovo* (The Free Word), a Toronto weekly that he edited with Ladislaus Biberovich during the 1960s.

Early in 1957, with parliamentary elections looming, Avramenko began to work on a film about Ukrainian Canadians. Encouraged and assisted by Progressive Conservative Party activist Paul Yuzyk, he filmed interviews with Ukrainian politicians, pioneers, and churchmen. One of the scenes showed Progressive Conservative leader John Diefenbaker and Ukrainian-Canadian MP Michael Starr greeting a Ukrainian delegation in Ottawa.[50] The film was not completed in time for the June election campaign, and an irate Yuzyk would remind Avramenko of this when he came looking for money a few years later.[51] When Avramenko tried to interest the NFB in his film, an official politely informed him that "I do not feel there is sufficient material of top quality to produce a film of the nature suitable for National Film Board distribution."[52]

The last of the grand festivals celebrating Avramenko's career was held at the Playhouse Theatre in Winnipeg on 30 January 1966 to mark the fortieth anniversary of his work in Canada and the forty-fifth anniversary of his career as a dance instructor. Arriving in Winnipeg in October 1965, Avramenko had lobbied friends, acquaintances, and the Ukrainian Canadian Committee to organize the festivities. He also gave interviews to the writer Irena Knysh, who was preparing a brief celebratory biographical sketch of the dance master for publication. The festival was produced by Myron Mason (Marian Masniak), one of Avramenko's pupils who had danced in *Cossacks in Exile,* sung with the Don Cossack Chorus, and worked on several CBC variety shows. It featured Ukrainian dancers trained by Meros Lechow, another Avramenko alumnus, as well as other dance ensembles, choirs, and instrumental groups.[53] While those in attendance included Ukrainian Catholic and Orthodox archbishops, Senator Paul Yuzyk, and Winnipeg's deputy mayor, Slaw Rebchuk, conspicuous by their absence were members of Rusalka, Winnipeg's premiere Ukrainian folk dancing ensemble. The group's absence reflected the fact that by the 1960s Avramenko was simply not a force to be reckoned with in contemporary Ukrainian-Canadian dance circles. Rusalka and other new dance ensembles, such as Yevshan in Saskatoon and Shumka in Edmonton, had outgrown the aging dance master and were more receptive to innovations introduced by Igor Moiseyev's and Pavlo Virsky's Soviet folk dance ensembles. When Avramenko subsequently tried to organize jubilee festivals in Saskatoon and Edmonton, his appeals were met with stony silence.[54]

By the mid-1960s, Ukrainian folk dancing in North America was trying to reinvent itself. Tours of North America by the Soviet Moiseyev Folk Dance Ensemble in 1958, and by the State Folk Dance Ensemble of the Ukrainian Soviet Socialist Republic under Pavlo Virsky and Mykola Bolotov in 1962, had been major salvos in the cultural Cold War and a triumph for the Soviet Union.[55] Over 500,000 North Americans had attended sold-out live performances by Moiseyev's dancers; 50 million had watched them on 29 June 1958 when they were the only act on the *Ed Sullivan Show;* and critics had referred to their performances as "fantastic," "superb," and "magnificent." Just as in London and Paris three years earlier, the *Hopak* from Moiseyev's *Ukrainian Suite* was a crowd favourite that always brought the house down. In 1962, Virsky's Ukrainian Folk Dance Ensemble, which had also dazzled crowds in London and Paris, made its North American debut with a three-week, sold-out booking at New York's Metropolitan Opera House. After the first performance on 24 April, the crowd gave the ensemble a fifteen-minute ovation and demanded numerous curtain calls. The *New York Times* critic described the group as "a rousing, jovial, utterly engaging horde of young people, dancing their hearts out and their heads off," and observed that the "national character" and the "marked individuality of the dancers" distinguished them from Moiseyev's ensemble. Those who did not enjoy the troupe's dancing were advised to "see their doctors about a spring check-up."[56]

The two ensembles that had done for the Soviet Union what Avramenko had hoped to do for the Ukrainian cause thirty years earlier had been established in 1937. Two years earlier Ukrainian ballet dancers had won the first

International Festival of the Folk Dance in London by performing a piece that blended the spontaneity and lyricism of the folk dance with the discipline and virtuosity of the ballet. The dance, which consisted of a *Kozachok* and a *Hopak*, had been choreographed by Leonid Zhukov of the Kyiv Ballet and Avramenko's mentor Vasyl Verkhovynets (who did not have an opportunity to bask in the glory of his achievement because, like so many other Ukrainian artists and intellectuals, he was arrested and executed in 1938). The Moiseyev and Virsky ensembles, based in Moscow and Kyiv, would combine the high professional standards, technical virtuosity, and poetic expressiveness of the ballet with the vitality, joy, and direct popular appeal of folk dancing.[57]

Igor Moiseyev and Pavlo Virsky had much in common. Moiseyev, the son of a Russian lawyer and his French wife, was born in Kyiv but grew up in Paris and Moscow. After graduating from the Bolshoi Theatre Ballet School in 1924, he became an accomplished character dancer and choreographer at the Bolshoi. Appointed head of choreography at the new Moscow Theatre of Folk Art in 1936, he hit upon the idea of establishing a professional company to perform folk dances. Virsky was born in Odessa and graduated from the city's Music and Drama School in 1927. After further studies in Moscow, he became a soloist and ballet master with the Odessa Ballet and ballet master with the Kharkiv, Dnipropetrovsk, and Kyiv opera and ballet theatres. Both men were professional ballet dancers and choreographers; they were not ethnographers or cultural purists determined to preserve folk dances in their pristine, traditional forms. Both were interested in the spirit of the folk dance. They were prepared to abandon constraints imposed by traditional dance steps and figures and to introduce elements from classical and character dances as well as pantomime and drama. Some of their dances featured "spectacular and acrobatic leaps and jumps," and they included mass scenes that gave prominence to the entire company. Nevertheless, both Virsky and Moiseyev made a genuine effort to maintain a balance "between authentic folk dance and theatrical effectiveness," and their choreography consistently drew and built on national folk dance traditions.[58] As Virsky wrote in 1966, "the main principle of our work is not just to copy ethnographic patterns of national dances, but to give them creative interpretation and enrich them."[59]

The appearance of the Moiseyev and Virsky ensembles in North America had a tremendous impact on Ukrainian folk dancing, provoking debates and encouraging the emergence of new amateur ensembles that focused on performance. Not everyone approved of their influence or regarded their performances as art rather than propaganda. Knowledgeable experts maintained that

> choreographers ... of Soviet dancing ensembles, in obeisance to the dictates of the Communist regime, have been knowingly distorting the original folk form and national characteristics of the Ukrainian folk dance through excessive stylization, acrobatics, pantomime and introduction of foreign elements borrowed from the dances of other nationalities of the Soviet Union. ... Soviet choreographers are themselves creating a new Soviet folklore, characterized mainly by themes on the life of the working people and portrayals of the "happy" life of the Soviet man; for example pseudo-folk dances *Na kukurudzianomu poli* (In the Cornfield), ... *Kolhospna polka* (The Collective Farm Polka), [and] *Zhovtneva lehenda* (October Legend), among others.[60]

Some Ukrainian émigré nationalists called for and carried out boycotts of both ensembles and demonstrated outside venues where they performed.

Academic and political debates aside, the dazzling performances of Ukrainian (-themed) dances by the two ensembles opened up "new vistas for audiences and dance groups alike." "Here," according to choreographer and dance historian Alexandra Pritz, "was a highly polished and theatrical form of Ukrainian dance, performed by trained professional dancers, that made all previous dance performances seem amateur and uninteresting by comparison."[61] Many Ukrainian Canadian dance groups attempted to pattern their performances on those of Virsky's ensemble, an option facilitated by the ready availability of new Soviet publications on all aspects of Ukrainian dance, including history, theory, music, costumes, and no fewer than 609 Ukrainian dance steps and movements relating to 140 dances. The results, as some ethnographers and historians observed, were a new "accent on high showmanship, vitality, sharp contrast, regimentation, and massiveness,"[62] and in some instances an uncritical acceptance of every Soviet dance trend and a concentration "only on their pyrotechnics."[63] As Ukrainian dance became more contemporary, and as its entertainment value and mass appeal grew, Avramenko, with his repertoire of eighteen dances choreographed between 1921 and 1928, was perceived as irrelevant, and he was marginalized even within the dance community.

Even before Moiseyev and Virsky brought their ensembles to North America as part of the post-Stalinist cultural exchange between the Soviet Union and the United States, many Ukrainian Americans had regarded Avramenko with greater ambivalence and suspicion than had their Canadian counterparts. Not only did he receive letters from people who had loaned money decades earlier and were still waiting for him to settle his debts, but also he continued to borrow large sums of money to pay for studio space, purchase a building, and finance his incessant travels. When he refused to settle a $2,500 debt in 1951, lawyer Theodore Swystun, who had sung one of the lead roles in *Natalka Poltavka,* threatened to publish an open letter in the Ukrainian press revealing that Avramenko habitually took money from widows under the pretext of Ukrainian patriotism and then failed to return it.[64] Three years later a Ukrainian Orthodox priest accused him of being a swindler when Avramenko proposed to return $8,000 borrowed from the priest's wife within thirty-two years![65] More significantly, in the United States, where prominent community leaders and organizations had refused to endorse any of his projects after 1933 and effectively ostracized him, there were no influential individuals with vested interests in embellishing his reputation. As a result, apart from special jubilee screenings of *Triumph of the Ukrainian Dance* organized by Avramenko and Biberovich in the spring of 1955, and modest celebrations in Chicago on the occasion of the thirtieth anniversary of his arrival in the United States, there were few if any festivities honouring Avramenko.

Nevertheless, in the fall of 1952, Avramenko had returned to New York City and opened his Academy of Dance and Film Studio in Nick Arseny's building at 4 St. Mark's Place in the East Village. This would be his primary American residence for the next decade, and there he and Arseny would offer several dance courses in 1952–53 and again in 1958–59.[66] Avramenko seems to have spent more of his time screening *Natalka Poltavka, Cossacks in Exile,* and *Marusia,* which he now advertised as one of his own productions. While he spent much of the decade travelling across the United States and Canada with old films, Avramenko also found time to offer brief dance courses in Chicago, Milwaukee, Minneapolis, Cleveland, Philadelphia, and several communities in New Jersey. From time to time, at the conclusion of a dance course, he would stage a recital that would be promoted as a "Prayer for America" or some variation on this theme.[67] In the spring of 1962, Avramenko moved his Dance and Film Studio into a building at 12 St. Mark's Place that he had purchased with a down payment of $19,000 that he had managed to borrow. Unable to make payments on the loans and the two mortgages that he had to take out, he soon sold the building to a group of elderly friends and supporters from whom he continued to rent the studio. Dance courses were offered at this location for the last time in 1961–62, and Avramenko's belongings remained in the building until it was sold in 1967.[68] His teaching career in the United States came to an end on the evening of 29 December 1962 when he broke his leg and sustained head and chest injuries in a traffic accident while on his way to a dance class in New Brunswick, New Jersey.[69] By this time, serious American students of Ukrainian folk dancing were turning to a new generation of professional dance instructors such as Roma Pryma-Bohachevsky, who had been trained in classical ballet and modern dance.[70]

Globetrotter

When his reputation and credibility began to wane among the new wave of Ukrainian immigrants in the United States and Canada, Avramenko decided to try his luck in Ukrainian communities overseas. As early as 1948–49, he had spent a full year in South America screening films, offering a few dance courses, staging several performances, and attempting to promote film projects that failed to get off the ground.[71] While he seems to have made a good impression on the pioneer settlers and Basilian missionaries in Prudentópolis and Paraná province,[72] this was not the case in Curitiba and São Paulo. By his own admission, Avramenko barely managed to get out of Brazil with his life, and apparently he was also obliged to beat a hasty retreat from Buenos Aires, Argentina, in the summer of 1949.[73] Although he rarely spoke about his South American trip, there is no doubt that it was another financial disaster. He borrowed $330 to pay his way home, and the man who made the loan was still trying to collect it twenty years later, complaining that no one wanted to purchase or attend screenings of the films that Avramenko had left as collateral.[74]

By the late 1950s, Avramenko was ready to go on the road once again. Highly successful tours of Europe and North America by Igor Moiseyev's State Folk Dance Ensemble of the USSR, featuring polished and theatrical renditions of several Ukrainian folk dances performed by talented and trained professionals, infuriated Avramenko.[75] He regarded such ensembles and tours as clever Soviet propaganda designed to conceal the suppression of Ukrainian culture in the USSR and thought that their spectacular choreography violated the spirit of the Ukrainian folk dance and amounted to little more than "clowning" and "circus acrobatics." Convinced that he alone could preserve the integrity of the Ukrainian dance, Avramenko resolved to "reply to Red Moscow and its shameless propagandist performances" by staging "a festival the likes of which the world has never seen."[76] The most appropriate venue for a performance of such gravity, he reasoned, would be London's Royal Albert Hall, "the biggest hall in the world's largest capital."[77] Although friends warned that, if such a performance failed to match the high professional standards set by the Soviet dancers, it would only embarrass and discredit the Ukrainian émigré community, Avramenko would not be deterred.

In October 1959, officers of the Association of Ukrainians in Great Britain (AUGB) were stunned by a letter announcing that Avramenko would be arriving aboard the *Queen Mary* on 17 November to join his colleague, Professor

Paul Yuzyk, on sabbatical leave in London.[78] Somewhat disoriented, the AUGB agreed to facilitate entry into the country for Avramenko by undertaking to provide him with "full accommodation and to cover all necessary expenses connected with his lectures."[79] As long as Avramenko confined himself to screening films and lecturing in Ukrainian communities, there was no trouble. However, when he insisted on staging a festival in the Royal Albert Hall regardless of the costs and began to display his "forceful personality" (misleading many to conclude that Yuzyk and prominent Canadian politicians and church leaders were behind the project), trouble ensued. Fearing that his Whitsun Festival of Ukrainian Folk Ballet, Song, and Music, featuring a special "Prayer for Great Britain," would be an artistic, financial, and public relations embarrassment for the Ukrainian community, the AUGB refused to endorse the event. AUGB executive director T.J. Kudlyk informed members that Avramenko lived on fantasies and did not care if his irresponsible actions compromised or destroyed the Ukrainian community in Great Britain.[80]

Left to his own devices, Avramenko decided to proceed with the festival even though some of the best choirs and the "Orlyk" dance ensemble, which had won first prize at the Edinburgh Festival, refused to participate.[81] He rented the Royal Albert Hall, organized a dance course in London, and brought in a Ukrainian filmmaker all the way from São Paulo, Brazil.[82] To finance the venture, he borrowed £1,115 from a dozen unsuspecting individuals by appealing to the central Ukrainian origins and Orthodox faith that he shared with them.[83] As collateral he put up prints of two films, a damaged projector, a screen, and some costumes. When it became obvious that the hall would be virtually empty on the day of the performance, Avramenko distributed complimentary tickets to nurses, off-duty policemen, and charitable organizations. After the festival, which took place on 5 June, he disappeared with gate receipts totalling £240 and only wrote to his creditors several weeks later from Germany, reassuring them that he was organizing dance courses and screening films in Munich. A priest, who had helped Avramenko to obtain the loans in good faith, accused him of having no conscience and thinking only of himself rather than the elderly, ailing, and unemployed people from whom he took the money.[84] Although Avramenko eventually settled his debts, he did so only after being threatened with exposure in the *Daily Mirror* and criticized in the Ukrainian press.[85] And even then years passed before he returned all of the money.[86]

After four months in Germany, Avramenko returned to New York City in November 1960. In the fall of 1963, he was off to Europe once again trying to capitalize on the recent release of Ukrainian Catholic archbishop Josyf Slipyj from eighteen years of captivity in the Soviet gulag.[87] Having obtained some money from two Ukrainian Catholic bishops in Canada,[88] and anticipating a cash settlement after his recent traffic accident, Avramenko reached an agreement with Australian filmmaker Yaroslav Kulynych and travelled to Rome.[89] There he proposed to film the Second Vatican Council and the venerable archbishop who had survived almost two decades in Siberian labour camps. Avramenko was convinced that the film would attract large audiences in Ukrainian communities all over the world and solve his chronic financial woes. During the next eighteen months, he travelled to Europe on several occasions, watching Kulynych film the Second Vatican Council in Rome, attending Slipyj's elevation to the rank of cardinal, and buying some footage of the Ukrainian seminary in Rome and Pope Paul VI's trip to Jerusalem from Italian filmmakers.[90] When he ran out of funds, Avramenko solicited loans and donations on a grand scale, using some of the money to settle debts in the United States. In Belgium alone, during a two-week period in 1964, he borrowed at least 90,000 Belgian francs (BEF), almost half of which he had yet to repay five years later.[91] Back in North America, Avramenko travelled from city to city screening the footage filmed by Kulynych and purchased from the Italians and organizing jubilee celebrations in his own honour.

The films brought back from Rome also enabled Avramenko to visit Australia for an extended period. He had been corresponding with local Ukrainian dance enthusiasts, including pupils from Kalisz and others who had studied with his followers in Lviv, since the early 1960s.[92] He had also become acquainted with the "Kuban Cossacks," three young Ukrainian Australians who were making names for themselves on American television and in Las Vegas with their acrobatic renditions of Ukrainian folk dances.[93] In spite of what had happened in London, the relentless sense of mission that had driven Avramenko all his life now drew him to Australia. Ignoring the advice of his Australian correspondents, he was once again determined to stage a festival that would "administer a knockout blow to Ukraine's enemies." Without revealing his ultimate objective, he persuaded the Federation of Ukrainian Associations in Australia (FUAA) and Ukrainian Catholic bishop Ivan Prashko to endorse a visit that would allow him to screen films, lecture, and offer dance lessons.[94] While making preparations for his departure, Avramenko tried to recruit Hollywood actors Jack Palance and Mike Mazurki, asking them to participate in his projects (though he barely knew the two men).[95]

Arriving in August 1966, Avramenko proceeded to lecture, screen films, and offer brief dance courses in and around Adelaide, Melbourne, Sydney, and Perth. Although up to 800 pupils enrolled in the courses, the films—a novelty in Australia—turned out to be his surest source of income.[96] Within weeks of his arrival, however, the seventy-one-year-old dance master's intolerance, arrogance, and belligerence, which seemed to increase as his arthritic limbs grew weaker and he became older, had alienated even his staunchest supporters. Avramenko screamed at his pupils, delivered long-winded homilies, criticized the three Ukrainian dance ensembles in Australia, accused them of contaminating the Ukrainian dance and folk costume with Russian influences, refused to work with local dancers and directors, and insulted individuals who had been loyal to him for years.[97] When he began to promote a series of festivals, culminating in a grand "Ukrainian Tribute to Australia" in Canberra, the FUAA became very apprehensive. Private recitals in church basements and suburban halls were acceptable, but the aging Avramenko was clearly past his prime and did not have a repertoire, dancers, or resources of the calibre required for a major performance "in front of foreigners" in the national capital.[98] Moreover, it would be a great embarrassment if Australian Ukrainians had to rely on an aging American citizen to produce a tribute to their new homeland.[99] Accordingly, Avramenko was informed that the FUAA would endorse his plans only if he was prepared to work with local performing arts groups.

In the spring of 1967, FUAA representatives began to make arrangements for the Canberra festival, but cooperation with Avramenko proved to be short-lived. By May, it became common knowledge that he had negotiated many personal loans in Tasmania and Wodonga to finance the festival, and soon rumours of the fiasco in London and his current debts in Belgium began to circulate. Asked to resign as festival director, Avramenko refused on the grounds that it was his project and that he wished to maintain its Ukrainian integrity.[100] In mid-June, however, Avramenko resigned and abandoned the project altogether after FUAA representatives rejected his program and approved one of their own.[101] Because a "Ukrainian National Festival" had already been publicized and prominent Australian politicians had agreed to participate, it went ahead on 26 August 1967 without Avramenko but with the participation of most Ukrainian-Australian performing arts groups. In the meantime, his creditors demanded that he return their money and appealed for assistance to the Ukrainian Catholic bishop, who had initially endorsed his lectures, screenings, and courses.[102]

During the summer of 1967, Avramenko kept a low profile, evaded creditors, and tried to launch a new project to settle the debts incurred by his Australian venture. In August, he wrote to the American ambassador in Australia and explained that he was a Ukrainian by birth, and an American citizen by choice, who had dedicated his life "to Ukrainian arts and to the worldwide struggle against communism." After claiming that his schools of Ukrainian folk dance had trained more than 100,000 people worldwide, and that he had produced a number of motion pictures, Avramenko revealed his plan: "My present wish is to go to Vietnam and to teach American, Australian, Korean or any other allied soldiers Ukrainian dancing." Because many of his students were already serving in Vietnam, he was sure to succeed and the army was sure to benefit because "the Ukrainian dance provides an excellent vehicle for instilling discipline, for promoting physical stamina and agility, and for providing entertainment and diversion." In addition, Avramenko offered to provide 100 Ukrainian costumes and stage "dance pageants in tribute to the American and Allied forces fighting in Vietnam … for the entertainment of service personnel."[103] After several interviews, officials at the embassy in Canberra managed to convince Avramenko, who had also proposed a trip to Thailand, that the government could not sponsor such trips, and they referred him to the Armed Forces Professional Entertainment Branch.[104]

Unable to get into Vietnam, by the fall of 1967 Avramenko was screening films and staging dance recitals once again, presumably in an effort to return at least some of the money that he had borrowed. While it is not clear to what extent he succeeded, it is clear that by the time he left Australia his reputation was in tatters. Shortly before Avramenko boarded the SS *Orcades* in Sydney on 4 February 1968 bound for Yokohama, Ukrainian Catholic bishop Ivan Prashko begged him to return all of the money that he had borrowed, admonished him for repeatedly taking advantage of the bishop's generosity, and implored him to stop destroying his own reputation by trying to stage grand spectacles and fighting with everyone who crossed his path.[105] In the months that followed, Avramenko would receive a number of letters asking him to settle his debts and offering the same advice.[106] One letter, from a woman who had known Avramenko decades earlier, concluded that "what you are doing now is worthless, and I know that it does not bring you any joy or money."[107]

When he returned to New York City in March 1968, the building at 12 St. Mark's Place had been sold, and Avramenko decided to move all of his belongings, including his massive personal archive, to Hollywood.[108] In September, he opened a Dancing Academy and Film Studio at 1675 Western Avenue and distributed flyers declaring that "Ukrainian dancing is an elixir. … Ukrainian dancing guarantees office workers youth and health."[109] After spending much of the fall and winter on the west coast (where he learned that his former wife, Pauline Garbolinsky, had passed away in New York), Avramenko spent the spring and summer of 1969 touring North America with his films.[110]

In September 1969, having borrowed money from friends, Avramenko returned to Rome determined to film Cardinal Josyf Slipyj and the new Ukrainian Catholic Cathedral of St. Sophia.[111] When nothing came of this project, he moved on to Germany, where he stayed a few days in Munich. Then he embarked on a trip that took him to Novyi Sad in Yugoslavia; Lyon, Paris, and Wissous in France; Linz, Austria; and Geneva, Switzerland. He came back to Munich in late January 1970 via Delmenhorst and Berlin. In Munich, he offered a brief dance course, and the Ukrainian Free University presented him with a special certificate in recognition of the fifty years that he had spent promoting Ukrainian folk dancing.[112] Instead of returning to North America, as had been anticipated, Avramenko travelled to Switzerland, where he tried to offer Ukrainian dancing lessons to Swiss Boy Scouts and spent a great deal of time in Geneva with Professor Mykhailo Yeremiiv, who had been a prominent member of the Ukrainian Central Rada in Kyiv in 1917. Polite and courteous to a fault, the eighty-one-year-old professor did not know how to rid himself of his house guest. Avramenko finally left in June when a film festival that Yeremiiv had been persuaded to arrange attracted only eleven people, all of them close friends of the professor.[113] Although he agreed to write a few articles about Avramenko's accomplishments in Europe, Yeremiiv subsequently informed friends that Avramenko "actually accomplished nothing in Europe, he just bustled about ... and incessantly berated everyone for no reason at all."[114]

For the remainder of the summer, Avramenko shuttled between Delmenhorst, Munich, and Lugano, staying with anyone willing to put him up for a few days or for several weeks. Then, after debating whether he should screen *Cossacks in Exile* at the site of the original encampment,[115] Avramenko decided to travel to Venice, where on 12 October 1970 he boarded a Greek vessel bound for Haifa, Israel. A week later he was in Tel Aviv and would remain in the Holy Land for almost one year.

In mid-November, Avramenko moved to Jerusalem and took up residence at the YMCA on King David Road. In the months that followed, he wrote letters in Ukrainian to Prime Minister Golda Meir, Moshe Dayan ("the Jewish Napoleon"), David Ben Gurion, Mayor Teddy Kollek, and countless other Israeli political figures, receiving polite acknowledgements from their secretaries.[116] He proposed to teach Ukrainian folk dancing to Israelis and once again announced plans to stage a "Great Ukrainian National Festival: Glory to Israel" that would pay tribute to Israel, Ukraine, the United States, Canada, and Great Britain. He also informed friends in Europe and North America that he wanted to film a performance of his solo dance *Hore Izraielia* (Woe of Israel) in front of the Wailing Wall. The performance would feature an Israeli choir and orchestra, twenty Jewish boys and girls trained in Ukrainian folk dancing by Avramenko, and several young dance soloists.[117] The spectacle had to be produced to refute accusations that Ukrainians were anti-Semitic and to celebrate the spirit of self-sacrifice that pervaded Israel as it struggled for statehood and survival. Acknowledging that Ukrainian units had participated in pogroms in Ukraine in 1918–21, Avramenko hoped to persuade Israelis that Symon Petliura, the man who had first encouraged him to use his art for the glory of Ukraine in 1917, had not instigated or encouraged the atrocities. He also wanted to inform them that many Ukrainians had saved Jews from Russian pogromshchiks and Nazi exterminators.[118] After accomplishing his mission and staging the performance, Avramenko was sure, the troupe would be booked for a tour of North America by a Jewish impresario.[119]

Avramenko devoted a great deal of time to corresponding with Ukrainian acquaintances all over the world, inviting them to participate in his festival and soliciting loans and donations. He supported himself by screening his films, which attracted Jewish immigrants from eastern Europe, and managed to get some exposure in the Israeli press. The *Jerusalem Post* published a brief story in the spring of 1971 noting that Avramenko spoke no Hebrew and little English, "but he makes up for his lack of verbal ability with extremely gracious manners, coupled with a highly aggressive personality."[120] At the same time, Avramenko received letters and moral support from a handful of Israelis, including elderly natives of Galicia who had been educated in Ukrainian secondary schools, several academics in Slavic studies, and students concerned about the fate of Soviet Jews.[121] Of course, no festival was held, though in October 1971, shortly before he left Israel, several Israeli students filmed Avramenko performing excerpts from *Hore Izraelia* in an amphitheatre.[122] A number of the Israelis that he befriended continued to correspond with him during the next few years, sending some of the warmest letters in his archive. But then Avramenko had been on his best behaviour during his Israeli sojourn because friends and several Ukrainian-American financial institutions had extended loans and donations lest he accumulate debts in Israel.[123]

Avramenko returned to Israel in May 1973 for twenty-fifth anniversary celebrations, and he spent the summer months in Europe, but by the mid-1970s he was eighty years old, and his days as a global traveller had come to an end.

Twilight

During the last decade of his life, Avramenko became increasingly bitter and disillusioned. After returning from Israel in November 1971, he resided at 1706 Sunset Boulevard in Hollywood, above a travel agency owned by a Ukrainian who had just co-produced *The Incredible Two-Headed Transplant,* one of the most implausible B movies released by American International Pictures.[124] During the next five years, Avramenko continued to roam around the continent on Greyhound buses with the old films that survived and new ones purchased in Europe and Israel. His circuit now included Los Angeles, Phoenix, San Francisco, Edmonton, Saskatoon, Winnipeg, Minneapolis (where his faithful old friend Andrii Kist had been a Ukrainian Orthodox pastor since 1940), Chicago, Detroit, Toronto, Montreal, New York City, Philadelphia, and Miami. But his tours were even less successful than in the past. In the aftermath of the 1972 summer tour, Avramenko admitted that almost no one had attended his screenings. During this tour, he had slept in parks and bus stations and endured harassment by the police. Apparently, he had even contemplated suicide but reconsidered because "Ukraine would not forgive me."[125]

In his spare time, Avramenko wrote letters to Senator Barry Goldwater, Richard Nixon, and Spiro Agnew informing them that he was praying for their election,[126] sent mementos of his Israeli trips to Pierre Trudeau and Pat Nixon,[127] and fantasized about a great festival featuring John Diefenbaker, Tricia Nixon, Cardinal Josyf Slipyj, and an orchestra conducted by Antin Rudnytsky, who had scored *Cossacks in Exile.*[128] In 1973, he even wrote to Argentinean president Juan Perón, mentioned mutual friends of the late Evita, and offered to organize a "Glory to Argentina" festival.[129] He also became increasingly obsessed with salvaging his massive personal archive and other materials of "great historical importance." These materials had been moved once again, to New York City's East Village, a neighbourhood being taken over by hippies, student radicals, black militants, punks, and drug addicts and abandoned by all local residents except aging Ukrainians.[130]

Nor could Avramenko comprehend the social turmoil unleashed in America by the Vietnam War. He complained about "the negroes (*nihry*) who boast they will destroy everything, including monuments and museums," and the "boorish" white students who were "demolishing classrooms and burning libraries instead of studying."[131] Even Canada, which he thought was different and which he believed would remain "Ukrainian" for a long time, had lost its attraction: crime was rampant, and the young generation, including young Ukrainians, horrified him: "These young people ... are the world's perdition. ... It appears that Sodom and Gomorrah are upon us. ... Such rabble does not deserve to live on Earth."[132]

And he continued to borrow money or, as one of his European visitors put it, "to tear it out of people's hands."[133] In the United States, Avramenko was totally dependent on personal friends and acquaintances. In Canada, though any popular support that he might have once enjoyed had disappeared as his peers passed away, he continued to enjoy the patronage of influential people and powerful community institutions. During his 1972 tour of Canada, he received a letter of reference from Senator Paul Yuzyk extolling his films and indicating that Yuzyk had personally known Avramenko for over forty years: "I am proud to have taken Ukrainian Folk Dancing courses under his direction when I was a youth," the senator informed all concerned.[134] Ukrainian Canadian Committee (UCC) executive director Simon J. Kalba wrote letters to former prime minister John Diefenbaker inviting him to attend screenings of Avramenko's films in Prince Albert.[135] And in October 1974, the UCC awarded Avramenko a Shevchenko Medal for services to the Ukrainian Canadian community.[136] A month later he received a $5,000 grant from the Shevchenko Foundation to work on *Zhyvy Ukraino!* (Long Live Ukraine!), a film about the Second World Congress of Free Ukrainians that he would ultimately complete with filmmaker Yaroslav Kulynych.[137] No doubt much of this official favour reflected pity for a homeless old man who simply could not give up the mission that had dominated, consumed, and ultimately destroyed his life. But it stood in sharp contrast to Avramenko's neglect in the United States, where past indiscretions had left their mark.

Celebrations of the fiftieth anniversary of Avramenko's work in North America did not quite live up to his expectations. Although the UCC issued a circular encouraging Ukrainian Canadians to mark the event and wildly exaggerated his achievements by crediting Avramenko with having trained 100,000 dancers,[138] this time there were no grand festivals: only a small banquet at Toronto's People's Home and a dance recital celebrating Avramenko's jubilee and the tenth anniversary of a new dance ensemble.[139] More important from Avramenko's point of view was the fact that his archive, totalling some 150 cubic feet of documents, photos, and films covering more than half a century, finally found a safe and secure home at the National Archives of Canada in Ottawa. In the United States, Avramenko was singled out for special mention by the Ukrainian Bicentennial Committee of New York City and named Man of the Year by a Ukrainian parish in Chicago in 1976.[140] Three years later Ivan Pihuliak, his most important collaborator during the glory days of the 1920s and early 1930s, published *Vasyl Avramenko a vidrodzhennia ukrainskoho tanku,* a brief monograph about Avramenko's career prior to 1925. This was hardly the type of recognition that would satisfy one who expected Ukrainian history to record his name "in golden letters" alongside those of Kotliarevsky, Shevchenko, Sadovsky, Verkhovynets, and Koshetz, but Avramenko appreciated his old colleague's gesture.

Avramenko spent the last years of his life in New York City. He continued to plan trips to distant lands, and he wrote to his few remaining correspondents about preparations to stage a grand pageant called "God Save Our America!"[141] He was usually present at Fourth of July celebrations in the East Village, clutching miniature flags of all the countries that he had visited, sometimes dancing a few turns on stage when introduced to the crowd. Every year on 22 March, his birthday, he visited the offices of the Ukrainian National Association and its daily *Svoboda,* the newspaper with which he had waged a bitter war in the 1930s. Now the eccentric old man was welcomed, and the staff wished him a happy birthday and sang "Mnohaia Lita."[142]

On Wednesday, 6 May 1981, at 11:25 a.m., Vasile Avramenko died, surrounded by a small circle of friends. Funeral services were held at the Fresh Ponds Crematorium in Queens on 9 May. In lieu of flowers, the public was asked to make donations for the "safeguarding of archival material" even though virtually all of Avramenko's archives had been transferred to the National Archives of Canada two years earlier.[143]

In the spring of 1993, Avramenko's remains were returned to Ukraine, and on 4 May, accompanied by a funeral cortege that included official representatives of the Ukrainian Ministry of Culture and the Institute of Ethnography at the Academy of Sciences, they were laid to rest in Stebliv, where Avramenko had been born almost a century earlier.[144]

THE LEGACY TOUR

EPILOGUE

In the summer of 2006, twenty-five years after his death, Vasile Avramenko was on a cross-Canada tour once again, and preparations were well under way to take the show to Ukraine. There were no dancers garbed in colourful folk costumes, no musicians playing violins, dulcimers, and banduras, and no female vocal trios singing Ukrainian lullabies on this tour. They, like the maestro, had been replaced by a double-sided, twenty-foot-long, serpentine pop-up display, consisting of eighteen eight-foot-tall graphic fabric panels bearing more than 180 blown-up photographs and images, as well as explanatory text in English, French, and Ukrainian to acquaint spectators with the life and career of the eccentric dance master and film producer.[1] A very enthusiastic curator and a twenty-minute QuickTime video accompanied the exhibit and enlivened the spectacle.

Sponsored by the Ukrainian Canadian Foundation of Taras Shevchenko, with additional funding from the governments of Alberta and Saskatchewan and the federal department of Canadian Heritage, the *Vasile Avramenko: A Legacy of Ukrainian Dance* commemorative travelling exhibit had been unveiled at the triennial Ukrainian Canadian Congress in Winnipeg in October 2004.[2] It had subsequently toured Alberta and Saskatchewan during their 2005 centennial celebrations, visited scores of cities and towns all across Canada, and travelled south to several American cities, including Minneapolis and Detroit.[3]

The exhibit, and the glossy, profusely illustrated, trilingual exhibition catalogue that accompanied it, tried to put the best possible face on Avramenko and his career. There were pictures of the dance master encouraging, embracing, and holding hands with his youngest pupils and captions reporting that he had been "supportive, gracious, polite, and forgiving of his students' shortcomings." The 1931 Metropolitan Opera House performance was depicted as a seminal event that "had put Ukrainian dance 'on the world stage,'" while Avramenko's ability to raise over $70,000 during the Depression to film

Natalka Poltavka was declared a "stunning feat." Nowhere was there the slightest hint of how Avramenko had raised the money, nor was there any mention of the fact that the 1931 performance at the Met had far greater resonance in central European Ukrainian émigré enclaves than it did in New York City and the United States, much less the world. The last thirty-five years of his life were glossed over and summarized as the work of a "self-styled ambassador for the Ukrainian cause," one who "offered seminars, established dance courses and organized special concerts." Above all, the exhibit and the catalogue characterized Avramenko as a "key figure" in an "identity revolution," a man who "launched a program of Ukrainization." "His teaching made a profound impact on the identity of generations of Ukrainian Canadians." After he came to Canada, "Ukrainian dance became highlighted on stages and took on a whole new meaning as a symbol of Ukrainian culture and Ukrainian identity. … [As a result,] dance has become one of the most important ways for young Ukrainian Canadians to connect with their Ukrainian identity and roots."[4] The maestro would have been absolutely delighted with this evaluation of his achievements.

In the fall of 2006, the travelling exhibit finally made its way to Avramenko's Ukrainian homeland. There it was on display in Lviv and Lutsk, two western Ukrainian cities where Avramenko had taught in 1922–23; in the state capital Kyiv, where it was housed at the Kyiv National University of Culture and the Arts; and in Avramenko's hometown, Stebliv.[5] After seventy years of being forced to venerate only those heroes who were endorsed by the Communist Party, newly independent Ukraine offered fertile soil for the growth of myths about native sons untainted by association with the discredited Soviet regime. Although not yet widely known in his homeland, Avramenko was already being mythologized by those who accepted information offered up in the celebratory Ukrainian-language booklets that had been published in the diaspora during his lifetime. The first volume of the authoritative *Encyclopedia of the History of Ukraine,* published in 2003, credited "Avramenko's ensemble" with many "triumphant concert tours" across the Americas and Great Britain during the 1930s and after the Second World War, and it referred to "very successful performances at World Fairs" in Toronto in 1926 [sic] and in Chicago in 1933 and at the White House in 1935.[6]

Needless to say, the touring Canadian exhibit did nothing to correct these misconceptions. If anything, it might have reinforced them. Popular articles published concurrently by Ukrainian journalists referred to Avramenko as a "dancer, ballet master, film producer, actor, who, without the slightest exaggeration, was known world-wide. It is enough to mention that the famous

'Hopak' that he choreographed on the stage of the Metropolitan Opera was received with a torrent of applause by spectators who would not allow the dancers to take their leave." They also intimated that film distributors in Great Britain, France, Germany, Czechoslovakia, and Lithuania had been very eager to obtain screening rights to Avramenko's feature films in 1939 and that the quasi-documentary *Triumph of the Ukrainian Dance,* screened in a few Ukrainian community halls, had been an enormous success in the movie theatres of America and Europe during the 1950s.[7] An article published in a scholarly review in 2010 repeated most of the inaccuracies and exaggerations mentioned above, and it went out of its way to equate Avramenko's work and achievements with those of Alexander Koshetz, though it contrasted the "explosive" and "imposing" personality of the choir conductor with the "quiet, gentle" dancer.[8] As recently as 2012, another Ukrainian academic credited Avramenko with "creating a qualitatively new genre of choreography. His spectacles approached the genre of ballet-poems, ballet-symphonies, which re-created the complex historical fate of the [Ukrainian] people.... The creativity of this astonishing man of genius who displayed the artistry of Ukrainian folk dancing to spectators in Europe, the USA, Canada, Australia, Brazil, Israel, Argentina, [and] Mexico [sic] is not yet adequately appreciated in his native Ukraine."[9]

Although Vasile Avramenko was not nearly as famous, accomplished, selfless, and idealistic as these glowing tributes suggest, it would be unjust to deny him a place in the history of Ukrainian performing arts and North American popular culture during the interwar years. Not only did he work with respected Ukrainian artists and performers such as Mykola Sadovsky and Alexander Koshetz, and Hollywood cult director Edgar G. Ulmer, whose career he helped to revive, but also his impact on Ukrainian popular culture in North America and on mainstream perceptions of Ukrainian Canadians, and to a much lesser extent Ukrainian Americans, was second to none.

Avramenko's role in institutionalizing Ukrainian folk dancing was of fundamental importance, and there can be no doubt that Avramenko deserves the title of "father of Ukrainian folk dancing" in Canada and the United States. During the 1920s and 1930s, he and his instructors taught Ukrainian folk dancing to more than 10,000 Ukrainian-Canadian and Ukrainian-American children and adolescents. They introduced a formal and disciplined approach to Ukrainian folk dancing and managed to train and motivate a cadre of dancers who continued and expanded the work of their mentors. As a result, between the late 1920s and the early 1940s, Ukrainian folk dancing was integrated into the cultural programs of many Ukrainian Canadian youth groups, including those affiliated with nation-wide organizations such as the Ukrainian Labour-Farmer Temple Association, the Ukrainian Self-Reliance League, and the Ukrainian National Federation.

The classes taught by Avramenko and his instructors also introduced a handful of talented and ambitious pupils to the world of dance and the performing arts. In western Ukraine, Yaroslav Chuperchuk, who became director of the "Halychyna" Ukrainian State Dance Ensemble in Lviv after the Second World War, had been one of Avramenko's first dance pupils.[10] In Canada, both Chester Kuc, founder of Edmonton's Shumka Dancers, and Peter Hladun, founder of Winnipeg's Rusalka Dancers, were initiated into Ukrainian folk dancing in Avramenko's dance courses.[11] In the United States, Michael Herman and Mary Ann Bodnar, who danced with Avramenko in the early 1930s, established Folk Dance House in New York City and played an important role in popularizing the International Folk Dancing movement, which focused on participatory and recreational dancing.[12] Other pupils whose interest in the performing arts might have been nurtured in Avramenko's dance classes included Hollywood film actor John Hodiak, who probably attended classes in Detroit in 1928 when he was a teenager. New York City and American Ballet Theater dancer, choreographer, and dance master John Taras, who worked closely with George Ballanchine and Jerome Robbins, enrolled in Avramenko's first New York City dance course at the age of nine in January 1929 and danced with the maestro for at least six years.[13]

On the other hand, Avramenko's artistic legacy—eighteen ensemble folk dances adapted for the stage and five relatively complex and demanding solo dances all choreographed during the 1920s—was modest. Avramenko had choreographed all but one of the dances before moving to North America, and it appears that by 1928 his creativity had been exhausted. This was not surprising since he always regarded Ukrainian folk dancing primarily as a tool for propaganda and the development of national consciousness rather than as a medium for artistic expression. His goals, as Ukrainian-Canadian ethnographer Andriy Nahachewsky has observed, were to polish and standardize a few representative Ukrainian folk dances; transform them into symbols of Ukrainian identity; and then use them to reinforce Ukrainian national unity and to acquaint foreigners with Ukrainians, their culture, and their political aspirations. Moreover, his belief that, once it had been standardized, the Ukrainian national dance corpus should remain forever unaltered meant that Avramenko was unwilling and unable to change with the times or to tolerate any experimentation and innovation. He stuck rigidly to his formulaic conception of "traditional" Ukrainian dance, and he tried to impose it on his acolytes and followers.[14] This approach stifled creativity, and by the 1950s and 1960s his repertoire no longer met the new standards for complexity and virtuosity established by Soviet Ukrainian dance master Pavlo Virsky and his disciples. Today Avramenko's repertoire survives in remote communities and is usually reserved for beginners and young children.

Avramenko's foray into motion picture production during the depths of the Depression was also problematic. Avramenko understood the power of motion pictures and wanted to use *Natalka Poltavka* and *Cossacks in Exile* to showcase all of the Ukrainian folk arts and to promote the Ukrainian cause on a global scale. Shot on tight budgets that Avramenko squandered on old debts and incessant travel, and dependent on an enthusiastic but uneven pool of talent, the films nevertheless retain much of the charm, humour, and musical élan that made the operettas on which they were based perennial favourites. Well reviewed in the film industry press and in major American and Canadian dailies, both pictures held their own among contemporary independently produced ethnic and Hollywood B movies. They certainly did not deserve the savage reviews penned by Avramenko's Ukrainian critics, including the venerable and highly accomplished, but embittered and elitist, Alexander Koshetz. Of course, whatever artistic and critical success the films enjoyed was directly attributable to the talented musical directors who arranged the scores; the veteran opera singers who carried off the lead roles with aplomb; the predominantly Jewish cameramen and technicians, who provided skills that simply were not available within the Ukrainian community; and the inimitable Edgar G. Ulmer, an Austrian Jew, who brought his many talents to bear on both films. Yet, without Avramenko, who managed to pull all of these elements together, the films would not have been made.

Avramenko also deserves credit for harnessing the Ukrainian-Canadian community's voluntarism and its zeal for the amateur arts in order to realize his vision of a Ukrainian Hollywood. The audacity of the undertaking and his ability to bring it to fruition by producing two feature films—a feat achieved only by Jews and African Americans during the Depression years—captivated Ukrainians on both sides of the forty-ninth parallel and in European émigré centres. Nevertheless, while both pictures were entertaining and made many Ukrainians feel proud and good about themselves, they were also major financial failures that ultimately destroyed his career and reputation. Nothing that Avramenko accomplished or attempted after 1940 would duplicate his interwar achievements or have any lasting significance.

Ultimately, his most important legacy was as a propagandist and showman who drew attention to the Ukrainian people and their struggle for independence by showcasing their folk culture. Promoting Ukrainian folk dancing at a time when the libidinous dances of the Jazz Age were causing offence to middle-class moral standards, Avramenko managed to attract a great deal of attention and to generate a fair amount of positive publicity in the mainstream press for Ukrainian Canadians with his energetic but chaste dances. By the time he left Canada in 1928, Ukrainian folk culture, particularly Ukrainian folk dancing, which had been the object of much opprobrium, was being celebrated as a pastime capable of upholding rather than destroying British and Canadian moral standards. At the same time, as folk dancing and the folk arts became the most important component of Ukrainian heritage connecting large numbers of young Ukrainian Canadians to their roots and to the ethnic community, Ukrainian-Canadian identity became synonymous with Ukrainian folk culture. This was an ambivalent legacy at best, one that not only stereotyped Ukrainian Canadians but also helped to straitjacket and constrict Ukrainian-Canadian cultural expression, especially in the prairie provinces.

Even more controversial than his artistic legacy are the methods that Avramenko used to stage his dance spectacles and produce his motion pictures. The relentless and fanatical determination with which he sought to realize his self-imposed mission was rooted in his formative experiences. Avramenko was an abused orphan and a homeless wanderer whose life finally acquired meaning and purpose in 1917 amid the tumult of war, revolution, and the struggle for Ukrainian independence. When his natural talent as a dancer and entertainer came to the attention of prominent Ukrainian politicians, they encouraged him to use his gifts for the glory of Ukraine. Avramenko never forgot this summons. Folk dancing and its deployment as a tool of Ukrainian propaganda became his passport to respectability, recognition, and fame. He spent the next sixty years trying to promote the "Ukrainian cause"—and his own reputation as a champion of that cause—with a grim and unwavering obstinacy. Convinced that the Ukrainian cause took precedence over everything else, Avramenko acted as if all means were justified to advance it. He had no qualms about promising personal wealth, pandering to popular prejudices, resorting to moral intimidation, and above all appealing to Ukrainian immigrants' yearning for political recognition and acceptance. Even at the age of seventy, well past his prime and decades after he had accomplished anything of value, Avramenko declared defiantly that he would not stop until God called him. He was prepared to march on bruised feet, with a flag in his hands, for the greater glory of Ukraine, as long as he had a heartbeat.

History offers one explanation for his compulsive behaviour and the methods that he chose to achieve his objectives. For centuries, Ukrainian lands had been, in the words of British historian Norman Davies, "the playground of power politics," a bone of contention among states that dominated eastern Europe.[15] The First World War and the collapse of the Russian and Austro-Hungarian Empires finally presented Ukrainian leaders with an opportunity to wrest freedom from the chaos of conflict. In 1918–19, they declared independence and proclaimed unification of the divided Ukrainian lands but were overpowered in the fighting that ensued. By 1923, Ukraine had been divided once again, this time by Soviet Russia, Poland, Romania, and Czechoslovakia.

For Ukrainian émigrés such as Avramenko, who had participated in the armed struggle, and for some Ukrainian community leaders in Canada and the United States, defeat was a bitter pill to swallow. They harboured feelings of grievance and resentment against those who had thwarted the creation of an independent and united Ukrainian state, and they pledged to continue the struggle and to promote the Ukrainian cause (*ukrainska sprava*) by all means at their disposal. During the interwar years, moderates published and distributed books and pamphlets on the "Ukrainian question"; sent delegates to international conferences; protested the violation of Ukrainian minority rights in Poland and Romania and the purges, show trials, and artificial famine that decimated the Ukrainian political and cultural elite and killed millions of Ukrainian peasants in the Soviet Union; and lobbied the Canadian, American, and British governments and the League of Nations. More extreme elements established the Ukrainian Military Organization (UVO) and its successor the Organization of Ukrainian Nationalists (OUN); declared that all means were justified in the struggle for Ukrainian independence; resorted to armed expropriations, sabotage, and assassinations; and sought out allies among Europe's revisionist powers, including Nazi Germany. Within this context, it fell to Avramenko to advance the Ukrainian cause as a showman and propagandist, and as we have seen he subordinated all considerations to this objective and carried out his mission no matter what the consequences for himself, his family, and the immigrants who entrusted him with their hard-earned money.

Psychology offers a second possible explanation. It should be apparent that there was more than a hint of narcissism in the personality of Avramenko. His grand sense of self-importance and life-long inability to change; his consistent failure to appreciate the challenges facing him; his excessive need for admiration and unwavering devotion; his utter refusal to listen to or take advice from anyone; his sense of entitlement and arrogant behaviour; his readiness to take advantage even of those closest to him; his striking lack of empathy for the victims of his numerous schemes and projects; and the fantasies that dominated the last years of his life were all symptomatic of the condition. Certainly, the abuse that he suffered at the hands of his brutal and alcoholic father; the sudden death of his protective and loving mother; the neglect and hostility displayed by his stepmother; and the need to fend for himself in an emotionally cold and hostile world from early childhood must have produced a growing sense of abandonment, betrayal, and humiliation and convinced young Vasile that most people were not dependable, trustworthy, and sincere but aggressive, violent, capricious, and unfair. To cope with this frightening reality, he turned inward, avoided strong emotional attachments, and gradually regressed into a world of fantasies about his uniqueness, importance, self-sufficiency, and omnipotence, a coping strategy that ultimately developed into narcissism.[16] The vast personal correspondence in Avramenko's archive offers a wealth of raw material and data for the psycho-historian who might wish to test this hypothesis.

Finally, Avramenko had much in common with some of the most prominent and successful show people of his era. Recent studies of Wild West Show founder William "Buffalo Bill" Cody, celebrity evangelist Aimee Semple McPherson, and dance impresario Sol Hurok suggest a number of parallels with the eccentric Ukrainian showman. Like Avramenko, all three possessed a restless drive and energy, an innate capacity for self-promotion, a yearning for public recognition and acclaim, and an ability to survive scandals and serious errors of judgement with relatively little damage to their reputations.

Cody drifted from job to job on America's western frontier, gained fame as an army scout and buffalo hunter, and played himself on the stage before conceiving the Wild West Show, a spectacle that dramatized and popularized the notion "that American identity was founded on the Western experience: triumphant conquest of wildness through virtue, skill, and firepower." Always on the road and rarely at home, Cody lived apart from his wife for many years before their marriage ended in a scandalous divorce. He performed until his death in 1917 not only to pay off debts but also to preserve the heroic persona that he had created for himself and to sustain "the narrative of his life." By that point, a series of popular dime novels celebrating his "heroic" deeds; millions of photos, leaflets, posters, and souvenirs churned out by his publicity machine; and countless tours of North America, Britain, and Europe had transformed Cody into America's first modern celebrity and the most famous American on Earth.[17]

Aimee Semple McPherson left her second husband in 1918 to become a barnstorming evangelist because she was convinced that a higher power had chosen her to preach the gospel. Displaying an extraordinary penchant for publicity, she used print, radio, gramophone records, and film to advance her evangelical mission. By 1923, when she settled down in Los Angeles and built the Angelus Temple, Sister Aimee had made nine transcontinental tours in her "gospel car" and established the foundations for the Church of the Foursquare Gospel—a hybrid of show business and "old-time religion." As with Avramenko, who claimed to work for the Ukrainian cause, her showmanship had a higher purpose (bringing sinners to Jesus), and she was able to raise prodigious sums of money for her projects by invoking "God's work." Because Sister Aimee believed that the ends justified the means, she did not shrink from integrating popular music, stage theatricals, and opera into her religious services. She employed Hollywood professionals, spent freely on elaborate stage sets, performed "illustrated sermons" in a plethora of costumes, and even attempted to carry the gospel "into the Babylon of Broadway" in 1934 by appearing at the Capitol Theater, a vaudeville landmark. By cultivating the aura of a movie star while also feeding and clothing the poor during the Great Depression, McPherson created a remarkably resilient persona that withstood two failed marriages, financial bickering with her mother and daughter, and an international scandal that resulted from her attempt to cover up a romantic tryst.[18]

Sol Hurok, the son of a Jewish hardware and tobacco merchant born north of Kharkiv on the boundary between Ukraine and Russia, immigrated to the United States in 1906 and had become the most successful international dance impresario in the country by the 1930s. Never a homebody, he spent little time with his wife and daughter and abandoned them during the 1920s, though, unlike Avramenko, he continued to provide very generously for their material needs. Like Avramenko, Hurok had "an insatiable thirst for applause and self-aggrandizement," and he always insisted that his name must appear above that of performers on billboards and advertisements. In other respects, Hurok was the antithesis of Avramenko. A businessman determined to make a profit by providing North American audiences with interesting, exotic, and novel performers, including singers and dancers from Russia and the Soviet Union, he did not allow political, religious, ethnic, or family loyalties to get in the way. Although he was fully cognizant of the persecution experienced by Jews, including members of his own family in the Soviet Union, "Hurok put business before honesty," according to his biographer, and refused to criticize the Soviet regime "in the hopes of getting attractions he wanted out of Russia." While this alienated some within the Jewish community, including the extremist Jewish Defence League, which bombed his New York City offices in 1972, Hurok is remembered as a great impresario who played an exceptional role in popularizing ballet, opera, and classical music in the United States. Among the entertainers whom he brought to North America during the Cold

War were the Soviet folk dance ensembles led by Igor Moiseyev and Pavlo Virsky whose highly acclaimed performances effectively ended Avramenko's career and influence in Ukrainian folk dancing circles.[19]

As his influence diminished during the postwar years, Avramenko's aggressive self-promotion established the foundations for a myth that drew very selectively on memories of his past achievements. Since his impact had always been greater in Canada than in the United States, and relatively few Ukrainian Canadians had been victimized by his projects, it was natural that the myth was fostered and took hold in Canada. Ukrainian-Canadian community leaders who had endorsed his projects and helped him to solicit funds in good faith wanted to put the best face possible on his accomplishments, as did Ukrainian-Canadian politicians, some of them former pupils, who were happy to be photographed in the company of Avramenko and costumed Ukrainian folk dancers. When representatives of both groups began to appear at the jubilee celebrations that Avramenko organized for himself, the legend began to take hold. During the last years of his life, the patronage of influential Ukrainian Canadians, the honours bestowed upon him by major community organizations, and the uncritical and celebratory books about his early life added credibility to the myth. Ultimately, the most enduring creation and the greatest work of art of Vasile Avramenko was the myth that he built and inspired during the interwar years and embellished during the Cold War years—that of the ballet master who brought the Ukrainian performing arts to Broadway; the Hollywood director who made successful Ukrainian talkies in the depths of the Great Depression; and the selfless Ukrainian patriot and activist who saved generations of North American Ukrainian youth from assimilation. This myth has outlived all of his other achievements.

ACKNOWLEDGEMENTS

This book could not have been written without the assistance of several institutions and many individuals. At the Canadian Institute of Ukrainian Studies (CIUS), University of Alberta, Jars Balan and Andrij Makuch, co-ordinators of the Ukrainian-Canadian Program, persuaded me to research and write a brief volume on Avramenko's career as part of my work on the history of Ukrainian Canadians during the interwar years. They offered enthusiastic encouragement, helpful suggestions, incisive comments and stylistic and editorial advice until the first draft of the monograph was completed. At the Centre for Ukrainian Canadian Studies (CUCS), University of Manitoba, where my research on Winnipeg's Ukrainian community was supported by the Mymka Research and Scholarship Endowment Fund, Dr. Denis Hlynka and Dr. Roman Yereniuk, the Centre's acting directors, were also very supportive. Denis offered me a sessional teaching appointment while I was writing the first draft and he encouraged me to complete and publish the finished product; Roman allowed me to focus on Avramenko for several months as I laboured to transform the manuscript into a publishable monograph. Dr. Robert Klymasz read and commented on the first draft, invited me to speak about Avramenko to his students, and never tired of asking when the book would be published.

Friends not affiliated with CIUS or CUCS, who read all or part of the manuscript, offered useful feedback and words of encouragement, or simply listened to my stories and revelations about Avramenko, include Borys Gengalo, Dr. Athanasius McVay, Peter Melnycky, Myron Momryk, Dr. Roman Onufrijchuk, John Paskievich, Dr. Myroslav Shkandrij and Ostap Skrypnyk. Irka Balan, who had permission to use all of my research notes while preparing an exhibit on Avramenko, kindly reciprocated by giving me a digital copy of Avramenko's first feature film, *Natalka Poltavka* (1936), which she obtained from the Immigration History Research Centre, University of Minnesota. I also owe a special debt of gratitude to Dr. Andriy Nahachewsky and Dr. Bohdan Nebesio, who read the first draft many years ago and offered comments on their respective fields of expertise – folk dance and film.

In addition to CIUS and CUCS, which employed me during the years I worked on the book, I would also like to acknowledge Winnipeg's Rusalka Ukrainian Dance Ensemble and the Department of Canadian Heritage for providing small grants that allowed me to plan the project and do some of the preliminary archival research.

Virtually all of the research was carried out at three institutions. At Library and Archives Canada (LAC), in Ottawa, Myron Momryk was unfailingly helpful and courteous on this occasion as on many other occasions in the past. At the Ukrainian Cultural and Educational Centre (Oseredok) in Winnipeg, Bohdana Bashuk, Sophia Kachor, Gloria Romaniuk, and Ken Romaniuk, were equally accommodating. At the University of Manitoba Archives and Special Collections, James Kominowski helped to locate and then digitized rare stills from Avramenko's film *Cossacks in Exile* (1938). Finally, if not for the generous hospitality provided by my old friend and classmate Borys Gengalo, who allowed an impecunious researcher from a chronically underfunded program to pitch camp in his living room/library for what must have seemed like an eternity, none of the research at LAC in Ottawa would have been possible.

Grateful acknowledgement is also made to the following individuals and institutions for permission to reproduce photographs: Oksana Loza, Executor, Vasile Avramenko Collection at Library and Archives Canada, Ottawa; Sophia Kachor, Executive Director and Chief of Collections, Ukrainian Cultural and Educational Centre (Oseredok), Winnipeg; Dr. Shelley Sweeney, University Archivist and Head of Archives and Special Collections, University of Manitoba; and Arianne Ulmer Cipes, for permission to reproduce the photograph of her father, Edgar G. Ulmer, held at the Academy of Motion Picture Arts and Sciences, Margaret Herrick Library, Hollywood.

At the University of Manitoba Press, I would like to thank David Carr for his interest in the project, for his enthusiasm, and for his sound advice concerning how to improve the final product. Without his involvement, Avramenko's story would still be a manuscript collecting dust in someone's office. I am also indebted to Glenn Bergen, for walking me through the publication process; to the copy editors and the design staff; and to the two anonymous readers (since identified as Dr. John Lehr and Dr. Marcia Ostashewski) for their evaluation and insightful comments.

A portion of Chapter 2 was published in a slightly different version as "'All that Jazz!': The Avramenko Phenomenon in Canada, 1925-1929," *Journal of Ukrainian Studies* 28, 2 (2003), 1-29.

All translations from Ukrainian are mine unless otherwise noted. Needless to say, I am responsible for any errors of fact and interpretation that remain.

The book is dedicated to my sister Tania and to my niece Alana. Although they were not involved in the production of this book in any way, and often expressed grave concern about my penchant for "hoarding" research materials (not to mention thousands of books and DVDs), they have always helped to keep me grounded and I have always relied on them for moral and emotional support. Now that the book has been published, they can read it and see what all the fuss was about.

Orest T. Martynowych
Winnipeg

ABBREVIATIONS

AUGB	—	Association of Ukrainians in Great Britain
BEF	—	Belgian franc
CBC	—	Canadian Broadcasting Corporation
CNE	—	Canadian National Exhibition
CNR	—	Canadian National Railway
CPR	—	Canadian Pacific Railway
DP	—	displaced person
FUAA	—	Federation of Ukrainian Associations in Australia
IMDb	—	Internet Movie Data Base
LAC	—	Library and Archives Canada
MGM	—	Metro-Goldwyn-Mayer
MLA	—	member of the Legislative Assembly
MP	—	member of Parliament
NBC	—	National Broadcasting Company
NFB	—	National Film Board (of Canada)
ODVU	—	Organization for the Rebirth of Ukraine
OUN	—	Organization of Ukrainian Nationalists
PRC	—	Producers' Releasing Corporation
RCA	—	Radio Corporation of America
RKO	—	Radio-Keith-Orpheum Pictures (RKO Radio Pictures Inc.)
SUMK	—	Canadian Ukrainian Youth Association (Soiuz Ukrainskoi Molodi Kanady)

UCC	—	Ukrainian Canadian Committee (since 1992 Ukrainian Canadian Congress)
UCECA	—	Ukrainian Cultural and Educational Centre Archive
ULFTA	—	Ukrainian Labour-Farmer Temple Association
UNA	—	Ukrainian National Association
UNF	—	Ukrainian National Federation
UNR	—	Ukrainian National Republic
USRL	—	Ukrainian Self-Reliance League
USSR	—	Union of Soviet Socialist Republics
UVO	—	Ukrainian Military Organization (Ukrainska Viiskova Orhanizatsiia)
VHS	—	Video Home System
VUFKU	—	All-Ukrainian Photo-Cinema Administration (Vse-Ukrainske Foto Kino Upravlinnia)
WASP	—	white Anglo-Saxon Protestant
YMCA	—	Young Men's Christian Association

NOTES

Chapter One: The Man and His Mission

1 Irena Knysh, *Zhyva dusha narodu: do iuvileiu ukrainskoho tanku* (Winnipeg: the author, 1966), and Ivan Pihuliak, *Vasyl Avramenko a vidrodzhennia ukrainskoho tanku* (Syracuse: the author, 1979), provide two brief and celebratory sketches of Avramenko's life and work prior to his arrival in Canada. Researchers may also wish to grapple with Avramenko's virtually undecipherable handwritten notes, "Moie zhyttia ta spohady, 1895–1915," at Library and Archives Canada (LAC), Ottawa, Vasile Avramenko Collection, MG 31 D 87, vol. 1, file 10.

2 O.L. Steshenko et al, eds., *Istoriia mist i sil Ukrainskoi RSR: Cherkaska oblast* (Kyiv: Instytut Istorii Akademii Nauk URSR, 1972), 397–400, contains a brief sketch of Stebliv at the turn of the twentieth century.

3 Paul Robert Magocsi, *A History of Ukraine* (Toronto: University of Toronto Press, 1996), 371–74, 380–81; Serhy Yekelchyk, *Ukraine: Birth of a Modern Nation* (New York: Oxford University Press, 2007), 29–31, 39–45, 54–61.

4 LAC, MG 31 D 87, vol. 9, file 1, contains Avramenko's revealing correspondence between 1928 and 1934 with Liuba Maistrenko.

5 LAC, MG 31 D 87, vol. 9, file 32, Avramenko's 1971 correspondence with Joseph Schwarz.

6 LAC, MG 31 D 87, vol. 18, file 3, Avramenko's brief undated note, "How I Conceived the Idea of Ukrainian Film" (in Ukrainian).

7 *Internet Encyclopedia of Ukraine*, http://www.encyclopediaofukraine.com/default.asp, maintained by the Canadian Institute of Ukrainian Studies, University of Alberta, contains concise and informative articles on the Ukrainian theatre and all of the personalities mentioned in this chapter.

8 M.T. Rylsky, ed., *Ukrainskyi dramatychnyi teatr: narysy istorii v dvokh tomakh,* vol. 1, *Dozhovtnevyi period* (Kyiv: Akademiia nauk Ukrainskoi RSR, 1967), 267–71, 330–32; Myron Shatulsky, *The Ukrainian Folk Dance* (Toronto: Kobzar, 1980), 48–49.

9 Orest Subtelny, *Ukraine: A History* (Toronto: University of Toronto Press, 1988), 305.

10 Valerian Revutsky, "Sadovsky's Theater," in *Internet Encyclopedia of Ukraine,* http://www.encyclopediaofukraine.com/display.asp?linkpath=/pages/s/a/sadovskystheater.htm.

11 George S.N. Luckyj, *Literary Politics in the Soviet Ukraine, 1917–1934,* revised and updated edition (Durham: Duke University Press, 1990), 129, citing the critic P. Rulin writing in 1929.

12 LAC, MG 31 D 87, vol. 1, file 31, brief undated "Biography of Vasile Avramenko."

13 Allan K. Wildman, *The End of the Russian Imperial Army: The Old Army and the Soldiers Revolt, March–April 1917* (Princeton, NJ: Princeton University Press, 1980), 101.

14 LAC, MG 31 D 87, vol. 9, file 32, Avramenko's letter to Joseph Schwarz, 1 February 1971.

15 Pihuliak, *Vasyl Avramenko,* 17.

16 V.M. Verkhovynets, *Teoriia ukrainskoho narodnoho tantsiu,* 5th ed. (Kyiv: Muzychna Ukraina, 1990), 13–35, contains an informative sketch of the life and career of the ethnographer and choreographer by Yaroslav Verkhovynets that is the source for the next few paragraphs.

17 Henry Abramson, *A Prayer for the Government: Ukrainians and Jews in Revolutionary Times, 1917–1920* (Cambridge, MA: Ukrainian Research Institute and Center for Jewish Studies, Harvard University, 1999), especially 134–40, which provide a balanced discussion of this episode.

18 LAC, MG 31 D 87, vol. 1, file 31, brief undated "Biography of Vasile Avramenko." Also see Vasyl Avramenko, "Ukrainskyi natsionalnyi tanok," in *Klenovyi lyst: kanadiiskyi almanakh* (Winnipeg: T-vo opiky nad ukrainskymy pereselentsiamy im. Sv. Rafaila v Kanadi, 1929), 11–17.

19 LAC, MG 31 D 87, vol. 15, file 9, "Tribute to Washington: Press Releases," 1932.

20 Pihuliak, *Vasyl Avramenko,* 17–62, provides the most thorough account of Avramenko's efforts to teach and popularize Ukrainian folk dancing in western Ukraine (then part of Poland), Czechoslovakia, and Germany between 1921 and 1925. The remainder of this chapter relies on his narrative.

21 o.H.P. "Soroklittia slavnoi diialnosty: Do biohrafii prof. O.A. Koshytsia," *Dnipro* (Philadephia), 1 and 8 March 1937.

22 Oleksandr Koshyts [Alexander Koshetz], *Z pisneiu cherez svit,* vol.1, *Podorozh Ukrainskoi respublikanskoi kapeli* (Winnipeg: Ukrainian Cultural and Educational Centre, 1952), and vol. 2, *Iz "shchodennyka" O. Koshytsia* (Winnipeg: Ukrainian Cultural and Educational Centre, 1970), contain descriptions of the tours. The Ukrainian Cultural and Educational Centre Archive (UCECA), Winnipeg, Alexander Koshetz Collection, box 15, contains an album full of reviews clipped from European newspapers.

23 *New York Tribune,* 1 October 1922.

24 *Winnipeg Evening Tribune,* 12 December 1923, citing reviews published recently in the American press.

25 *Manitoba Free Press,* 12 December 1923.

26 UCECA, Alexander Koshetz Collection, box 14, "Shchodennyk."

27 LAC, MG 31 D 87, vol. 7, file 19, Avramenko's correspondence with Ivan Bobersky (1925–34); vol. 12, files 1–28, announcements, programs, and brochures; vol. 16, files 4–14, schools; and UCECA, Ivan Bobersky Collection, box 1a, contain a wealth of information about Avramenko's teaching and performing in western Ukraine and Czechoslovakia.

28 Subtelny, *Ukraine,* 427.

29 Yekelchyk, *Ukraine,* 121–34, provides a concise and cogent analysis of Ukrainian-Polish relations during the interwar years.

30 Pihuliak, *Vasyl Avramenko,* 36.

31 LAC, MG 31 D 87, vol. 8, file 11, Avramenko's correspondence with Andrii Kist (1922–27).

32 LAC, MG 31 D 87, vol. 7, file 19, Bobersky's letters to Avramenko and Hassan, 21 January to 5 October 1925; vol. 8, file 3, Hassan's letters to Avramenko, 30 April to 2 November 1925; vol. 7, file 11, Biberovich's letters to Avramenko and Hassan, 13 July to 6 October 1925.

Chapter 2: Dance Master

1 *Toronto Evening Telegram*, 27 February 1926.

2 For a discussion of Canadian imperial sentiment, see Carl Berger, *The Sense of Power: Studies in the Ideas of Canadian Imperialism, 1867–1914* (Toronto: University of Toronto Press, 1970).

3 E.D. McLaren, "On National Aspirations," in *Empire Club Speeches: Being Addresses before the Empire Club of Canada* (Ottawa: Dent, 1906), 136.

4 Reverend James Robertson, a Presbyterian, cited in Michael Owen, "'Keeping Canada God's Country': Presbyterian School Homes for Ruthenian Children," in Dennis L. Butcher et al., eds., *Prairie Spirit: Perspectives on the Heritage of the United Church of Canada in the West* (Winnipeg: University of Manitoba Press, 1985), 186–87.

5 Cited in Vivian Olender, "The Canadian Methodist Church and the Gospel of Assimilation, 1900–1925," *Journal of Ukrainian Studies* 7, 2 (1982): 68.

6 Jonathan F. Vance, *A History of Canadian Culture* (Toronto: Oxford University Press, 2009), 177–80, 277–80.

7 LAC, MG 31 D 87, vol. 7, file 19, Avramenko's letter to Ivan Bobersky, 17 November 1927.

8 See, for example, Vasyl Avramenko, "Ukrainskyi natsionalnyi tanok," in *Klenovyi lyst:kanadiiskyi almanakh* (Winnipeg: T-vo opiky nad ukrainskymy pereselentsiamy im. Sv. Rafaila v Kanadi, 1929), 11–17, the text of a speech that he delivered in countless Ukrainian community halls.

9 LAC, MG 31 D 87, vol. 8, file 3, Hassan's letters to Avramenko, 25 June, 22 August, 7–13 September, 4 October, 2 and 25 November 1925.

10 *Ukrainskyi holos* (Ukrainian Voice; Winnipeg), 27 January 1926.

11 LAC, MG 31 D 87, vol. 8, file 11, P.V. Kukhta, "Vasyl Avramenko: Ioho diialnist vid pryizdu do Kanady."

12 LAC, MG 31 D 87, vol. 16, file 19, "Toronto."

13 For example, see Florence Randal Livesay, "Songs of Ukraine Preserve Spirit of Its People," *Musical America* (12 June 1926), and "Songs and Dances of the Ukraine," *Canadian Magazine* (January 1927), which also contained two photographs of Avramenko.

14 Alexandra Pritz, "Ukrainian Dance in Canada: The First Fifty Years, 1924–1974," in Jaroslav Rozumnyj, ed., *New Soil—Old Roots: The Ukrainian Experience in Canada* (Winnipeg: Ukrainian Academy of Arts and Sciences in Canada, 1983), 129–30.

15 LAC, MG 31 D 87, vol. 15, file 40, "Ballet Schools: Rules and Regulations."

16 Andriy Nahachewsky, "First Existence Folk Dance Forms among Ukrainians in Smoky Lake, Alberta and Swan Plain, Saskatchewan" (MA thesis, University of Alberta, 1985), 193–94. Avramenko's brochure *Ukrainski natsionalni tanky: opys* (Winnipeg: Shkoly ukrainskoho natsionalnoho tanku, 1928) contained descriptions of the eighteen dances that Avramenko choreographed and taught.

17 Andriy Nahachewsky, *Ukrainian Dance: A Cross-Cultural Approach* (Jefferson, NC: McFarland and Company, 2012), 104.

18 *Toronto Evening Telegram,* 25–27 February 1926; *Toronto Daily Star,* 25–26 February 1926.

19 *Ukrainskyi holos,* 28 June and 30 July 1926, reported that Matthew Popovych and his wife were touring southwestern Ontario with a group of ULFTA dancers who had been trained by Avramenko.

20 *Toronto Evening Telegram,* 28 August 1926.

21 *Toronto Daily Star,* 7 September 1926. These were also the qualities attributed to Native Canadians by contemporaries. Writing about Quebec's tercentenary in 1908, historian H.V. Nelles observed that, "Indians in costume added colour to otherwise drab, black-coated, celluloid-collared, speech-drowned, formalities. Indians brought joy, innocence, spontaneity, and mystery – the carnivalesque dimensions – to the celebration." See his *The Art of Nation-Building: Pageantry and Spectacle at Quebec's Tercentenary* (Toronto: University of Toronto Press, 2000), 172.

22 LAC, MG 31 D 87, vol. 8, file 11, P.V. Kukhta, "Vasyl Avramenko: ioho diialnist vid pryizdu do Kanady," lists the periodicals that carried items on Avramenko during his sojourn in Toronto.

23 LAC, MG 31 D 87, vol. 2, files 5 and 6, and vol. 6, file 25, contain Avramenko's correspondence with Darkovych from May through September 1926.

24 LAC, MG 31 D 87, vol. 16, file 17, "Fort William, Port Arthur, Ontario"; *Ukrainskyi holos,* 13 October, 3 and 10 November 1926.

25 LAC, MG 31 D 87, vol. 2, file 5, Hryhorii Hanuliak's letter to Avramenko, 21 October 1926; vol. 8, file 3, Yuri Hassan's letter to Avramenko, January 1927.

26 UCECA, Alexander Koshetz Collection, box 15, "Shchodennyk"; *Ukrainskyi holos,* 17 and 24 November, 1 December 1926.

27 *Fort William Times Journal,* 2 December 1926; *Ukrainskyi holos,* 22 and 29 December 1926, 5 January 1927; LAC, MG 31 D 87, vol. 16, file 18, "Kenora."

28 Barry McCarten, "History and Live Theatre in Winnipeg," *Manitoba History* 16 (1988): 21–22; Jim Blanchard, *Winnipeg 1912* (Winnipeg: University of Manitoba Press, 2005), 35–38; Alan Artibise, *Winnipeg: An Illustrated History* (Toronto: James Lorimer and Company, 1977), 109–62.

29 *Ukrainskyi holos,* 26 January 1927, and *Kanadyiskyi farmer* (Canadian Farmer; Winnipeg), 2 February 1927, published enthusiastic reviews.

30 LAC, MG 31 D 87, vol. 16, file 21, "Winnipeg, Manitoba."

31 *Ukrainskyi holos,* 26 January 1927, reported that on the same day ULFTA dancers put on a recital of their own at the Ukrainian Labour Temple, three blocks north, at the corner of McGregor and Pritchard, to draw away spectators from Avramenko's performance.

32 *Ukrainskyi holos,* 26 January, 9 and 16 February, 2 March 1927.

33 *Kanadyiskyi farmer,* 9 March 1927.

34 *Manitoba Free Press,* 2 May 1927, and *Winnipeg Evening Tribune,* 2 and 4 May 1927, published reviews.

35 *Manitoba Free Press,* 4 June 1927.

36 *Winnipeg Evening Tribune,* 2 July 1927; *Edmonton Journal,* 2 July 1927; *Kanadyiskyi farmer,* 6 July 1927; *Ukrainskyi holos,* 6 July 1927.

37 LAC, MG 31 D 87, vol. 8, file 3, Yuri Hassan's letter to Avramenko, 1 July 1927.

38 LAC, MG 31 D 87, vol. 8, file 25, copy of Atkinson's letter to Koohtow (Kukhta), 7 February 1927; vol. 8, file 3, Hassan's letter to Avramenko, 27 April 1927.

39 Orest T. Martynowych, *Ukrainians in Canada: The Formative Period, 1891–1924* (Edmonton: Canadian Institute of Ukrainian Studies Press, 1991), 277–84.

40 Andrij Makuch, "Narodni Domy in East Central Europe," and Andriy Nahachewsky, "Ukrainian Performing Arts in Alberta," both in Manoly R. Lupul, ed., *Continuity and Change: The Cultural Life of Alberta's First Ukrainians* (Edmonton: CIUS Press, 1988), 202–10 and 211–20.

41 Jars Balan, "Backdrop to an Era: The Ukrainian Canadian Stage in the Interwar Years," *Journal of Ukrainian Studies* 16, 1–2 (1991): 89–113, is the source for the next three paragraphs.

42 *Ukrainskyi holos,* 10 and 17 August 1927; *Kanadyiskyi farmer,* 17 and 31 August 1927.

43 LAC, MG 31 D 87, vol. 12, files 64–67, concert advertisements, and vol. 44, file 5, ticket sales and expenditures, provide vital financial data about the tour.

44 Pritz, "Ukrainian Dance in Canada," 129.

45 *Ukrainskyi holos,* 28 December 1927.

46 *Edmonton Journal,* 27 November 1927.

47 LAC, MG 31 D 87, vol. 16, files 15 and 16, "Canora, Yorkton, Saskatoon" and "Edmonton."

48 *Ukrainskyi holos,* 22 February 1928, reported on the incident at St. Joseph's College; LAC, MG 31 D 87, vol. 16, file 15, H.F. Stratiichuk to Avramenko, 8 March 1928, explained the opposition of devout Ukrainian Orthodox students in Canora to participation in a dance performance during Lent.

49 It appears that such teachers were expected to forward 25 percent of their earnings to Avramenko and could issue certificates only after he or one of his authorized assistants had examined their pupils. See LAC, MG 31 D 87, vol. 8, file 12, Kist's letters to Avramenko, 24 July and 8 August 1928, and vol. 9, file 18, Avramenko's letter to Pihuliak, 12 February 1929.

50 LAC, MG 31 D 87, vol. 9, file 17, letters exchanged by Pihuliak and Kist, 26 and 30 January 1928.

51 LAC, MG 31 D 87, vol. 8, file 3, letters exchanged by Hassan and Avramenko, 10–15 June 1927, 13–26 September 1927, 22 December 1927–3 January 1928, 8 February–2 March 1928; vol. 8, file 12, Kist's letters to Avramenko, 10 and 12 February 1928; vol. 9, file 17, Kist's letter to Pihuliak, 30 January 1928; and vol. 10, file 13, Stephan Tychowecky's letter to Avramenko, 11 February 1928, all concern the rumours circulating in Winnipeg.

52 The Chicago Woman's World's Fair was an annual event between 1925 and 1928 that showcased "women's ideas, work and products" and raised funds in support of the women's Republican Party organizations that sponsored the event. See "Woman's World's Fair 1925," in *Encyclopedia of Chicago,* http://encyclopedia.chicagohistory.org/pages/1374.html.

53 LAC, MG 31 D 87, vol. 7, file 25, letters exchanged by Stephanie Cymbalist and Avramenko, 10 and 18 April 1928.

54 LAC, MG 31 D 87, vol. 9, file 17, Kist's letter to Pihuliak, 17 May 1928.

55 *Ukrainskyi holos,* 30 May 1928.

56 LAC, MG 31 D 87, vol. 8, file 12, Kist's letters to Avramenko, 21, 28, and 31 May, 4 and 14 June, and 6 July 1928, trace the Garbolinsky family's reactions to the episode, from shock and dismay to acceptance.

57 LAC, MG 31, D 87, vol. 8, file 12, Kist's letters to Avramenko, 2–17 July 1928, and vol. 9, file 18, Kist's letters to Pihuliak, 11 and 13 July 1928, contain information about Avramenko's ultimately unsuccessful efforts to organize and finance the tour.

58 LAC, MG 31 D 87, vol. 16, file 3, "Avramenko Schools of Ukrainian Folk Ballet in the USA."

59 LAC, MG 31 D 87, vol. 8, file 12, Kist's letters to Avramenko, 25 September and 1 October 1928.

60 LAC, MG 31 D 87, vol. 9, file 18, letters exchanged by Avramenko and Pihuliak, 16 and 18 January 1929.

61 LAC, MG 31 D 87, vol. 9, file 19, Pihuliak's letters to Avramenko, 30 March, 4 and 11 April 1929.

62 Montreal *Gazette,* 15 April 1929; also see *Montreal Daily Star,* 15 April 1929.

63 LAC, MG 31 D 87, vol. 9, file 28, Olena Serdechna's letters to Avramenko, 26 January–20 February 1927.

64 LAC, MG 31 D 87, vol. 2, file 12, Petro Bilon's letter to Avramenko, 11 April 1928.

65 LAC, MG 31 D 87, vol. 2, file 10, Ivan Bodrug's letter to Avramenko, 24 February 1928.

66 LAC, MG 31 D 87, vol. 8, file 14, as related in Kist's letter to Avramenko, 30 December 1930.

67 Steve Freund, "Movie Industry," and Michael Hartman, "Popular Culture," both in Garry B. Nash, gen. ed., *Encyclopedia of American History,* vol. 7, *The Emergence of Modern America 1900–1928* (New York: Facts On File, 2010), 214–16 and 263–66.

68 John Herd Thompson and Allen Seager, *Canada 1922–1939: Decades of Discord* (Toronto: McClelland and Stewart, 1985), 180–81.

69 Scott Eyman, *The Speed of Sound: Hollywood and the Talkie Revolution, 1926–1930* (Baltimore: Johns Hopkins University Press, 1997), places these developments in context.

70 Peter Morris, *Embattled Shadows: A History of Canadian Cinema, 1895–1939* (Montreal: McGill-Queen's University Press, 1978), 57–62, 95–121.

71 *Microsoft Encarta Reference Library 2004 Plus DVD* contains descriptions and definitions of these dances.

72 Peter Ling, "Sex and the Automobile in the Jazz Age," *History Today* 39, 11 (1989): 18–24.

73 Kathy Peiss, "Making Up, Making Over: Cosmetics, Consumer Culture, and Women's Identity," in Victoria de Grazia and Ellen Furlough, eds., *The Sex of Things: Gender and Consumption in Historical Perspective* (Berkeley: University of California Press, 1996), 311–36.

74 Paula S. Fass, *The Damned and the Beautiful: American Youth in the 1920s* (New York: Oxford University Press, 1977), 22–23, 303.

75 *Ukrainskyi holos,* 17 November 1926, published an article under the title "Concerning the Issue of Our Native Music," in which Peter Lazarowich and Honore Ewach, two recent university graduates, lamented that "our weddings and other pastimes are accompanied by the bellowing of modern jazz rather than the sounds of our native music." As a result, traditional forms of Ukrainian instrumental and dance music were threatened with extinction. Previously, traditional Ukrainian melodies and the instrumentalists who performed them were well known in Canada; "however, since jazz became the ideal inducement to dance, all of these old musicians have fallen silent. Now a musician who dared to play a *kolomyika* in public would only provoke laughter."

76 LAC, MG 30 D 307, vol. 1, file 10, acc.84/392, Julian Stechishin Collection, "Diary." All passages from the diary have been translated from Ukrainian by the author.

77 For the published version, see Vasyl Avramenko, "Ukrainskyi natsionalnyi tanok," in *Klenovyi lyst: kanadiiskyi almanakh* (Winnipeg: T-vo opiky nad ukrainskymy pereselentsiamy im. Sv. Rafaila v Kanadi, 1929), 11–17.

78 LAC, MG 31 D 87, vol. 7, file 24, Yevhen Chykalenko's letter to Avramenko, 10 January 1928.

79 *Toronto Evening Telegram*, 25 February 1926.

80 *Toronto Evening Telegram*, 28 August 1926.

81 LAC, MG 30 D 307, vol. 1, file 11, acc.84/392, "Diary."

82 Ibid.

83 *Kanadyiskyi farmer*, 29 June 1927, review of Winnipeg Playhouse performance.

84 LAC, MG 31 D 87, vol. 8, file 25, Kukhta's letter to Avramenko, 15 January 1928.

85 LAC, MG 31 D 87, vol. 7, file 19, Bobersky's letter to Avramenko, 19 April 1929.

86 LAC, MG 31 D 87, vol. 7, file 19, especially Bobersky's humorous letters to Avramenko, 2, 11, and 16 November 1927; vol. 8, file 12, Kist's letter to Avramenko, 3 June 1928; vol. 8, file 25, Kukhta's letter to Avramenko, 3 March 1928.

87 LAC, MG 31 D 87, vol. 2, file 8, document dated 3 June 1927.

88 LAC, MG 31 D 87, vol. 10, file 11, Avramenko's letter to J. Sytnyk, 27 December 1927.

89 LAC, MG 31 D 87, vol. 7, file 3, Avramenko's letter to his brother Havrylo Avramenko, 19 January 1929. In 1929, the average annual wage in Canada was $1,200, and fewer than 5 percent of Canadians earned more than $2,500 annually. See Thompson and Seager, *Canada 1922–1939*, 138.

90 William A. Everett and Paul R. Laird, *Historical Dictionary of the Broadway Musical* (Lanham, MD: Scarecrow Press, 2008), xvii–xix, 311–13.

91 Marcia B. Siegel, *The Shapes of Change: Images of American Dance* (Berkeley: University of California Press, 1985), and Julia L. Foulkes, *Modern Bodies: Dance and American Modernism from Martha Graham to Alvin Ailey* (Chapel Hill: University of North Carolina Press, 2002), cover the history of modern dance in America.

92 Scott Yanow, *Jazz: A Regional Exploration* (Westport, CT: Greenwood, 2005), 29–97, provides an accessible overview of the jazz scene in interwar New York.

93 Malcolm Bradbury, ed., *The Atlas of Literature* (London: Prospero, 1996), 186–89.

94 Robert Hughes, *American Visions: The Epic History of Art in America* (New York: Alfred A. Knopf, 1997), 323–35, 353–65.

95 Irving Howe, *World of Our Fathers: The Journey of the East European Jews to America and the Life They Found and Made* (New York: Touchstone, 1976), 556–73, discusses Jewish entertainers.

96 Albert Fried, *The Rise and Fall of the Jewish Gangster in America* (New York: Columbia University Press, 1980), and Jenna Weissman Joselit, *Our Gang: Jewish Crime and the New York Jewish Community, 1900–1940* (Bloomington: Indiana University Press, 1983), are the standard works on the subject.

97 LAC, MG 31 D 87, vol. 16, file 3, "Avramenko Schools of Ukrainian Folk Ballet in the USA."

98 LAC, MG 31 D 87, vol. 8, file 3, Avramenko's letters to Hassan, 28 January–12 February 1929; vol. 2, file 20, Avramenko's letter to Koshetz, 20 June 1931.

99 Ethan Wolff, *Frommer's Memorable Walks in New York* (New York: Wiley Publishing, 2006), 97. In 1911, gangster Big Jack Zelig, the last leader of the Monk Eastman Gang, killed one of his adversaries in the casino. By the 1940s, it was a haven for jazz lovers; today it is the Ukrainian National Home.

100 LAC, MG 31 D 87, vol. 16, file 3, "Avramenko Schools of Ukrainian Folk Ballet in the USA." A complete list of instructors would include those who taught in Canada (1925–40)—Victor Moshuk, Ivan Pihuliak, Andrii Kist, Stefan Yemchuk, Sam Hancharyk, Ivan Pasichniak, Paul Tkachuk, Illia Kosikovsky, Osyp Tatarniuk, Teodor Zalopany, Hryhorii Tyzhuk, Paul Yavorsky, Ivan Tokaryk, Mariian Masniak (Myron Mason), and Ivan Kalyniuk—and those who taught in the United States (1929–37)—Ivan Pihuliak, Andrii Kist, Peter Smook, Ivan Zablotsky, John Ewanchuk, Mykhailo Hyra, Roman Fenchynsky, Ivan Shylo, Stepan Musiichuk, Teddy Rakowiecki, S. Herman, Volodymyr Shemerdiak, Ivan Savchyn, Myroslaw Zelechiwsky, Stefan Yemchuk, Orest Pankiv, Reverend Alexis Revera, and Nick Arseny.

101 LAC, MG 31 D 87, vol. 2, file 19; vol. 3, file 1; and vol. 3, file 29, Tyzhuk's letters to Avramenko, 19 September, 16–19 October, and 30 November 1931; 8, 11, and 16 February 1932; and 20 June 1933, provide interesting information on the instructor and his schools in western Canada.

102 Richard Spottswood, "Ethnic and Popular Style in America," in William Ferris and Mary L. Hart, eds., *Folk Music and Modern Sound* (Jackson: University Press of Mississippi, 1982), 66, and Pekka Gronow and Ilpo Saunio, *An International History of the Recording Industry* (London: Cassell, 1998), 46–47, provide information on Humeniuk, Columbia Records, and the origins of the ethnic recording industry in North America.

103 LAC, MG 31, D 87, vol. 10, file 5, Smook's letter to Avramenko, 13 November 1929, and Avramenko's letter to Smook, 8 January 1930.

104 LAC, MG 31 D 87, vol. 11, file 9, "Ballet Schools: Financial Matters," 31 January 1930.

105 LAC, MG 31 D 87, vol. 10, file 9, Avramenko's letter to Lev Sorochynsky, 17 January 1930.

106 LAC, MG 31 D 87, vol. 10, file 41, "Ukrainian Military Organization (UVO)," 7 July 1929.

107 LAC, MG 31 D 87, vol. 8, file 14, Kist's letter to Avramenko, 16 July 1930.

108 LAC, MG 31 D 87, vol. 8, file 13, Kist's letter to Pauline (Garbolinsky) Avramenko, 5 September 1929, and Kist's letter to Avramenko, 7 September 1930.

109 LAC, MG 31 D 87, vol. 9, file 19, Pihuliak's letter to Avramenko, 14 August 1929; vol. 8, file 29, Kalenik Lissiuk's letters to Avramenko, 14–20 August 1930.

110 Gerald Early, "The Birth of Mass Culture," in Lorraine Glennon and John A. Garraty, eds., *Our Times: The Illustrated History of the 20th Century* (Atlanta: Turner Publishing, 1995), 146–51.

111 Dmytro M. Shtohryn, *Ukrainians in North America: A Biographical Directory* (Champaign, IL: Association for the Advancement of Ukrainian Studies, 1975), 185, provides a brief biographical sketch. In his later years, Lissiuk was involved with various right-wing groups, including Wake Up America, the Congress of Freedom, and the John Birch Society. His papers are located at the Harvard Ukrainian Research Institute in Cambridge; see http://hollis.harvard.edu/?itemid=%7Clibrary/m/aleph%7C009499647.

112 LAC, MG 31 D 87, vol. 10, file 3, Avramenko's letter to Reverend W. Sliuzar, 17 September 1929, and vol. 13, file 27, leaflet, dated 20 December 1931, provide information on Jacoby and Avramenko's performances for Jacoby and his friends.

113 *Svoboda* (New York), 22 May 1929.

114 *New York Times,* 20 May 1929.

115 LAC, MG 31 D 87, vol. 10, file 14, Avramenko's letter to James Tymochko, 22 May 1929.

116 LAC, MG 31 D 87, vol. 1, file 50, "Ukrainian Dance in America," draft of Avramenko's reply to a critical article published by I. Bodnar in *Svoboda,* 6 August 1930.

117 UCECA, Alexander Koshetz Collection, box 7, Rev. W.A. Kaskiw's letter to Alexander Koshetz, 19 March 1931.

118 LAC, MG 31 D 87, vol. 15, file 3, "Metropolitan Opera: Correspondence and Communiques," letter to parents of School of Ukrainian Folk Dance and Ballet pupils.

119 *New York Evening Post,* 27 April 1931; *The Advertiser,* 1 May 1931, also published an enthusiastic review.

120 *Svoboda,* 14 May 1931.

121 *Narodna volia* (People's Freedom; Scranton, PA) 50 (1931) (unidentified clipping with the periodical's name and exact date missing; located in the inaccessible materials of the Avramenko Collection at LAC). I am grateful to LAC archivist Myron Momryk for taking me into the vaults to see this and other clippings. LAC, MG 31 D 87, vol. 2, file 19, Mykhailo Seleshko's letter to Avramenko, 10 October 1931, reveals that Avramenko was very concerned by the "attacks" on him published in *Narodna volia.* Seleshko, an émigré nationalist living in Berlin, tried to explain that this was the price of "American freedom of the press." In 1932, *Narodna volia* refused to publish Avramenko's article on preparations for the Washington bicentennial tour because Avramenko had never purchased ad space in the periodical (vol. 2, file 24, *Narodna volia* editor's letter to Avramenko, 23 January 1932).

122 *New York Times,* 22–27 April 1931.

123 *New York Times,* 26 April 1931.

124 LAC, MG 31 D 87, vol. 10, file 30, Konovalets's letter to Avramenko, 8 May 1931.

125 LAC, MG 31 D 87, vol. 2, file 19, Seleshko's letter to Avramenko, 10 November 1931.

126 *Narodne slovo* (People's Word; Pittsburgh), 24 March 1932.

127 LAC, MG 31 D 87, vol. 8, file 14, Avramenko's letter to Kist, 18 July 1931; vol. 10, file 19, Avramenko's letter to Ivan Yedenak, 28 July 1931.

128 LAC, MG 31 D 87, vol. 7, file 6, Avramenko's letter to his wife, Pauline (Garbolinsky) Avramenko, 2 January 1932; vol. 8, file 15, Avramenko's letter to Kist, 5 January 1932.

129 LAC, MG 31 D 87, vol. 3, file 3, Avramenko's letter to the Ukrainian National Association executive, 16 February 1932, reveals that Avramenko estimated at least $15,000 would be required to finance all of the preparations for the tour.

130 UCECA, Alexander Koshetz Collection, box 7, Koshetz's letter to Mykhailo Yeremiiv, 14 January 1932. The Koshetz Collection, box 16, contains unsigned copies of agreements proposed to Koshetz by Avramenko dated 18 January 1932 and 27 April 1932.

131 The Washington bicentennial tour dates were Washington, DC, 1 May; Baltimore, MD, 3 May; Wilmington, DE, 4 May; Allentown, PA, 5 May; Philadelphia, PA, 6 May; New York City, 8 May (matinee and evening); Boston, MA, 10 May; Holyoke, MA, 11 May; New Haven, CT, 12 May; Hartford, CT, 13 May; Troy, NY, 14 May; Utica, NY, 15 May; Syracuse, NY, 16 May; Rochester, NY, 17 May; Buffalo, NY, 18 May; Pittsburgh, PA, 20 May; Youngstown, OH, 21 May;, Cleveland, OH, 22 May; Toledo, OH, 23 May; Detroit, MI, 24 May; Grand Rapids, MI, 26 May; Muskegon, MI, 27 May; and Chicago, IL, 28 May.

132 LAC, MG 31 D 87, vol. 9, file 16, Pihuliak's letter to Avramenko, 28 April 1932. Ultimately, the Ukrainian delegation had to settle for a tour of the White House provided by members of the presidential staff.

133 LAC, MG 31 D 87, vol. 9, file 20, Pihuliak's letter to Avramenko, 27 April 1932.

134 LAC, MG 31 D 87, vol. 11, file 10, "Financial Records of Concerts, 1929–33."

135 UCECA, Alexander Koshetz Collection, box 17, "Shchodennyk podorozhi 1932." The choir conductor's personal journal with its scathing commentary appears to be the only extant record of the tour.

136 *New York Evening Post,* 9 May 1932.

137 *New York Times,* 9 May 1932.

138 *Brooklyn Daily Eagle,* 9 May 1932.

139 *Boston Globe,* 11 May 1932.

140 *Baltimore Sun,* 4 May 1932.

141 *Philadelphia Public Ledger,* 7 May 1932.

142 *New York World-Telegram,* 9 May 1932.

143 *Boston Evening Transcript,* 11 May 1932.

144 LAC, MG 31 D 87, vol. 8, file 3, Avramenko's letters to Hassan, 19 August–26 September 1932 and 21 December 1933; vol. 8, file 15, Avramenko's letter to Kist, 27 August 1932; and vol. 10, file 9, Avramenko's letter to his brother Havrylo Avramenko, 3 September 1932, reveal that he had paid Koshetz and the choir the $10,000 that they had been promised, but he was left with a personal debt of almost $15,000, which matched the sum that he had borrowed to finance the tour.

145 UCECA, Alexander Koshetz Collection, box 17, "Shchodennyk podorozhi 1932."

146 LAC, MG 31 D 87, vol. 7, file 6, Pauline (Garbolinsky) Avramenko's letter to Avramenko, 15 November 1932, informing him that gossip, rumours, and reports about the disparaging comments and threats that he was making during his travels had reached New York City.

147 LAC, vol. 13, files 58–59, "New England States Concert Tour, 1933"; vol. 9, file 11, Avramenko's correspondence with Mykola Novak, February–June 1933; vol. 9, file 20, Avramenko's correspondence with Pihuliak, February–June 1933.

148 LAC, MG 31 D 87, vol. 11, file 26, "Agreement," 12 May 1933.

149 LAC, MG 31 D 87, vol. 13, file 61, "Chicago, Illinois, August 1933," contains advertisements and programs concerning the event.

150 *Svoboda,* 24 August 1933.

151 LAC, MG 31 D 87, vol. 11, file 10, "Financial Records of Concerts, 1929–33." Avramenko's personal loss might have been only $1,500: LAC, MG 31 D 87, vol. 3, file 31, Avramenko's letter to the Ukrainian Chicago World's Fair Exhibit Corporation, 26 August 1933.

152 LAC, MG 31 D 87, vol. 3, file 32, Avramenko's letter to Dr. Luka Myshuga (*Svoboda* editor), 26 August 1933.

153 David M. Kennedy, *Freedom from Fear: The American People in Depression and War, 1929–1945* (New York: Oxford University Press, 1999), 163–67.

154 LAC, MG 31 D 87, vol. 7, file 1, Nick Arseny's letter to Avramenko, 6 September 1932.

155 LAC, MG 31 D 87, vol. 10, file 9, Lev Sorochynsky's letter to Avramenko, 5 August 1927, and vol. 8, file 12, Kist's letter to Avramenko, 12 February 1928, raised these issues and rejected Avramenko's behaviour.

156 LAC, MG 31 D 87, vol. 8, file 3, Avramenko's letter to Hassan, 4 May 1928.

157 LAC, MG 31 D 87, vol. 8, file 3, Avramenko's letter to Hassan, 2 February 1928.

158 LAC, MG 31 D 87, vol. 8, file 12, Avramenko's letter to Kist, 10 July 1928.

159 LAC, MG 31 D 87, vol. 9, file 18, Kist's letter to Ivan Pihuliak, 11 July 1928.

160 LAC, MG 31 D 87, vol. 10, file 5, Avramenko's letter to Smook, October 1932, and Smook's letters to Avramenko, 17 January and 17 February 1933; in July 1933, Smook turned down an offer to work with Avramenko at the Chicago World's Fair.

161 LAC, MG 31 D 87, vol. 9, file 20, Pihuliak's letter to Avramenko, 26 August 1933; vol. 9, file 16, Pihuliak's letter to Avramenko, 4 October 1933.

162 LAC, MG 31 D 87, vol. 9, file 18, Kist's letter to Avramenko, 7 September 1929, begged Avramenko to stop lecturing and to focus on dance lessons.

163 For a perceptive discussion of how Ukrainophiles used the folk costume to create a national mythology and resist the Russian imperial regime, see Serhy Yekelchyk, "The Body and the National Myth: Motifs from the Ukrainian National Revival in the Nineteenth Century," *Australian Slavonic and East European Studies* 7, 2 (1993): 31–59. Unlike Avramenko, the Ukrainophiles had confined use of the folk costume to festive occasions.

164 LAC, MG 31 D 87, vol. 8, file 25, Avramenko's letter to Kukhta, 17 February 1928.

165 LAC, MG 31 D 87, vol. 10, file 21, Avramenko's correspondence with Vasyl Yemets (bandura virtuoso), 29 January–1 March 1929, took issue with Ukrainian artists being photographed in frock coats rather than embroidered shirts.

166 LAC, MG 31 D 87, vol. 4, file 6, Reverend Alexis Revera's letter to Avramenko, 2 November 1936.

167 LAC, MG 31 D 87, vol. 13, file 73, leaflet advertising the event, April 1935; vol. 4, file 4, contains a copy of an April 1935 letter from Avramenko to White House officials suggesting that his pupils be invited to participate. *Svoboda,* 3 May 1935, published two reports on the event. The children performed several dances for Mrs. Roosevelt in the White House garden and presented her with a basket of Ukrainian Easter eggs. Other participants in the festivities asked the dancers who they were and where they came from. The *Washington Evening Star* made positive reference to the Ukrainian dancers in its coverage of the Easter Egg Roll.

168 LAC, MG 31, D 87, vol. 9, file 8, Pauline (Garbolinsky) Avramenko's letter to Mrs. Mykytiuk, 17 April 1929.

169 LAC, MG 31 D 87, vol. 7, file 6, Pauline (Garbolinsky) Avramenko's letters to Avramenko, 28 July–15 September 1929.

170 LAC, MG 31 D 87, vol. 7, file 6, Avramenko's letter to Pauline (Garbolinsky) Avramenko, 2 January 1932.

171 LAC, MG 31 D 87, vol. 7, file 6, Pauline (Garbolinsky) Avramenko's letter to Avramenko, 14 August 1933.

172 LAC, MG 31 D 87, vol. 7, file 27, Avramenko's letter to Mrs. Teklia Danys, 20 December 1933.

173 LAC, MG 31 D 87, vol. 8, file 1, letters exchanged by Avramenko and Fred Garbolinsky, 6–8 September 1934.

174 LAC, MG 31 D 87, vol. 7, file 6, Pauline (Garbolinsky) Avramenko's letter to Avramenko, 5 September 1933, in which Pauline implores him not to borrow any more money from her father, and Avramenko's letter to Pauline, 5 May 1935, in which Avramenko states that going out to work is inappropriate.

175 LAC, MG 31 D 87, vol. 7, file 6, Pauline (Garbolinsky) Avramenko's letter to Avramenko, 21 August 1929.

176 LAC, MG 31 D 87, vol. 8, file 1, Avramenko's letter to Fred Garbolinsky, 6 March 1935.

177 LAC, MG 31 D 87, vol. 7, file 6, Avramenko's letter to Pauline (Garbolinsky) Avramenko, 18 December 1934, enumerates a veritable litany of his wife's alleged transgressions.

178 LAC, MG 31 D 87, vol. 7, file 6, Avramenko's letter to Pauline (Garbolinsky) Avramenko, 4 March 1935; letters exchanged by Avramenko and Pauline, 5 May–24 August 1935 and 19–28 February 1936.

179 LAC, MG 31 D 87, vol. 4, files 1, 3, and 6, Olena Kulchytska's letters to Avramenko, 8–10 November 1934, 9 May and 16 August 1935, and 20 January 1936.

180 LAC, MG 31 D 87, vol. 3, file 32, Avramenko's letters to Mr. Hirchytsia and Mr. Smygelsky, 22 December 1933, informing them that Avramenko was unable to settle the $500 debt that he had incurred with each; vol. 4, file 6, Reverend Volodymyr Sliuzar's letter to Avramenko, 21 July 1936, on behalf of Avramenko's creditor, Mr. Hukalo, on the verge of bankruptcy; vol. 4, file 6, Vasyl and Pavlyna Korpak's letter to Avramenko, 11 November 1936, informing him that they were about to lose their house; vol. 4, file 6, Michael Sardinski's letter to Avramenko, November 1936; vol. 4, file 6, in particular, contains many more letters from irate and despondent creditors.

Chapter 3: Motion Picture Producer

1 Donald Spoto, *Blue Angel: The Life of Marlene Dietrich* (New York: Doubleday, 1992), 108–23.

2 Cited by Roger Ebert, "The Scarlet Empress," in *The Great Movies III* (Chicago: University of Chicago Press, 2010), 347–51.

3 John Baxter, *Von Sternberg* (Lexington: University of Kentucky Press, 2010), 180.

4 Garry Morris, "Mother Russia! Von Sternberg's *The Scarlet Empress* on DVD," *Bright Lights Film Journal* 33 (2001), http://brightlightsfilm.com/33/scarletempress.php.

5 *Ukrainian Weekly,* 6 October 1933; *Svoboda,* 20 October 1933.

6 LAC, MG 31 D 87, vol. 19, file 48, "Scenario" (in Ukrainian; for the film *Triumph of Ukrainian Dance,* 1954).

7 LAC, MG 31 D 87, vol. 18, file 3, Avramenko's two-page undated note, "How I Conceived the Idea of Ukrainian Film" (in Ukrainian).

8 Ivan Pihuliak, *Vasyl Avramenko a vidrodzhennia ukrainskoho tanku* (Syracuse: the author, 1979), 24.

9 LAC, MG 31 D 87, vol. 8, file 11, Andrii Kist's letter to an unidentified recipient, 18 August 1926; vol. 8, file 3, Yuri Hassan's letter to Avramenko, 19 September 1926.

10 UCECA, Alexander Koshetz Collection, box 16, Koshetz's letter to Sid Grauman, 11 January 1927.

11 UCECA, Alexander Koshetz Collection, box 8, Ivan Lampart's letter to Koshetz, 2 October 1928; box 13, Dmytro Yakubenko's letter to Koshetz, 18 April 1931.

12 LAC, MG 31 D 87, vol. 10, file 16, Yakubenko's letter to Avramenko, 24 December 1928, and Avramenko's letter to Yakubenko, 5 January 1929. A very interesting discussion of the transition from silent films to talkies is in Scott Eyman, *The Speed of Sound: Hollywood and the Talkie Revolution, 1926–1930* (Baltimore: Johns Hopkins University Press, 1997).

13 LAC, MG 31 D 87, vol. 10, file 16, letters exchanged by Avramenko and Yakubenko, 27 September–16 October 1929.

14 LAC, MG 31 D 87, vol. 9, file 18, correspondence between Pihuliak and Avramenko, 22–26 January 1929; vol. 8, file 3, Avramenko's letter to Hassan, 28 January 1929.

15 LAC, MG 31 D 87, vol. 8, file 3, Avramenko's letter to Hassan, 12 February 1929.

16 Heorhii V. Zhurov, *Z mynuloho kino na Ukraini, 1896–1917* (Kyiv: Vyd-vo Akademiï nauk UkrRSR, 1959); Volodymyr Myslavsky, "Pershe desiatylittia isnuvannia

ihrovohoho kinematohrafa v Ukraini (1907–1917)," in Viktor Sydorenko, ed., *Narysy z istorii kinomystetstva Ukrainy* (Kyiv: Intertekhnolohiia, 2006), 9–52.

17 Ivan Koshelivets, "Film," in *Encyclopedia of Ukraine*, vol. 1 (Toronto: University of Toronto Press, 1984), 884–86; "Kinomystetstvo," in *Ukrainska radianska entsyklopediia*, vol. 5, 2nd ed. (Kyiv: Vyd-vo Akademiï nauk UkrRSR, 1977–85), 192–94.

18 Heorhii V. Zhurov, *Kyivska kinostudiia imeni O. Dovzenka* (Kyiv: Derzhavne vyd-vo obrazotvorchoho mystetstva UkrRSR, 1962); Serhii Trymbach, "Istoriia ukrainskoho kino 1910–1920-ti roky," in Sydorenko, *Narysy z istorii kinomystetstva Ukrainy*, 53–76; Jeremy Hicks, *Dziga Vertov: Defining Documentary Film* (London: I.B. Tauris, 2007), 53–70.

19 Eric A. Goldman, *Visions, Images, and Dreams: Yiddish Film, Past and Present* (Teaneck, NJ: Ergo, 1988), 33–54.

20 George O. Liber, "Death, Birth Order and Alexander Dovzhenko's Cinematic Visions," *Kinema: A Journal for Film and Audiovisual Media* 8, 1 (2000), http://www.kinema.uwaterloo.ca/article.php?id=306&feature; George O. Liber, *Alexander Dovzhenko: A Life in Soviet Film* (London: British Film Institute, 2002); Jay Leyda, *Kino: A History of the Russian and Soviet Film*, 3rd ed. (Princeton, NJ: Princeton University Press, 1983), 242–46, 252–55, 275–76.

21 LAC, MG 31 D 87, vol. 8, file 12, Kist's letter to Avramenko, 9 August 1928.

22 LAC, MG 31 D 87, vol. 8, file 12, Kist's letters to Avramenko, 26 and 28 August, 1 September 1928.

23 LAC, MG 30 D 87, vol. 8, file 15, Kist's letter to Avramenko, 26 April 1934; vol. 18, files 4 and 34, Vasyl (Vasile) Avramenko, "New Ukrainian Films for 1940" (in Ukrainian) and "List of Property Needed for Scenery."

24 LAC, MG 31 D 87, vol. 1, file 31, "Biography of Vasile Avramenko," undated.

25 LAC, MG 31 D 87, vol. 13, file 28, leaflet advertising screening at the St. Michael's Church Hall, 123 Park Street, New Haven, Connecticut, 24 January 1932; vol. 8, file 21, Avramenko's letter to Alexander Koshetz inviting him to attend a screening in Ansonia, Connecticut, 22 January 1932.

26 LAC, MG 31 D 87, vol. 2, file 20, Avramenko's letter to Alexander Koshetz, 20 June 1931; vol. 8, file 14, Avramenko's letter to Kist, 18 July 1931.

27 LAC, MG 31 D 87, vol. 7, file 17, and vol. 9, file 11, Avramenko's letters to Mykola Novak and Walter (Volodymyr) Blondynenko, August 1932.

28 LAC, MG 31 D 87, vol. 7, file 27, Avramenko's letter to Mrs. Teklia Danys, 24 March 1934.

29 LAC, MG 31 D 87, vol. 7, file 17, Walter Blondynenko to Avramenko, 26 May 1934.

30 LAC, MG 31 D 87, vol. 3, file 32, Avramenko's letter to Ivan (Shchyt-) Orlyk and his wife, Tania, one-time members of Koshetz's Ukrainian National Chorus, 2 September 1933.

31 LAC, MG 31 D 87, vol. 7, file 27, Avramenko's letters to Mrs. Teklia Danys, 2–10 September 1933; vol. 8, file 1, Avramenko's letter to Fred Garbolinsky, 6 September 1933; vol. 10, file 24, Avramenko's letters to Mrs. Anna Jonker, wife of a Winnipeg physician, 6 and 19 September 1933; vol. 3, file 32, Avramenko's letter to Miss Mary Korecki, a Winnipeg school teacher, 6 September 1933; vol. 9, file 6, Avramenko's letter to Dr. Milojevich, 19 October 1933.

32 LAC, MG 31 D 87, vol. 18, file 3, Avramenko's two-page undated note, "How I Conceived the Idea of Ukrainian Film" (in Ukrainian). Avramenko visited and planned lectures at Bellfield, Kiew, Butte, Mes, Kildare, and Gorham, North Dakota. LAC, MG 31 D 87, vol. 3, file 32, Avramenko's letter to Mr. Romanyk, 30 November 1933.

33 Lary May, *The Big Tomorrow: Hollywood and the Politics of the American Way* (Chicago: University of Chicago Press, 2000), 121–24 and fig. 27, "Weekly Admissions to Movies in the United States, 1929–1940," 290.

34 LAC, MG 31 D 87, vol. 18, file 3, Avramenko's two-page undated note, "How I Conceived the Idea of Ukrainian Film" (in Ukrainian).

35 LAC, MG 31 D 87, vol. 7, file 29, Roman Fenchynsky's letter to Avramenko, 20 February 1934; vol. 18, file 2, "Notes on Films and Film Production, 1935"; vol. 18, file 3, Avramenko's two-page undated note, "How I Conceived the Idea of Ukrainian Film" (in Ukrainian).

36 LAC, MG 31 D 87, vol. 4, file 2, Avramenko's letter to the UNA Central Executive, 10 May 1934.

37 LAC, MG 31 D 87, vol. 18, file 12, advertisement for 1 January 1935 screening; vol. 4, file 3, financial accounts of screenings submitted by Teodor Fedus, 5 May 1935.

38 LAC, MG 31 D 87, vol. 18, file 3, Avramenko's two-page undated note, "How I Conceived the Idea of Ukrainian Film" (in Ukrainian). When the executive officers of the UNA saw the film, they concluded that it "would under no circumstances serve to propagandize" the association and asked Avramenko to hand over all prints. *Svoboda,* 4 May 1935, supplement.

39 LAC, MG 31 D 87, vol. 4, file 4, Avramenko's letter to Anna Sten, 9 February 1935.

40 A good actress, Sten is remembered as "Goldwyn's folly," and the studio's efforts to improve her English diction were immortalized by Cole Porter in his song *Anything Goes:* "When Sam Goldwyn can with great conviction // Instruct Anna Sten in diction // Then Anna Shows // Anything Goes." On Goldwyn's failed attempt to make another Greta Garbo or Marlene Dietrich out of Anna Sten, see A. Scott Berg, *Goldwyn: A Biography* (New York: Riverhead Books, 1998), Chapter 14. On Anna Sten, see the informative obituary published in *The Independent* (London), 19 November 1993, http://www.independent.co.uk/news/people/obituary-anna-sten-1505253.html, and T. Luciw, "Is Anna Sten a Ukrainian?," *Ukrainian Weekly,* 24 December 1937, which reveals that the actress spoke only Ukrainian until the age of twelve, when she moved to Moscow.

41 Greg Merritt, *Celluloid Mavericks: A History of American Independent Film* (New York: Thunder's Mouth Press, 2000), 12–13, 24–32, 84–88; Frances K. Gateward, "African American Cinema," in Barry Keith Grant, ed., *Schirmer Encyclopedia of Film,* vol. 1 (Farmington Hills, MI: Thompson Gale, 2007), 59–70.

42 Goldman, *Visions, Images, and Dreams,* 55–110; Merritt, *Celluloid Mavericks,* 80–84.

43 Goldman, *Visions, Images, and Dreams,* 112–13.

44 UCECA, Lev Sorochynsky Collection, box 4, Avramenko's letters to Lev Sorochynsky, 6 and 23 October 1935.

45 LAC, MG 31 D 87, vol. 13, file 77, "New York, New York, January 1936," leaflet advertising the 12 January 1936 opening.

46 LAC, MG 31 D 87, vol. 7, file 6, letters exchanged by Pauline (Garbolinsky) Avramenko and Avramenko, 19–28 February, 2 April, and 29 November 1936, reveal that Avramenko tried to convince Pauline that he should have custody of their daughter because directors at Paramount and MGM wanted him to make a film with Oksana; Pauline refused because she did not believe him and suspected that he wanted to exploit the child. Although he did provide child support of about five dollars per week between March 1935 and February 1936 (MG 31 D 87, vol. 11, file 1), by April 1936 he was no longer doing so. In November 1936, he indicated that there would be no more child support payments because Pauline had violated their separation agreement by

having Oksana baptized into the (Ukrainian) Greek Catholic (rather than Ukrainian Orthodox) faith so that she could attend a Catholic school.

47 LAC, MG 31 D 87, vol. 22, file 21, "Promin, New York 1936," contains a copy of the solitary April 1936 issue, which contains Avramenko's arguments for the creation of a "Ukrainian Hollywood" and surveys what Avramenko and his associates had already accomplished.

48 Basil A. Stevens, "Help Build the Ukrainian Hollywood," *Promin* 1 (1936): 12–14 (in English).

49 Mykola P. Novak, *Na storozhi Ukrainy: Vlasni spohady, istorychni materiialy, dokumenty, lystuvannia, arkhiv* (Los Angeles: the author, 1979), 132–33. Novak was an employee but not a shareholder of Avramenko Film Production Incorporated in 1936.

50 LAC, MG 31 D 87, vol. 9, file 3, Ladislaus (Vladyslav) Biberovich's letter to Avramenko, 15 July 1938, recalling the inclusion of "inappropriate" scenes in the film version of *Natalka Poltavka.*

51 LAC, MG 31 D 87, vol. 19, file 13, Michael Gann, "Response to Criticism of 'Natalka Poltavka,' 1937."

52 LAC, MG 31 D 87, vol. 10, file 9, and UCECA, Lev Sorochynsky Collection, box 4, letters exchanged by Avramenko and Sorochynsky, 27–29 May 1936.

53 LAC, MG 31 D 87, vol. 19, file 11, "Publicity" files for *Natalka Poltavka,* including leaflets and program.

54 Ibid.

55 For a résumé, see his filmography, http://www.imdb.com/name/nm0119886/, and list of stage plays directed, http://www.imdb.com/name/nm0119886/otherworks, at the Internet Movie Data Base (IMDb).

56 Gary D. Rhodes, ed., *Edgar G. Ulmer: Detour on Poverty Row* (Lanham, MD: Lexington Books, 2008); Bernd Herzogenrath, ed., *Edgar G. Ulmer: Essays on the King of the B's* (Jefferson, NC: McFarland, 2009); Bernd Herzogenrath, ed., *The Films of Edgar G. Ulmer* (Lanham, MD: Scarecrow Press, 2009); and Tom Weaver, Michael Brunas, and John Brunas, *Universal Horrors: The Studio's Classic Films, 1931–1946* (Jefferson, NC: McFarland, 2009), are just some of the recent works that examine Ulmer's work. For a brief introduction to his life and work, see Noah Isenberg, "Perennial Detour: The Cinema of Edgar G. Ulmer and the Experience of Exile," *Cinema Journal* 43, 2 (2004): 3–25.

57 David Kalat, "*Detour*'s Detour," in Herzogenrath, ed., *The Films of Edgar G. Ulmer,* 139.

58 Gregory William Mank, *Bela Lugosi and Boris Karloff: The Expanded Story of a Haunting Collaboration* (Jefferson, NC: McFarland, 2009), 153–200, provides a lively and thorough account of Ulmer and the making of *The Black Cat* in February–May 1934.

59 D.J. Turner, "From Nine to Nine," in Herzogenrath, ed., *The Films of Edgar G. Ulmer,* 53–60.

60 "Shirley Ulmer: Queen of B-Movies, as Screenplay Writer and Script Girl," *The Guardian,* 4 September 2000, http://www.guardian.co.uk/news/2000/sep/04/guardianobituaries3.

61 LAC, MG 31 D 87, vol. 19, file 9, "Draft of Lease for Filming Location."

62 Peter Bogdanovich, "Edgar G. Ulmer: An Interview," *Film Culture* 58–60 (1974), especially 209–16.

63 Ibid.

64 LAC, MG 31 D 87, vol. 4, file 6, press release, 8 December 1936; vol. 4, file 7, Avramenko's letters to Vasyl Trylovsky, 11 October 1936, and to Mykola Pevny, 3 November 1936.

65 LAC, MG 31, D 87, vol. 19, file 11, "Publicity."

66 A copy of a relatively good print of the film survives at the Immigration History Research Center, University of Minnesota. I am grateful to Irka Balan (Winnipeg) for sharing her DVD copy of the film.

67 *Svoboda,* 16 January 1939, compared the Soviet version with Avramenko's production.

68 *Variety,* 17 February 1937, cited in Alan Gevinson, ed., *Within Our Gates: Ethnicity in American Feature Films, 1911–1960* (Berkeley: University of California Press, 1997), 700–01.

69 *New York Times,* 15 February 1937.

70 *New York American,* 15 February 1937; *New York Daily News,* 15 February 1937.

71 *Ukrainskyi holos* (Ukrainian Voice; Winnipeg), 10 March 1937.

72 *Winnipeg Free Press,* 5 March 1937; also see the brief review in *Winnipeg Evening Tribune,* 5 March 1937.

73 *Toronto Daily Star,* 30 March 1937.

74 *Toronto Evening Telegram,* 30 March 1937.

75 *Los Angeles Daily News,* 29 May 1937.

76 *Svoboda,* 16 January 1939.

77 *Novyi shliakh* (The New Pathway; Saskatoon), 2 March 1937.

78 *Svoboda,* 12–15 April 1937.

79 LAC, MG 31 D 87, vol. 7, file 6, Pauline (Garbolinsky) Avramenko's letter to Avramenko, 15 November 1932; Avramenko's letter to Pauline, 18 December 1934; vol. 4, file 10, Avramenko Film Corporation's letter to the UNA Central Executive complaining that its organ, *Svoboda,* and especially Dr. Luka Myshuga, its editor, refused to publish any reports and articles about Avramenko's work and his new film studio; 12 May 1937; vol. 8, file 4, Avramenko's undated letter to H. Herman, blaming Myshuga for sending Pauline "down a very bad path."

80 *Svoboda,* 30 April 1937, published an editorial defending Koshetz and reproduced both letters submitted by Avramenko.

81 *Svoboda,* 29 April 1937.

82 LAC, MG 31 D 87, vol. 19, file 13, "M. Gann, 'Response to Criticism of *Natalka Poltavka,*'" 12 pages (in Ukrainian).

83 UCECA, Alexander Koshetz Collection, box 18, letters exchanged by Koshetz and Dr. Luka Myshuga, 19, 21, and 25 May 1937; box 13, letter from Andrii and Oleksandr Chekhivsky (Paris) to Myshuga, 4 June 1937; box 6, letters exchanged between Koshetz and Ivan Atamanets, 29 June, 4 July, and 19 August 1937.

84 John Wyver, *The Moving Image: An International History of the Film, Television, and Video* (Oxford: Basil Blackwell, 1989), 123–37; Blair Davis, *The Battle for the Bs: 1950s Hollywood and the Rebirth of Low-Budget Cinema* (New Brunswick, NJ: Rutgers University Press, 2012), 21–22.

85 Eric Schaefer, *"Bold! Daring! Shocking! True!" A History of Exploitation Films, 1919–1959* (Durham: Duke University Press, 1999), 96–103.

86 LAC, MG 31 D 87, vol. 4, file 11, correspondence with Rebush's Kinotrade, 723–7th Avenue, New York City, March 1937; vol. 7, file 13, Rebush's letter to Avramenko, 23 November 1938, explaining why efforts by the latter to distribute *Natalka Poltavka* in 1937 had failed.

87 LAC, MG 31 D 87, vol. 9, file 11, Novak's letter to Avramenko, 24 May 1937.

88 Novak, *Na storozhi Ukrainy,* 143–45.

89 LAC, MG 31 D 87, vol. 4, file 8, Stepan Doroshchuk's letter to Avramenko, 9 May 1937.

90 On the Yiddish film industry, see J. Hoberman, *Bridge of Light: Yiddish Film between Two Worlds* (Philadelphia: Temple University Press, 1991), Chapter 18; Sylvia Paskin, ed., *When Joseph Met Molly: A Reader on Yiddish Film* (Nottingham, UK: Five Leaves Publications, 1999); Eric A. Goldman, *Visions, Images, and Dreams: Yiddish Film, Past and Present* (Teaneck, NJ: Ergo Media, 1988).

91 LAC, MG 31 D 87, vol. 4, file 8, Avramenko's letter to the board of directors of Avramenko Film Production Incorporated, 24 March 1937.

92 Novak, *Na storozhi Ukrainy,* 133.

93 LAC, MG 31 D 87, vol. 8, file 15, Andrii Kist's letters to Avramenko, 5 and 27 October 1937.

94 *Ukrainskyi holos,* 10 March 1937; *Pravda* (The Truth; Winnipeg), 17 March 1937.

95 LAC, MG 31 D 87, vol. 3, file 1, Hryhorii Tyzhuk's letter to Avramenko, 11 February 1932.

96 LAC, MG 31 D 87, vol. 8, file 14, Volodymyr Kedrovsky, co-editor of *Svoboda,* cited in Andrii Kist's letter to Avramenko, 11 December 1930.

97 *Ukrainskyi holos,* 13 October 1937, and subsequent issues; also see *Zaporozhets za Dunaiem: vistnyk ukrainskoi filmovoi studii Vasylia Avramenka* 1 (1938), the "herald" of Avramenko's film studio, which published promotional material penned by Avramenko.

98 *Ukrainskyi holos,* 20 October 1937.

99 *Ukrainskyi holos,* 27 October 1937; "Iak rozpochato spravu 'Zaporozhtsia' v Kanadi?," *Zaporozhets za Dunaiem* 1 (1938): 6–8.

100 *Ukrainskyi holos,* 27 October 1937.

101 "Pryniattia v chest Vasylia Avramenka," *Zaporozhets za Dunaiem* 1 (1938): 19. For a study of Charles Thorson, see Gene Walz, *Cartoon Charlie: The Life and Art of Animation Pioneer Charles Thorson* (Winnipeg: Great Plains Publications, 1998).

102 *Ukrainskyi holos,* 27 October 1937; "Iak rozpochato spravu 'Zaporozhtsia' v Kanadi?," *Zaporozhets za Dunaiem* 1 (1938): 6–8.

103 *Ukrainskyi holos,* 10 November 1937, published a letter from Ivan Petrowsky, head of Ukrafilm, revealing these developments.

104 *Ukrainskyi holos,* 17 November 1937; *Kanadyiskyi farmer,* 17 November 1937.

105 *Ukrainskyi holos,* 24 November 1937.

106 LAC, MG 31 D 87, vol. 8, file 15, Andrii Kist's letter to Avramenko, 19 November 1937; UCECA, Alexander Koshetz Collection, box 6, Koshetz's letter to Ivan Atamanets, 3 December 1937.

107 LAC, MG 31 D 87, vol. 7, file 30, letters exchanged by Avramenko and Gann, 24 November–12 December 1937; UCECA, Mykyta Mandryka Collection, box "Avramenko Film Company," 10 January 1938.

108 LAC, MG 31 D 87, vol. 8, file 15, Andrii Kist's letter to Avramenko, 19 November 1937, mentioned that, while Gann was still with Ukrafilm, he had opposed hiring Ulmer to direct *Marusia* and supported the company's decision to go with Leo Bulgakov.

109 LAC, MG 31 D 87, vol. 18, file 7, "Avramenko Film Company Limited: Prospectus."

110 Mykhailo H. Marunchak, *Biohrafichnyi dovidnyk do istorii ukraintsiv Kanady* (Winnipeg: Ukrainian Academy of Arts and Sciences in Canada, 1986), 57, 413–14, has brief biographical entries on Biberovich and Mandryka; the latter is also listed in Dmytro M. Shtohryn, ed., *Ukrainians in North America: A Biographical Directory*

(Champaign, IL: Association for the Advancement of Ukrainian Studies, 1975), 197. Biberovich had known Avramenko since July 1925, when, as an employee of the Scandinavian-American Line, he tried to obtain a visa for Avramenko, who was still in central Europe. LAC, MG 31 D 87, vol. 7, file 11, Biberovich's letter to Avramenko, 13 July 1925.

111 LAC, MG 31 D 87, vol. 9, file 3, Mandryka's letter to Avramenko and Biberovich, 26 July 1938, mentions these episodes during the past winter.

112 LAC, MG 31 D 87, vol. 9, file 2, Mandryka's letter to Biberovich, 28 May 1938.

113 LAC, MG 31 D 87, vol. 9, file 2, Mandryka's letters to Biberovich, 15 April, 4, 6, and 17 May, and 27–28 June 1938; vol. 10, file 18, Yavorsky's letters to Mandryka, 6 June–5 July 1938; vol. 7, file 12, Dmytro Mykytiuk's letter to Biberovich, 21 October 1938. Yavorsky's side of this episode is found in the Paul Yavorsky Papers, LAC, MG 31 D 123, vol. 1, file "Diary: Tour with V. Avramenko," which, however, focus on events after July 1938. Darene Roma Yavorsky, *"Show Them What You Can Do": Building the Ukrainian Spirit across Canada: An Illustrated Biography of Pavlo Romanovich Yavorsky* (Hensall, ON: Word and Image Studio, 2007), is a daughter's attractive and well-illustrated but uncritical tribute to her father.

114 LAC, MG 31 D 87, vol. 9, file 2, Mandryka's letters to Avramenko, 19 April and 4 June 1938.

115 *Ukrainskyi holos,* 16 March 1938.

116 LAC, MG 31 D 87, vol. 9, file 3, Mandryka's letter to Biberovich and Avramenko, 6 July 1938; vol. 9, file 3, Mandryka's letter to Biberovich, 1 November 1938; vol. 7, file 13, Mandryka's letter to Biberovich, 8 November 1938.

117 LAC, MG 31 D 87, vol. 9, file 2, Mandryka's letter to Biberovich, 20 June 1938.

118 LAC, MG 31 D 87, vol. 9, file 2, letters exchanged by Mandryka and Biberovich, 4 May, 25–28 May, and 9–10 and 27 June 1938. The prospective purchaser was William Kieryliuk, a Vegreville department store owner; by June, Ukrafilm agents were working actively to discourage Kieryliuk.

119 UCECA, Mykhailo Seleshko Collection, box 7(b), letter from Ya. Dyrembach to W. Topolnytsky, 15 January 1938.

120 *Kanadyiskyi farmer,* 23 February 1938. For a brief essay on Bobby Breen, whose Jewish family emigrated from Kyiv shortly after the revolution, see Charles Foster, *Once Upon a Time in Paradise: Canadians in the Golden Age of Hollywood* (Toronto: Dundurn Press, 2003), 37–55.

121 LAC, MG 31 D 87, vol. 7, file 12, Dmytro Mykytiuk's letter to Biberovich, 27 May 1938, concerning plans to pull money (*vytiahnuty hroshi*) out of parents of Winnipeg dance school children who were being prepared to perform in the film.

122 LAC, MG 31 D 87, vol. 9, file 2, Mandryka's letter to Avramenko, 4 June 1938.

123 LAC, MG 31, D 87, vol. 4, file 12, Peter Ratuski's letter to Avramenko, 1 March 1938, mentioned what Ratuski had heard on his travels across eastern Canada.

124 LAC, MG 31 D 87, vol. 4, file 12, V. Tulevitriv's letter to Avramenko, 7 December 1938.

125 LAC, MG 31 D 87, vol. 9, file 2, Mandryka's letters to Biberovich, 14 April and 2 June 1938.

126 LAC, MG 31 D 87, vol. 9, file 2, Mandryka's letter to Avramenko, 26 February 1938.

127 LAC, MG 31 D 87, vol. 9, file 2, Biberovich's letter to Mandryka, 9 June 1938.

128 Shtohryn, ed., *Ukrainians in North America,* 279–80 and 316, contains biographical sketches. Their sons, Roman (b. 1942) and Dorian (b. 1944), graduated from Juilliard and had successful careers as a pianist and a cellist respectively. Dorian was a founder

and member of the New York Rock and Roll Ensemble, exponents of "classical baroque rock" (1967–73).

129 LAC, MG 31 D 87, vol. 7, file 30, Michael Gann's letter to Avramenko, 15 December 1937, agreeing to speak with Sokil and Rudnytsky about participation in the film project. The two had arrived in the port of New York on 8 December, according to *Ukrainskyi holos*, 22 December 1937.

130 LAC, MG 31 D 87, vol. 4, file 12, Antin Rudnytsky's letter to Avramenko, 12 April 1938, reveals that Rudnytsky was already working on the score. For the composer's side of the episode, see Antin Rudnytsky, "Iak povstala filma 'Zaporozhets za Dunaiem,'" *Dilo* (The Deed; Lviv), 28 August 1938.

131 Rudnytsky, "Iak povstala filma 'Zaporozhets za Dunaiem'"; LAC, MG 31 D 87, vol. 9, file 2, Mandryka's letter to Biberovich, 26 May 1938.

132 LAC, MG 31 D 87, vol. 4, file 13, Avramenko's letter to Biberovich and Gann, 5 August 1938; vol. 7, file 12, Avramenko's letter to Biberovich, 8 August 1938. Photos and brief notes about the principal actors/singers and musicians (as well as donors) are found in *Zaporozhets za Dunaiem: Vistnyk ukrainskoi filmovoi studii Vasylia Avramenka* 3 (1938).

133 LAC, MG 31 D 87, vol. 7, file 12, Biberovich's letters to Avramenko and Mandryka, 28 and 30 October 1938, indicating that the general's rambling improvised speech would have to be edited down from three minutes to one.

134 *Kanadyiskyi farmer*, 15 June 1938; LAC, MG 31 D 87, vol. 9, file 2, Biberovich's letter to Mandryka, 29 May 1938, revealed that $2,530 would be required to pay the musicians and another $400 for the choir and other incidental costs.

135 *Kanadyiskyi farmer*, 22 June 1938, published the letter from dissatisfied Ukrainian professional musicians.

136 *Kanadyiskyi farmer*, 20 July 1938.

137 Bogdanovich, "Edgar G. Ulmer," 215–16. The only articles that attempt to examine the production and filming of *Cossacks in Exile* and *The Singing Blacksmith* are Bohdan Y. Nebesio, "*Zaporozhets za Dunaiem* (1938): The Production of the First Ukrainian-Language Feature Film in Canada," *Journal of Ukrainian Studies* 16, 1–2 (1991): 115–29, and Claudia Pummer, "At the Border: Edgar G. Ulmer's Foreign Language Productions: *The Singing Blacksmith* and *Cossacks in Exile*," in Rhodes, ed., *Edgar G. Ulmer*, 41–57.

138 Cited by Hoberman, *Bridge of Light*, 267– 68.

139 LAC, MG 31 D 87, vol. 9, file 8, Biberovich's letter to Vasyl Mykytiuk, 19 July 1938.

140 LAC, MG 31 D 87, vol. 9, file 3, Biberovich's letter to Mandryka, 13 August 1938.

141 LAC, MG 31 D 87, vol. 9, file 3, Mandryka's letter to Biberovich, 6 July 1938; *Winnipeg Free Press*, 6 July 1938, published a photo of the Winnipeg contingent; *Kanadyiskyi farmer*, 6 July 1938, published a photo of dance soloist William Yacyna; *Ukrainskyi holos*, 13 July 1938.

142 LAC, MG 31 D 87, vol. 9, file 3, Biberovich's letter to Mandryka, 9 July 1938.

143 Rudnytsky, "Iak povstala filma 'Zaporozhets za Dunaiem.'"

144 LAC, MG 31 D 87, vol. 7, file 12, Biberovich's letter to Mandryka, 21 July 1938, expressing incredulity that an "immoral girl" with a terrible reputation had been allowed to be part of the Winnipeg contingent.

145 LAC, MG 31 D 87, vol. 7, file 12, Avramenko's letter to Biberovich, 29 October 1938.

146 LAC, MG 31 D 87, vol. 4, file 12, Dmytro Mykytiuk's letter to Avramenko, 19 August 1938.

147 LAC, MG 31 D 87, vol. 9, file 3, Mandryka's letter to Biberovich, 22 August 1938.

148 LAC, MG 31 D 87, vol. 7, file 12, Avramenko's letters to Biberovich, 19 and 23 August 1938; vol. 7, file 30, Mandryka's letter to Michael Gann, 29 August 1938.

149 LAC, MG 31 D 87, vol. 4, file 13, Avramenko's letter to Biberovich, 30 August 1938, indicated that Avramenko was trying to obtain money from D. Vorona and Fred Pelech, the head and manager of Beaver Bread Limited (Bread and Cakes), 103 Lightbourne Avenue, Toronto. He would use Pelech's money on his next film project.

150 LAC, MG 31 D 87, vol. 9, file 3, Biberovich's letter to Mandryka, 8 August 1938.

151 LAC, MG 31 D 87, vol. 9, file 3, Biberovich's letter to Danylo Budka, 25 August 1938.

152 LAC, MG 31 D 87, vol. 9, file 8, Mykytiuk's letter to Biberovich, 4 October 1938.

153 LAC, MG 31 D 123, vol. 1, file (Paul Yavorsky's) "Diary 1938," entry for 12 September 1938; LAC, MG 31 D 87, vol. 7, file 1, Nick Arseny's telegram to Avramenko, 14 September 1938.

154 LAC, MG 31 D 123, vol. 1, file (Paul Yavorsky's) "Diary 1938," entries for 12–29 September 1938.

155 LAC, MG 31 D 87, vol. 7, file 13, Biberovich's letter to Mandryka, 1 November 1938.

156 LAC, MG 31 D 87, vol. 9, file 3, Mandryka's letter to Biberovich, 18 October 1938; vol. 7, file 12, Biberovich's letter to Mandryka, 22 October 1938; letters exchanged by Avramenko and Mandryka in Winnipeg, and Gann and Biberovich in New York, 25 October–9 November 1938.

157 LAC, MG 31 D 87, vol. 7, file 13, Biberovich's letters to Mandryka, 11–12 November 1938; vol. 9, file 37, Dr. H.G. Skehar to Avramenko, 27 November 1938.

158 UCECA, Mykyta Mandryka Collection, box "Avramenko Film Company," Dr. H.G. Skehar's letters to Mandryka, 5 and 9 December 1938.

159 LAC, MG 31 D 87, vol. 9, file 3, letters exchanged by Mandryka and Biberovich, 4–5 July 1938, indicate that the Soviet film was already being screened in Winnipeg and New York and that Ulmer had already had an opportunity to see it; vol. 9, file 8, Mykytiuk's letter to Biberovich, 4 October 1938, reveals that the film was attracting large audiences in Ukrainian colonies in rural Manitoba.

160 LAC, MG 31 D 87, vol. 9, file 8, Mykytiuk's letter to Biberovich, 4 October 1938, described the ad campaign launched by local distribution managers William Scraba and Meros Lechow's father; vol. 7, file 12, Mandryka's letter to Biberovich, 30 October 1938, opined that "*Marusia* is not a film, it is s - - t. People laugh out loud during the tragic moments. ... It is on the same level as the plays put on by the Ukrainian school on [Winnipeg's] Euclid Avenue. ..." *Ukrainskyi holos,* 12 November 1938, described the film's Winnipeg premiere reverentially. For a detached assessment, see Gevinson, ed., *Within Our Gates,* 645.

161 LAC, MG 31 D 87, vol. 7, file 13, Avramenko's letter to Biberovich, 25 November 1938.

162 LAC, MG 31 D 87, vol. 7, file 13, Biberovich's letter to Mandryka, 26 November 1938.

163 *Winnipeg Free Press,* 6 December 1938; *Ukrainskyi holos,* 7 December 1938; *Kanadyiskyi farmer,* 7 December 1938.

164 Gevinson, ed., *Within Our Gates,* 226–27, has a brief synopsis and overview of reviews; the official program, *Ukrainian Operatic Film Cossacks in Exile,* also contains a synopsis and many stills. A copy of a deteriorated and apparently incomplete print of the film is available on a VHS videocassette at LAC in Ottawa and at UCECA in Winnipeg.

165 *Winnipeg Free Press,* 5 December 1938.

166 *Winnipeg Evening Tribune,* 5 December 1938.

167 LAC, MG 31 D 87, vol. 10, file 18, Paul Yavorsky's letter to Winnipeg office, 3 January 1939.

168 LAC, MG 31 D 123, vol. 1, file (Paul Yavorsky's) "Diary 1938," entry for 7 December 1938; apparently, 150 of the 2,700 who saw the movie in Saskatoon were "English."

169 Ibid., entry for 23–24 December 1938; *Edmonton Journal*, 23 December 1938.

170 LAC, MG 31 D 87, vol. 4, file 12, Ivan Danylchuk's letter to Avramenko, 23 December 1938.

171 LAC, MG 31 D 87, vol. 4, file 12, Peter Lazarowich's letter to Avramenko, 23 December 1938.

172 LAC, MG 31 D 87, vol. 7, file 13, Mandryka's letter to Biberovich, 8 November 1938, while very critical as always of Avramenko's personal and fiscal habits, conceded that Avramenko was "a nucleus of fiery energy, … a creative impetus for the inert masses, … the mobilizer of sleepy resources … whose original but real idealism … is a treasure."

173 LAC, MG 31 D 87, vol. 7, file 14, Peter Ratuski's letter to Biberovich, 13 January 1939.

174 *Toronto Daily Star*, 12 January 1939.

175 *Toronto Evening Telegram*, 12 January 1939.

176 LAC, MG 31 D 87, vol. 7, file 14, Mandryka's letter to Biberovich, 2 February 1939.

177 *New York Times*, 28 January 1939.

178 *New York Daily News*, 28 January 1939.

179 *Brooklyn Eagle*, 28 January 1939; *New York Herald-Tribune*, 30 January 1939.

180 UCECA, Alexander Koshetz Collection, box 18, undated clipping from *Novoe russkoe slovo*.

181 UCECA, Alexander Koshetz Collection, box 6, Koshetz's letters to Ivan Atamanets, early (undated) and 14 February 1939.

182 UCECA, Mykyta Mandryka Collection, box "Avramenko Film Company," "Prybutky i vydatky kompanii za rik vid 9-oho hrudnia 1937 do 31-oho hrudnia 1938."

183 LAC, MG 31 D 87, vol. 9, file 2, Biberovich's letter to Mandryka, 23 June 1938; vol. 7, file 12, Biberovich's letters to Mandryka, 18–20 and 26 October 1938; vol. 7, file 13, letters exchanged by Biberovich and Mandryka, 2, 8, and 15 November 1938.

184 LAC, MG 31 D 87, vol. 4, file 12, Pavlo Lysiak's letter to Biberovich, 1 September 1938; vol. 7, file 13, Biberovich's letters to Mykytiuk, 20–21 December 1938.

185 LAC, MG 31 D 87, vol. 7, file 13, letters exchanged by Eugene Deslaw and Biberovich, 7 November and 27 December 1938; UCECA, Alexander Koshetz Collection, box 7, letters exchanged by Eugene Deslaw and Koshetz, 27 November and 19 December 1938. On Deslaw, who also worked with Boris Kaufman (Dziga Vertov's brother and a future Oscar winner for his cinematography in *On the Waterfront*), Luis Buñuel, Marcel Carné, and Fred Zinnemann, see Jaroslaw Zurowsky, "Ievhen Deslav: A Forgotten Ukrainian Filmmaker," *Journal of Ukrainian Studies* 9, 2 (1984): 87–92, and the film credits on the IMDb website, http://www.imdb.com/name/nm0221342/. *Montparnasse* (1929), a sample of his early work, is on the Turner Classic Movies website, http://fan.tcm.com/_Montparnasse-1929-Eugene-Deslaw/video/1657676/66470.html?createPassive=true.

186 LAC, MG 31 D 87, vol. 9, file 3, Biberovich's letter to Mandryka, 8 July 1938.

187 LAC, MG 31 D 87, vol. 7, file 13, Eugene Deslaw's letter to Biberovich, 7 November 1938.

188 LAC, MG 31 D 87, vol. 4, file 12, letter from Indian film distributor to Gann's Musart Film Productions, 28 September 1938.

189 LAC, MG 31 D 87, vol. 7, file 14, and UCECA, Mykyta Mandryka Collection, box "Avramenko Film Company," Mandryka's letters to Biberovich, 28 February 1939.

190 LAC, MG 31 D 87, vol. 7, file 14, Mandryka's letter to Biberovich, 14 January 1939.

191 LAC, MG 31 D 87, vol. 7, files 13 and 14, Biberovich's letter to Avramenko, 19 December 1938, and Mandryka's letter to Biberovich, 20 January 1939.

192 LAC, MG 31 D 87, vol. 7, file 14, Mandryka's letter to Biberovich, 28 February 1939.

193 UCECA, Mykyta Mandryka Collection, box "Avramenko Film Company," Mandryka's letter to Avramenko, 6 March 1939, and Michael Gann's letter to Mandryka, 6 April 1939.

194 LAC, MG 31 D 87, vol. 7, file 14, Biberovich's letter to Mandryka, 6 January 1939.

195 LAC, MG 31 D 87, vol. 7, file 14, Biberovich's letters to Mandryka and to Avramenko, 2 and 6 March 1939.

196 LAC, MG 31 D 87, vol. 7, file 14, Biberovich's letters to Mandryka, 8 and 10 February 1939.

197 LAC, MG 31 D 87, vol. 7, file 14, Biberovich's letters to Avramenko and Mandryka, 6 and 8 March 1939.

198 UCECA, Mykyta Mandryka Collection, box "Avramenko Film Company," Michael Gann's letter to Mandryka, 23 April 1939.

199 LAC, MG 31 D 87, vol. 7, file 14, Avramenko's letter to Biberovich and Gann, 9 February 1939; UCECA, Mykyta Mandryka Collection, box "Avramenko Film Company," Mandryka's letter to Avramenko, 8 March 1939.

200 LAC, MG 31 D 87, vol. 7, file 14, Biberovich's letter to Mandryka, 6 March 1939; UCECA, Mykyta Mandryka Collection, box "Avramenko Film Company," Biberovich's letter to Avramenko, 9 March 1939.

201 LAC, MG 31 D 87, vol. 18, file 8, Avramenko Film Company Limited, "Zvit z richnykh zboriv" (annual report; in Ukrainian), 31 March 1939.

202 LAC, MG 31 D 87, vol. 7, file 14, Biberovich's letters to Mandryka, 10–11 and 20 March 1939; Mandryka's letter to Biberovich, 21 March 1939; Biberovich's letters to Avramenko, 13–14 and 17 March 1939; Biberovich's letter to J.T. Thorson, 22 March 1939; UCECA, Mykyta Mandryka Collection, box "Avramenko Film Company," Mandryka's letter to Avramenko, 8 March 1939, and Biberovich's letter to Mandryka, 23 March 1939. Biberovich left because, in his opinion, Mandryka had handed control of the film company to the "self-interested" Gann. Mandryka maintained that the company's controllers had lost confidence in Biberovich because he had not submitted any reports for January and February and the screenings during that period.

203 LAC, MG 31 D 87, vol. 18, file 35, undated notes.

204 LAC, MG 31 D 87, vol. 4, file 12, Antin Rudnytsky's letter to Avramenko, 12 April 1938; vol. 7, file 13, Biberovich's letters to Avramenko, 11 and 14 December 1938; vol. 7, file 14, Biberovich's letter to Avramenko, 7 January 1939.

205 LAC, MG 31 D 87, vol. 7, file 30, Avramenko's letter to Michael Gann, 4 November 1938; vol. 7, file 13, Mandryka's letter to Biberovich, 8 November 1938; vol. 10, file 18, Paul Yavorsky's letters to Avramenko, 12 and 17 November 1938; vol. 4, file 12, Ivan Danylchuk's letter to Avramenko, 7 December 1938; vol. 7, file 14, Avramenko's letter to Michael Gann, 4 February 1939; UCECA, Mykyta Mandryka Collection, box "Avramenko Film Company," undated document "Umovy na novi filmy," which listed new film projects, set fees for distribution rights, and stipulated rewards for donors and lenders.

206 LAC, MG 31 D 87, vol. 10, file 18, Paul Yavorsky's letters to Avramenko, 17, 22, and 30 November 1938; vol. 4, file 12, Savella Stechishin's letter to Avramenko, 28 November 1938; LAC, MG 31 D 123, vol. 1, file "Diary: Avramenko SUMK Film Studio," entries dated 1 and 2 November.

207 LAC, MG 31 D 87, vol. 10, file 18, Paul Yavorsky's letters to Avramenko, 10 and 29 December 1938, and 3, 6, 18, 19, and 27–28 January 1939; LAC, MG 31 D 123, vol. 1, file "Diary: Avramenko SUMK Film Studio," entries dated 7–28 December 1938 and 16 January 1939. Both sources chronicle the partly successful effort to persuade the recently widowed Mrs. Sofia Greschuk and her son Ivan, both of Saskatoon, to invest their inheritance of several thousand dollars in the Avramenko SUMK Film Studio.

208 LAC, MG 31 D 87, vol. 10, file 18, Paul Yavorsky's letters to Avramenko, 6, 13, and 18 January 1939.

209 Paul Robert Magocsi, *The Shaping of a National Identity: Subcarpathian Rus': 1848–1948* (Cambridge, MA: Harvard University Press, 1978), 234–46, provides a concise introduction to this episode.

210 LAC, MG 31 D 87, vol. 18, files 15–16, "Kobzar Film Corporation: Certification of Incorporation, 1939," and "Kobzar Film Corporation: Minutes and Bylaws of Meetings, 1939–40"; vol. 11, file 3, Michael Gann's letter to Theodore Humeniuk, 23 October 1939; vol. 11, file 26, "Contracts and Agreements," agreement with Thomas S. Dwyer and Maria Procai, 21 December 1939; vol. 11, file 29, "Kobzar Film Corporation: Accounts, 1939–41."

211 LAC, MG 31 D 87, vol. 8, file 29, Avramenko's letter to Lissiuk, 19 May 1939; vol. 11, file 26, "Contracts and Agreements," sales contract with Lissiuk, 24 June 1939; vol. 9, file 4, Avramenko's letters to Mandryka, 22, 23, and 28 December 1939; vol. 18, file 17, "Dnipro Film Corporation: Agreement with Kobzar Film Corporation," 17 January 1940.

212 LAC, MG 31 D 87, vol. 44, unnumbered file, 1939 loan receipt book.

213 For a brief synopsis, see Gevinson, ed., *Within Our Gates*, 1060–61. The film is available in seven segments on YouTube starting at http://www.youtube.com/watch?v=iS1U3RcUQSY.

214 LAC, MG 31 D 87, vol. 18, file 38, "Fighters for Freedom of Carpatho-Ukraine (Povstantsi)—Description of Scenes, 1939," contains information on the staged scenes filmed with actors after the events. Also see Volodymyr Viatrovych, "Karpatska Ukraina ta ii armiia u fotohrafiakh Kalenyka Lysiuka," on the *Istorychna Pravda* website, http://www.istpravda.com.ua/artefacts/2011/03/16/31888/.

215 LAC, MG 31 D 87, vol. 8, file 1, Lissiuk to Avramenko, 24 December 1940.

216 LAC, MG 31 D 87, vol. 4, file 16, Mykhailo Zakhopy's [?] letter to Avramenko, 25 February 1940.

217 LAC, MG 31 D 87, vol. 4, file 18, Theodore Humeniuk's letter to Avramenko, 14 January 1941.

218 LAC, MG 31 D 87, vol. 4, file 17, Avramenko's letters to Mr. Shabatura and Mrs. Sofia Greschuk, 24 and 28 December 1940.

219 LAC, MG 31 D 87, vol. 4, file 8, Paul Molava's letter to Avramenko, 28 May 1937, demanding return of his loan; vol. 4, file 12, Mrs. Kornacka's letter to Avramenko, 12 December 1938, imploring that he return at least $200 because she could not make her mortgage payments; vol. 4, file 14, Anna Kohut's letter to Avramenko, 17 January 1939, asking him to return her loan because she was unemployed with a sick and elderly mother to look after; vol. 4, file 16, Mrs. E. McDermich's letter to Avramenko, 13 January 1940, asking him to return her money; vol. 4, file 16, Roman Betza's letter to Avramenko, 21 November 1940, asking for his money because his property was being auctioned off for debt; et cetera. An undated note (ca. 1940) in vol. 18, file 35, indicates that *Cossacks in Exile* had cost $75,000 to produce. Of this sum, $35,000 had been returned to creditors, $30,000 was still owed to Canadian creditors, and a $10,000 US mortgage had been taken out on the film.

Chapter 4: Fugitive

1 Edith L. Blumhofer, *Aimee Semple McPherson: Everybody's Sister* (Grand Rapids, MI: Wm. B. Eerdmans Publishing, 1993); Daniel Mark Epstein, *Sister Aimee: The Life of Aimee Semple McPherson* (New York: Houghton Mifflin Harcourt, 1994); and Matthew Avery Sutton, *Aimee Semple McPherson and the Resurrection of Christian America* (Cambridge, MA: Harvard University Press, 2007) are the most reliable studies of McPherson.

2 LAC, MG 31 D 87, vol. 4, file 23, Avramenko's letter to Aimee Semple McPherson, 24 May 1943.

3 Edward T. James, Janet Wilson James, and Paul S. Boyer, eds., *Notable American Women, 1607–1950: A Biographical Dictionary,* vol. 2 (Cambridge, MA: Harvard University Press, 1971), 479.

4 Margarita Agreneva-Slaviansky was the twelfth and youngest child of Dmitri Aleksandrovich Agrenev-Slaviansky (1834–1908), a Russian singer and choir conductor of noble birth who had done much to preserve and popularize Russian folk songs. In 1926, she defected from the Soviet Union and immigrated to the United States via China. She founded a Russian chorus in New York and toured North America after 1930, often on the Chautauqua circuit. See Margaret Tsuda, "Slavic Song in New York Hills," *Christian Science Monitor,* 22 May 1990, http://www.csmonitor.com/1990/0522/uslav.html, and the brochure advertising Princess Agreneva-Slaviansky's Royal Russian Company and its first American tour in 1930, http://sdrc.lib.uiowa.edu/traveling-culture/chau1/pdf/princessa/1/brochure.pdf.

5 LAC, MG 31 D 87, vol. 4, file 17, Avramenko's letter to Margarita Agreneva-Slaviansky, 20 October 1940; vol. 4, file 19, Avramenko's letter to John (Ivan) Baran, manager of the Slavic Festival, 24 January 1941, indicates that rumours about Avramenko's past and character were causing Agreneva-Slaviansky "much grief."

6 LAC, MG 31 D 87, vol. 13, file 85, "Chicago, March 1941," Slavic Festival leaflets; vol. 8, file 29, Kalenik Lissiuk's letters to Avramenko, 19–26 February and 21–28 March 1941, provide insights into why the festival failed.

7 LAC, MG 31 D 87, vol. 4, file 18, Mrs. Slavka Vesela's letters to Avramenko, undated and 10 September 1941.

8 LAC, MG 31 D 87, vol. 4, file 23, Avramenko's letter to John Baran, 4 April 1943.

9 LAC, MG 31 D 87, vol. 4, file 21, Avramenko's letter to the Los Angeles Police Department, 15 July 1942, reporting that he had closed his Ballet-Film Studio "temporarily on account of lack of students."

10 *Ukrainskyi holos,* 14 May 1941, citing an article in the San Francisco Russian-language periodical *Novaia zaria* (New Star), 26 April 1941; copies of both articles are at UCECA, Alexander Koshetz Collection, box 5.

11 LAC, MG 31 D 87, vol. 4, file 19, Avramenko's letter to Serge Jaroff (Sergei Zharov), 16 August 1941.

12 LAC, MG 31 D 87, vol. 4, file 19, Avramenko's letter to V.B. Sergievsky, 26 August 1941.

13 LAC, MG 31 D 87, vol. 4, file 23, Avramenko's letters to Margarita Agreneva-Slaviansky, 8 and 13 January 1943.

14 UCECA, Alexander Koshetz Collection, box 5, contains an undated clipping from the *Novoe russkoe slovo* (New Russian Word) about Avramenko and other guests present at the opening of the first Russian Theater Bureau run by Mary Bran in Hollywood; LAC, MG 31 D 87, vol. 7, file 30, Avramenko's letter to Michael Gann, 13 August 1944.

15 LAC, MG 31 D 87, vol. 4, file 20, leaflet/notice dated April 1942; vol. 4, file 23, Avramenko's letter to Margarita Agreneva-Slaviansky, 8 January 1943.

16 LAC, MG 31 D 87, vol. 7, file 15, letters exchanged by Avramenko and Biberovich, 29 July and 7 September 1942. On the origins and history of the NFB, see Zoë Druick, *Projecting Canada: Government Policy and Documentary Film at the National Film Board of Canada* (Montreal: McGill-Queen's University Press, 2007).

17 Ulmer left PRC in 1947 after United Artists asked him to direct *The Strange Woman,* a costume piece about a conniving female social climber starring Hedy Lamarr and George Sanders. The same year he also directed *Carnegie Hall* for United Artists, the story of an aspiring concert pianist featuring performances by Arthur Rubinstein, Jascha Heifetz, and Lily Pons, and *Ruthless,* a melodrama about the rise and fall of an unscrupulous financier starring Zachary Scott and Sydney Greenstreet. After another swashbuckler, *The Pirates of Capri* (1949) in Italy, Ulmer directed *The Man from Planet X* (1951). It was the first film about alien visitors and helped to launch the science fiction film craze. Of ten other films made during the decade, only *The Naked Dawn* (1954), a western, and *Hannibal* (1960), an Italian costume drama starring Victor Mature as the Carthaginian general, stand out. *Babes in Bagdad* (1952), featuring Paulette Goddard, Gypsy Rose Lee, and Sebastian Cabot, was apparently the worst. His career came to an end in the 1960s when television finally killed B movies. Ulmer directed low-budget science fiction films such as *Beyond the Time Barrier* (1960), *The Amazing Transparent Man* (1960), and *L'Atlantide* (1961), and he concluded his career with *The Cavern* (1965), a drama about six soldiers trapped in a cave with a beautiful woman. Larry Hagman, who would find fame as J.R. Ewing on the television serial *Dallas,* had one of the supporting roles. Ulmer died in Los Angeles in September 1972. Although French "new wave" filmmakers, including François Truffaut, had discovered him during the 1950s, it was only after his death that he gained a degree of recognition in his adopted land. In recent years, Martin Scorsese, John Landis, and Peter Bogdanovich have championed his best work, and *Detour* has been named to the National Film Registry by the Library of Congress. For an overview of Ulmer's work after 1940, see the essays in Bernd Herzogenrath, ed., *The Films of Edgar G. Ulmer* (Lanham, MD: Scarecrow Press, 2009); Vincent Brook, *Driven to Darkness: Jewish Émigré Directors and the Rise of Film Noir* (New Brunswick, NJ: Rutgers University Press, 2009), 145–66; Eric Ulman, "Edgar G. Ulmer," *Senses of Cinema* 24 (2003), http://sensesofcinema.com/2003/great-directors/ulmer/; and Noah Isenberg, *Edgar G. Ulmer: A Filmmaker at the Margins* (Berkeley: University of California Press, 2014).

18 LAC, MG 31 D 87, vol. 7, file 30, letters exchanged by Avramenko and Michael Gann, 22 May 1942 and 28 January and 2 February 1943; vol. 4, file 23, Avramenko's letter to Producers' Releasing Corporation of America, 20 February 1943.

19 LAC, MG 31 D 87, vol. 7, file 30, Avramenko's letter to Michael Gann, 29 April 1944, reported that Avramenko had already visited with Montgomery's siblings.

20 LAC, MG 31 D 87, vol. 4, file 25, Avramenko's letter to John Hodiak, 26 June 1944, and his letter to Mr. Wasyl Hodiak, 28 December 1944.

21 LAC, MG 31 D 87, vol. 4, file 25, Avramenko's letters to Mr. Dmytryk, 19 and 26 September 1944.

22 LAC, MG 31, D 87, vol. 4, file 27, Avramenko's letter to Myron Surmach, 6 February 1945.

23 LAC, MG 31 D 87, vol. 11, file 28, "Legal Documents and Certificates, 1936–1965," document dated 15 May 1943; vol. 7, file 27, Avramenko's letter to Mrs. Teklia Danys, 11 May 1943.

24 LAC, MG 31 D 87, vol. 1, file 17, "Industrial Accident, Los Angeles, 1943."

25 LAC, MG 31 D 87, vol. 7, file 30, Avramenko's letter to Michael Gann, 22 November 1943.

26 LAC, MG 31 D 87, vol. 7, files 4 and 6, Avramenko's letters to Oksana Avramenko, 25 June 1943, and Pauline (Garbolinsky) Avramenko, 2 June 1943.

27 LAC, MG 31 D 87, vol. 4, file 21, Avramenko's letter to Michael Gann, 24 June 1942, and vol. 7, file 27, Avramenko's letter to Mrs. Teklia Danys, which admitted that Avramenko had not sent Pauline any child support since the spring of 1941.

28 LAC, MG 31 D 87, vol. 9, file 4, Avramenko's letter to Mandryka, 15 February 1944; vol. 7, file 30, Avramenko's letter to Michael Gann, 13 August 1944.

29 LAC, MG 31 D 87, vol. 7, file 15, Avramenko's letter to Biberovich, 22 January 1945.

30 LAC, MG 31 D 87, vol. 7, file 27, Avramenko's letter to Mrs. Teklia Danys, 23 October 1944; vol. 8, file 17, Avramenko's letter to Andrii Kist, 22 January 1945.

31 Michael Sayers and Albert E. Kahn, *Sabotage! The Secret War against America* (New York: Harper and Brothers, 1942), Chapter 5. A Russian-language translation was published in Moscow in 1947.

32 LAC, MG 31 D 87, vol. 5, file 31, Avramenko's application to replace a lost passport, 14 July 1964, indicated that Avramenko had received his American certificate of naturalization on 27 November 1961 (#8260102).

33 Yury Boshyk, Wsevolod Isajiw, and Roman Senkus, eds., *The Refugee Experience: Ukrainian Displaced Persons after World War II* (Edmonton: Canadian Institute of Ukrainian Studies Press, University of Alberta, 1992), is the standard reference work on the topic.

34 LAC, MG 31 D 87, vol. 4, files 25 and 27, letters exchanged between Avramenko and Myron Surmach, 17–18 June 1945; vol. 7, file 30, Avramenko's letter to Michael Gann, 17 June 1945.

35 LAC, MG 31 D 87, vol. 9, file 4, Avramenko's letter to Mandryka, 17 October 1945; vol. 13, files 88–97, concert announcements, programs, leaflets, October 1945–May 1947.

36 Jillian Dawn Staniec, "Cossacks and Wallflowers: Ukrainian Stage Dance, Identity, and Politics in Saskatchewan from the 1920s to the Present" (MA thesis, University of Saskatchewan, 2007), 53.

37 *Toronto Evening Telegram*, 7, 11, and 12 February 1946.

38 William Kurelek, *Someone with Me: The Autobiography of William Kurelek* (Niagara Falls, ON: Niagara Falls Art Gallery, Kurelek Collection, 1988), 171–75.

39 *Winnipeg Tribune*, 1 September 1946.

40 LAC, MG 31 D 87, vol. 13, file 95, leaflet advertising 14–15 December 1946 banquet and dance recital in honour of Avramenko's twenty-fifth anniversary as a dance instructor, Winnipeg.

41 LAC, MG 31 D 87, vol. 1, file 19, "Greetings on the 25th Anniversary of Avramenko's Community and Artistic Activities"; vol. 23, file 3, *Ukrainskyi Tantsiuryst*, Toronto, 1951 (brochure).

42 LAC, MG 31 D 87, vol. 14, files 4–100, announcements, leaflets, programs, 1951–76, suggest the number of jubilee celebrations held during these years.

43 LAC, MG 31 D 87, vol. 6, file 15, Mykola Novak's letter to Avramenko, 24 April 1973.

44 In 1966, envelopes were distributed prior to the fortieth anniversary of Ukrainian dance in North America inviting recipients to send a jubilee gift (*iuvileinyi dar*) to the Avramenko School of Ukrainian Dance at 12 St. Mark's Place, New York City, or 36 Gardenvale Road, Toronto.

45 *Winnipeg Tribune*, 21 January 1957, published an article about one such celebration emceed by Yuzyk and attended by Hryhorczuk and Juba. LAC, MG 31 D 87, vol. 16, file 21, "Schools of Ukrainian Folk Ballet," Winnipeg, reveals that Juba's sister had

been enrolled in Avramenko's 1927 Winnipeg dance school; vol. 16, file 15, Saskatoon, lists Michael Hryhorczuk, future Manitoba Liberal Progressive MLA (1949–66) and attorney general (1955–58), as a pupil in Saskatoon in 1928; and vol. 16, file 16, Edmonton, mentions Ambrose Holowach (b. 1914), who would become a Social Credit MP (1953–58) and MLA (1959–71) for Edmonton, among Avramenko's dance pupils in 1928.

46 LAC, MG 31 D 87, vol. 11, file 32, "Triumph of Ukrainian Dance: Estimate," undated; Avramenko seemed to believe that the film could be put together for about $12,200 to $14,700.

47 LAC, MG 31 D 87, vol. 9, file 13, G.B.R. Panchuk's letters to Avramenko, 20 July–3 August 1954, expressing dismay that Avramenko was working on the film without a plan or scenario; vol. 9, file 23, Avramenko's letters to Stephan Rosocha, 19–22 November 1954; vol. 5, file 11, Avramenko's letter to the Montreal Ukrainian Folk Dance Jubilee Committee, 22 December 1954.

48 LAC, MG 31 D 87, vol. 9, file 23, Avramenko's letter to Stephan Rosocha, 23 January 1954, asked him to be the Canadian administrator of the film project; letters exchanged between Avramenko and Rosocha, 26 and 28 October 1954, concern the tour.

49 LAC, MG 31 D 87, vol. 9, file 23, Stephan Rosocha's letter to Avramenko, 28 October 1954, explaining how a collection for a jubilee gift would be taken at screenings of the film.

50 LAC, MG 31 D 87, vol. 19, files 60–61, "Ukrainian Pioneers in Canada, 1957," synopsis and miscellaneous notes. A rough cut of the film, titled *Ukrainian Pioneers and Politicians,* was screened at the Ukrainian People's Home, 191 Lipincott Avenue, Toronto, on 1 May 1957. It presented a Whiggish interpretation of Ukrainian Canadian history as sixty years of progress. In one of the scenes, Avramenko was shown placing a wreath at the war memorial monument in Ottawa.

51 LAC, MG 31 D 87, vol. 10, file 25, Paul Yuzyk's letters to Avramenko, 5 June 1958 and 11 May 1959. In the second letter, Yuzyk regretted that Avramenko's film had not been ready two years earlier when the Conservative Party was seeking election. At that time, he intimated, he would have been able to help Avramenko.

52 LAC, MG 31 D 87, vol. 5, file 16, Grant McLean's letter to Avramenko, 11 December 1957.

53 LAC, MG 31 D 87, vol. 14, file 60, "Winnipeg, Manitoba, January 1966," Grand Jubilee Festival program.

54 LAC, MG 31 D 87, vol. 8, file 20, Avramenko's letter to Irena Knysh, 2 June 1966.

55 Victoria Hallinan, "The 1958 Tour of the Moiseyev Dance Company: A Window into American Perception," *Journal of History and Cultures* 1 (2012): 51–64.

56 *Ukrainian Weekly,* 5 and 12 May 1962, quoting *New York Times* critic John Martin.

57 Andriy Nahachewsky, *Ukrainian Dance: A Cross-Cultural Approach* (Jefferson, NC: McFarland, 2012), 202–12.

58 "Moiseyev, Igor," http://universalium.academic.ru/279467/Moiseyev,_Igor.

59 Staniec, "Cossacks and Wallflowers," 90, quotes Virsky.

60 M. Pasternakova, "The Folk and Art Dance," in Volodymyr Kubijovyc, ed., *Ukraine: A Concise Encyclopedia,* vol. 1 (Toronto: University of Toronto Press, 1963), 609.

61 Alexandra Pritz, "Ukrainian Dance in Canada: The First Fifty Years, 1924–1974," in Jaroslav Rozumnyj, ed., *New Soil—Old Roots: The Ukrainian Experience in Canada* (Winnipeg: Ukrainian Academy of Arts and Sciences in Canada, 1983), 144.

62 Robert B. Klymasz, "The Fine Arts," in Manoly R. Lupul, ed., *A Heritage in Transition: Essays in the History of Ukrainians in Canada* (Toronto: McClelland and Stewart, 1982), 285.

63 Pritz, "Ukrainian Dance in Canada," 145.

64 LAC, MG 31 D 87, vol. 5, file 4, Theodore Swystun's letter to Avramenko, 18 January 1951, on behalf of his client, Mrs. Evfrozyna Khomichak.

65 LAC, MG 31 D 87, vol. 5, file 10, legal firm Arthur, Arthur & Arthur's letter to Avramenko, 1 October 1954, on behalf of their client, Mrs. Maria Shoppey-Sawka, and Rev. Demetrius T. Sawka's letter to Avramenko, 2 November 1954.

66 LAC, MG 31 D 87, vol. 14, file 6, leaflets announcing grand opening of Avramenko's Academy of Dance and Film Studio, 27–29 September 1952.

67 LAC, MG 31 D 87, vol. 14, file 49, leaflet advertising "A Prayer for America, Canada, Ukraine, and All the Nations" at the Willimantic State Teachers' College Auditorium in Willimantic, Connecticut.

68 LAC, MG 31 D 87, vol. 11, file 6, financial notes, undated (ca. 1962); vol. 1, file 72, miscellaneous.

69 LAC, MG 31 D 87, vol. 20, file 36, leaflet "Maiestro Vasyl Avramenko pokalichenyi," which informed the Ukrainian public about Avramenko's accident.

70 On Roma Pryma-Bohachevsky (1927–2004), who studied with Agrippina Vaganova and Martha Graham, see http://www.syzokryli.com/roma.php, and her obituary in the *Ukrainian Weekly,* 30 May 2004.

71 LAC, MG 31 D 87, vol. 1, file 2, "Documents and Identification, 1942–1975," document dated 7 July 1948. It appears that Avramenko went to South America at the invitation of the Association of Supporters of Ukrainian Culture (Tovarystvo Prykhylnykiv Ukrainskoi Kultury); see vol. 4, file 32, letters to Avramenko, January 1948. His entry into Argentina was facilitated by the Prosvita Society in Buenos Aires; see vol. 5, file 1, Prosvita Society's letter to Avramenko, 18 March 1949. The staff of *Nash klych* (Our Slogan), an OUN-affiliated weekly published in Buenos Aires, also offered to help Avramenko get into Argentina, via Paraguay, on a temporary tourist pass; vol. 5, file 1, Mykhailo Pohoretsky's letters to Avramenko, 24–26 March 1949.

72 LAC, MG 31 D 87, vol. 5, file 1, letter from Fr. Yosyf Martynets OSBM to Avramenko, 22 March 1949.

73 LAC, MG 31 D 87, vol. 5, file 4, Avramenko's letter to Mr. Zaparyniuk, 16 August 1951; vol. 5, file 38, Yakiv Riznyk's letter to Avramenko, 28 August 1967, citing a recent letter about this episode from Kalenik Lissiuk.

74 LAC, MG 31 D 87, vol. 5, file 4, Osyp Burban's letter to Avramenko, 28 August 1951; vol. 5, file 14, Osyp Burban's letter to Avramenko, 16 February 1956; vol. 5, file 31, Avramenko's letter to Bishop Andrii Sapeliak, 30 May 1964, stating that Avramenko had every intention to settle his debt with Osyp Burban; vol. 5, file 33, Osyp Burban's letter to Avramenko, 26 November 1965; vol. 5, file 35, Osyp Burban's letter to Avramenko, 1 January 1966.

75 LAC, MG 31 D 87, vol. 7, file 15, Biberovich's letter to Avramenko, 23 August 1958, pointing out that Avramenko could not compete with Moiseyev's choreography and dancers.

76 LAC, MG 31 D 87, vol. 5, file 19, Avramenko's letter to Petro Dnistrovyk, 9 October 1958; vol. 5, file 21, Avramenko's letter to Soiuz Ukraintsiv Brytanii (Association of Ukrainians in Great Britain; AUGB), 3 October 1959; vol. 10, file 25, Avramenko's letter to Paul Yuzyk, 23 October 1959.

77 LAC, MG 31 D 87, vol. 15, file 16, "Whitsun Festival, London, England: Communique 1960."

78 LAC, MG 31 D 87, vol. 5, file 21, Avramenko's letter to Soiuz Ukraintsiv Brytanii (AUGB), 3 October 1959; vol. 5, file 20, AUGB executive director Theodore J. Kudlyk's letter to Avramenko, 9 October 1959.

79 LAC, MG 31 D 87, vol. 5, file 20, Theodore J. Kudlyk's letter to Avramenko, 3 November 1959.

80 LAC, MG 31 D 87, vol. 5, file 22, Theodore J. Kudlyk's letter to Prof. Pasika-Hordij, 12 May 1960.

81 LAC, MG 31 D 87, vol. 5, file 22, Petro Dnistrovyk's letter to Avramenko, 26 May 1960.

82 LAC, MG 31 D 87, vol. 5, file 22, George Tamarski's letter to Avramenko, 8 January 1960. His participation cost Avramenko £275 for travel expenses, £102 for film and battery, and £38 for food and other expenses: vol. 11, file 6, "Financial Notes," two-page document titled "Pozychky iaki mnoiu zatiahneni na ulashtuvannia festivaliu v Roial Albert Hol … Pryblyzni vydatky. …"

83 LAC, MG 31 D 87, vol. 5, file 23, Ya. Ivaniuk's letter to an unidentified priest (Fr. Ihor), 19 September 1960, contains a list of the lenders.

84 LAC, MG 31 D 87, vol. 5, file 22, Rev. Konstantyn Kalinovsky's letters to Avramenko, 29 June and 19 July 1960. Also see the letters to Avramenko from M. Sydorenko (1 July 1960), Luba Yawtushenko (27 September 1960), and Rev. Vladimir Pellech, writing on behalf of Mrs. Alyna Oleksyn, who had been left homeless (18 November 1960), all in vol. 5, file 22; and the letter from invalids Mr. and Mrs. Oliynyk to Avramenko, 10 November 1962, in vol. 5, file 26.

85 LAC, MG 31 D 87, vol. 5, file 23, M. Sydorenko's letter to Mr. Kochaniwskyj of the Whitsun Festival Committee, 29 August 1960; the London weekly *Ukrainska dumka* (Ukrainian Thought), 8 September 1960, published an article by Ya. Havryliv describing Avramenko as a swindler.

86 LAC, MG 31 D 87, vol. 5, file 37, Ivan Hrushetsky's letter to S. Miskiw, 5 June 1967, reporting that he had seen documents proving that Avramenko had paid off his English debts. At the time, Avramenko was in Australia, and his English creditors were prepared to surrender the films and equipment that he had left as collateral.

87 Jaroslav Pelikan, *Confessor between East and West: A Portrait of Ukrainian Cardinal Josyf Slipyj* (Grand Rapids, MI: William B. Eerdmans, 1990), tells Slipyj's story. His release inspired a novel by Morris L. West and the 1968 Hollywood film *The Shoes of the Fisherman,* starring Anthony Quinn and Laurence Olivier.

88 LAC, MG 31 D 87, vol. 7, file 15, Avramenko's letter to Biberovich, 18 September 1963, identified his benefactors as Metropolitan Maxim Hermaniuk of Winnipeg and Bishop Andrew (probably Roborecky, of Saskatoon).

89 LAC, MG 31 D 87, vol. 5, file 30, Avramenko's letter to Ukrainian Catholic archbishop Ivan Buchko, 23 September 1963.

90 LAC, MG 31 D 87, vol. 5, files 31 and 32, Avramenko's letter to Bishop Andrii Sapeliak, 30 May 1964, and Fr. Vasyl Sapeliak's letter to Avramenko, 17 June 1964.

91 LAC, MG 31 D 87, vol. 5, file 33, Ivan Savaryn's letter to Avramenko, 5 January 1965, concerning the terms of the initial loan; vol. 5, file 37, Marika Halaburda's letter to Avramenko, 31 December 1967, reminding Avramenko that he still owed his Belgian creditors 20,000 BEF; vol. 6, file 6, letter to Avramenko, 13 August 1969, stating that he still owed 32,229 BEF ($644 US) to seven people in Zwartberg, Belgium.

92 LAC, MG 31 D 87, vol. 5, file 28, Yaroslav Bulka's letters to Avramenko, 1 June and 25 July 1963; vol. 5, file 29, Liuba (Matskevych) Oliinyk's letter to Avramenko, 6 August

1963; vol. 5, file 32, Dmytro Denysenko's letter to Avramenko, 12 April 1964; vol. 5, file 32, Nina Denysenko's letter to Avramenko, 4 June 1964; vol. 5, file 28, Nina Denysenko's letter to Avramenko 14 December 1965; vol. 5, file 34, Avramenko's letter to Nina Denysenko, 28 December 1965, reporting that he planned to tour Australia in 1966; vol. 5, file 35, Dmytro Denysenko's letter to Avramenko, 14 March 1966.

93 LAC, MG 31 D 87, vol. 5, file 28, Yaroslav Bulka's letter to Avramenko, 1 June 1963, indicated that Bulka, who had studied Ukrainian folk dancing with Avramenko's pupils in Lviv during the 1920s, had taught Wasyl Kowalenko and the three Kumpan brothers who billed themselves as the Kuban Cossacks. Avramenko's correspondence with the group's agents is in vol. 5, file 32, letters to Avramenko, April and 21 May 1964. The Kuban Cossacks were featured on the *Hollywood Palace* variety show in 1965, 1966, and 1970 and on the *Ed Sullivan Show* in 1968.

94 LAC, MG 31 D 87, vol. 5, file 35, Lidia Haievska-Denys's letter to Avramenko, 18 May 1966, promising the federation's support, and Bishop Ivan Prashko's letter of recommendation, 9 June 1966.

95 LAC, MG 31 D 87, vol. 5, file 35, Rodion Slipyj's letters to Avramenko, 9–20 August 1966, indicating that Rodion Slipyj, could not come to Australia with Palance and Mazurki; vol. 5, file 36, Avramenko's letters to Jack Palance, 12 August and 15 September 1966, asking him and Mike Mazurki to join him in Australia.

96 LAC, MG 31 D 87, vol. 14, files 66–72, announcements, programs, brochures of performances, and screenings, Australia, 1966–67; vol. 5, file 38, Ivan Hrushetsky's letter to Yaroslav Bulka, 7 July 1967, estimating that Avramenko's dance classes had been attended by 800 pupils; vol. 5, file 38, Yakiv Riznyk's letter to Avramenko, stating that it was his film screenings, especially the Catholic footage of Rome and the Second Vatican Council, that had saved Avramenko from bankruptcy in Australia.

97 LAC, MG 31 D 87, vol. 5, file 34, Avramenko's letter to M. Boliukh, FUAA president, 14 November 1966; vol. 5, file 35, Lidia Haievska-Denys's letter to Avramenko, 8 December 1966; vol. 5, file 38, Mr. Pasichynsky's letter to Avramenko, 25 April 1967; vol. 5, file 38, Dmytro Denysenko's letter to Avramenko, 9 May 1967.

98 LAC, MG 31 D 87, vol. 5, file 35, Canberra concert committee's letter to Avramenko, 9 November 1966.

99 LAC, MG 31 D 87, vol. 5, files 37 and 38, Ivan Hrushetsky's letters to S. Miskiw and Yaroslav Bulka, 5 June and 7 July 1967.

100 LAC, MG 31 D 87, vol. 6, file 1, Avramenko's letter to S. Miskiw, 6 May 1967, and Avramenko's letter to FUAA executive, 4 June 1967; vol. 5, file 37, Ivan Hrushetsky's letter to S. Miskiw, 5 June 1967.

101 LAC, MG 31 D 87, vol. 1, file 28, "Australia," document dated 11 June 1967.

102 LAC, MG 31 D 87, vol. 5, file 37, Bishop Ivan Prashko's letter to Avramenko, 27 July 1967.

103 UCECA, Vasile Avramenko Collection, box 4, copy of Avramenko's letter to Edward A. Clark, US ambassador to Australia, summer 1967; LAC, MG 31 D 87, vol. 1, file 30, "Proposed Trip to Vietnam and Thailand: Correspondence, 1967."

104 LAC, MG 31 D 87, vol. 5, file 37, Robert L. Johnson, US Army representative, Melbourne, report on visit with Avramenko, 15 August 1967; Col. W.A. Divers's (Canberra) letter to Col. William Ward, US Embassy (Bangkok, Thailand), 31 October 1967; vol. 5, file 38, Col. M.V. Talbot's (US Military Assistance Command, Vietnam) letter to the US Embassy in Canberra, 29 September 1967.

105 LAC, MG 31 D 87, vol. 6, file 3, Bishop Ivan Prashko's letter to Avramenko, 22 January 1968.

106 LAC, MG 31 D 87, vol. 5, file 37, I. Didokha's letter to Avramenko, 3 September 1967, imploring him to return a $500 loan; Mykhailo and Tania Bohoslavsky's letters to Avramenko, 10–14 October 1967, asking him to return at least $500 of the sum that they had loaned to him; Lesia Novytska's letter to Avramenko, 23 October 1967, asking him to settle his small debt; Anton Ohloblyn's letter to Avramenko, 27 November 1967, asking him to return his $100; B. Ihnativ's letter to Avramenko, 16 December 1967, asking him to settle his bill for 5,000 specially printed envelopes; et cetera.

107 LAC, MG 31 D 87, vol. 6, file 4, Babunia's (Grandmother's) letter to Avramenko, 23 October 1968. The anonymous woman, who lived in Lidcombe, New South Wales, Australia, begged Avramenko to stop destroying his reputation at his advanced age, to forget about performing on the stage, and to stop fooling people with tales of his Academy of Dance and Film Studio.

108 LAC, MG 31 D 87, vol. 6, file 3, Myron Sitnicki's letter to Mykola Teslevych, 4 March 1968.

109 LAC, MG 31 D 87, vol. 14, file 77, leaflet dated 15 September 1968; UCECA, Vasile Avramenko Collection, box 2, leaflet, 1968.

110 LAC, MG 31 D 87, vol. 6, file 4, Fedor Braznyk's (Braznick's) letter to Avramenko, 9 December 1968. Pauline had succumbed to cancer. Their daughter, Oksana, who resided in Detroit with her large family, was at Pauline's bedside when her mother died.

111 LAC, MG 31 D 87, vol. 8, file 31, Wolodymyr Luciw's letter to Avramenko, 9 August 1969; vol. 10, file 30, letter from the Association for a Patriarchate of the Ukrainian Greek Catholic Church to Cardinal Josyf Slipyj, 19 August 1969, informing him that Avramenko was eager to film the blessing of the St. Sophia Church in Rome.

112 LAC, MG 31 D 87, vol. 14, file 81, leaflet dated 6–8 February 1970.

113 LAC, MG 31 D 87, vol. 10, file 22, Mykhailo Yeremiiv's letters to Avramenko, 13 April and 29 June 1970.

114 LAC, MG 31 D 87, vol. 9, file 7, Mykhailo Yeremiiv's letter to Sofia Moravetzka, undated (1970s).

115 LAC, MG 31 D 87, vol. 8, file 31, Avramenko's letter to Wolodymyr Luciw, 7 October 1970.

116 LAC, MG 31 D 87, vol. 6, file 10, letter from Shulamit Nardi (assistant to the president) to Avramenko, 1 March 1971, informing Avramenko that "President Shazar truly regrets that because of his trip abroad he will not have the time to see you"; note from Teddy Kollek to Avramenko, 20 April 1971, thanking Avramenko for his kind Passover wishes; vol. 8, file 22, letter from Eli Mizrachi (assistant in the prime minister's office) to Avramenko, 12 November 1970, indicating that Golda Meir "very much enjoyed looking at the pictures of your Dancing Group."

117 LAC, MG 31 D 87, vol. 8, file 20, Avramenko's letter to Irena Knysh, 1 November 1970; vol. 9, file 29, Avramenko's letter to Peter Shelly (Shelepiuk), 5 January 1971.

118 LAC, MG 31 D 87, vol. 8, file 20, Avramenko's letters to Irena Knysh, 11 December 1970 and 5, 11, and 18 January, 6 February, 20 March, and 21 September 1971; vol. 9, file 22, Avramenko's letters to Joseph Shwarz, 1 and 19 February 1971.

119 LAC, MG 31 D 87, vol. 9, file 29, Avramenko's letter to Peter Shelly (Shelepiuk), 5 January 1971. By the time he was ready to leave Israel, and after having purchased what he referred to as "shocking" footage of the Holocaust, Avramenko was making plans to create an epic film with the aid of Jewish producers; see vol. 9, file 22, Avramenko's letter to Julian Revaj, 18 August 1971.

120 *Jerusalem Post,* 19 April 1971; *Ukrainian Weekly,* 22 May 1971 (article in Ukrainian). Russian- and Polish-language (*Nowiny Kurier;* Tel Aviv) Israeli periodicals also published stories about Avramenko.

121 LAC, MG 31 D 87, vol. 6, file 10, Prof. Dov Noy's letter to Avramenko, 1 December 1971; M. Ben Jakow's letter to Avramenko, 16 February 1971; Miriam Michaeli's letter to Avramenko, 4 December 1971.

122 LAC, MG 31 D 87, vol. 6, file 10, letters from members of Ramah Programs in Israel (Shira, Angela, Francesca, and Gerry) to Avramenko, 17 and 24 November 1971; vol. 9, file 22, Avramenko's letter to Julian Revaj, 15 October 1971; vol. 9, file 23, Avramenko's letter to Stephan Rosocha, 28 September 1971.

123 LAC, MG 31 D 87, vol. 6, file 10, letter from UNA executive to Avramenko, 9 September 1971, with $200 to cover hospital expenses; vol. 9, file 22, Julian Revaj's letter to Avramenko, informing him that his old credit union would loan him $300. The singer and bandurist Wolodymyr Luciw, with Avramenko in Israel in the spring of 1971, mentions his friend's publicity stunts and efforts to teach Ukrainian folk dancing to Arab Eastern rite Christian seminarians. See Volodymyr Lutsiv, "Nezabutnii maiestro Vasyl Avramenko u moii pamiati," in *Almanakh Ukrainskoho narodnoho soiuzu 1987* (Jersey City, NJ: Ukrainian National Association, 1986), 154–67.

124 LAC, MG 31 D 87, vol. 8, file 22, Wolodymyr Kowal's letter to Avramenko, 22 July 1970. Kowal, the producer of the film, also owned Ace Travel Service at 1706 Sunset Boulevard, Hollywood, where Avramenko resided. *The Incredible Two-Headed Transplant* starred Bruce Dern and radio host Casey Kasem. See Gary A. Smith, *The American International Pictures Video Guide* (Jefferson, NC: McFarland , 2009), 97–98. It can be viewed at http://www.youtube.com/watch?v=u3ysiREoxFI or on a 2004 MGM *Midnite Movies Double Feature* DVD that also features *The Thing with Two Heads* (1972).

125 LAC, MG 31 D 87, vol. 8, file 5, Avramenko's letter to Halyna Hoover, 3 August 1972; vol. 8, file 20, Avramenko's letters to Irena Knysh, 14 and 16 September 1972 and 20 February 1973.

126 LAC, MG 31 D 87, vol. 10, file 30, Avramenko's letters to Richard Nixon, Spiro Agnew, and Barry Goldwater, 3 November 1968; Avramenko's letter to Richard Nixon, 26 November 1968, requesting that his "Company of World Festival Dancers" be permitted to perform at the presidential inauguration in January 1969.

127 LAC, MG 31 D 87, vol. 10, file 30, letter from Henry Alan Lawless (PMO) to Avramenko, 15 June 1973, thanking him for the "message from Jerusalem and also for the gifts you so kindly sent to [the prime minister] and Mrs. Trudeau"; letter from Pat Nixon to Avramenko, 19 June 1973, thanking him for the "warm greetings from the Holy Land and ... the symbolically designed gifts for both of us."

128 LAC, MG 31 D 87, vol. 8, file 31, Avramenko's letter to Wolodymyr Luciw, 20 February 1973.

129 LAC, MG 31 D 87, vol. 6, file 16, Avramenko's letter to Juan Perón (in Ukrainian), 25 September 1973.

130 LAC, MG 31 D 87, vol. 8, file 31, Avramenko's letter to Wolodymyr Luciw, 21 June 1972.

131 LAC, MG 31 D 87, vol. 8, files 5 and 31, Avramenko's letters to Halyna Hoover and Wolodymyr Luciw, 21 and 22 June 1972.

132 LAC, MG 31 D 87, vol. 8, file 5, Avramenko's letter to Halyna Hoover and Teklia Danys, 26 October 1972.

133 LAC, MG 31 D 87, vol. 10, file 22, Mykhailo Yeremiiv's letter to Sofia Moravetzka, undated (ca. 1973).

134 LAC, MG 31 D 87, vol. 10, file 25, Paul Yuzyk's letter To Whom It May Concern, 28 July 1972.

135 LAC, MG 31 D 87, vol. 6, file 13, copy of Simon J. Kalba's letter to John G. Diefenbaker, 29 September 1972.

136 LAC, MG 31 D 87, vol. 6, file 17, Simon J. Kalba's letter to Avramenko, 19 September 1974.

137 LAC, MG 31 D 87, vol. 8, file 5, Avramenko's letter to Halyna Hoover, 17 December 1974. This film should not be confused with the Soviet Ukrainian documentary of the same name released in 1957.

138 LAC, MG 31 D 87, vol. 6, file 19, UCC circular, dated 22 December 1975. The circular claimed that Avramenko and his instructors had trained 30,000 folk dancers in Canada, 50,000 in the United States, and 20,000 in other parts of the world.

139 LAC, MG 31 D 87, vol. 14, file 95, leaflet, 1977; *Ukrainian Weekly,* 27 March and 3 April 1977.

140 LAC, MG 31 D 87, vol. 10, file 30, copy of letter from Senator Paul Yuzyk to Myron B. Kuropas, special assistant to the president, 17 May 1976, suggesting that Avramenko "could also be featured at some of the Ukrainian [American Bicentennial] celebrations in the USA." Yuzyk observed that the "celebration of the American Bi-centennial and the centennial of the Ukrainians in your country should not neglect to include in the programs some aspects of Avramenko's contributions, i.e., Ukrainian folk-dancing and films."

141 LAC, MG 31 D 87, vol. 8, file 20, Avramenko's letter to Irena Knysh, 6 March 1978.

142 *Svoboda,* 8 and 14 May 1981; *Ukrainian Weekly,* 27 March 1977, 10 and 17 May 1981.

143 *Svoboda,* 8 May 1981; *Ukrainian Weekly,* 10 May 1981.

144 Lidia Korsun, "Vasyl Avramenko—lytsar ukrainskoho tantsiu," *Chas i podii* (Chicago), 19 March 2009, http://www.chasipodii.net/article/4451/?vsid=040067543ce11ae55eb2b2b33fa4b7d8.

Epilogue: The Legacy Tour

1 "Ukrainian Canadian Federation Pop-Up Display," http://www.creativedisplay.ca/portfolio/ukrainian-canadian-federation-pop-up#col-1, has a description and photo of part of the exhibit. For more photos, see "The Legacy of Vasile Avramenko: The History of Ukrainian Dance in Canada," http://www.stvladimirs.com/vasilea.htm, the website of St. Vladimir's Ukrainian Cultural Centre in Windsor, Ontario.

2 *Vasile Avramenko: A Legacy of Ukrainian Dance,* researched, compiled, and curated by Irka Balan (Winnipeg: Ukrainian Canadian Foundation of Taras Shevchenko, 2006).

3 "Avramenko Exhibit Marks Provincial Centennials," in *Centrepieces: A Publication of the Ukrainian Resource and Development Centre* (Edmonton: Grant MacEwan College, 2005), 3.

4 *Vasile Avramenko,* iv–v, 20–24, 32, 35–36, 39–40, 43, 63–64.

5 Lidiia Korsun, "Vasyl Avramenko—lytsar ukrainskoho tantsiu," *Chas i podii* (Time and Events; Chicago), 19 March 2009, http://www.chasipodii.net/article/4451/, the third part of a lengthy and fundamentally uncritical celebration of Avramenko; the first two parts appeared in the 5 and 12 March 2009 issues of *Chas i podii.*

6 O.O. Kovalchuk, "Avramenko Vasyl Kyrylovych," in V.A. Smolii, ed., *Entsyklopediia istorii Ukrainy,* vol. 1 (Kyiv: Naukova dumka, 2003), 16. The encyclopedia was produced by the Institute of Ukrainian History at the Ukrainian National Academy of Sciences.

7 Olha Melnyk, "Vasyl Avramenko—tantsivnyk iakoho znav tsilyi svit," *Personal-plius,* 6–12 October 2006, http://www.personal-plus.net/191/1260.html.

8 Mariia Zahaikevych, "Mystetski paraleli: velych i paradoksy doli Oleksandra Koshytsia i Vasylia Avramenka," *Studii mystetstvoznavchi* 31, 3 (Kyiv: Instytut mystetstvoznavstva, folklorystyky ta etnolohii im. M.T. Rylskoho, 2010), 34–40. The article also contained a photo of Koshetz with the Mexican composer and conductor Miguel Lerdo de Tejada, incorrectly identified as Avramenko!

9 Valentyna Korotia-Kovalska, "Ukrainskyi narodnyi tanets iak nevidiemna chastyna svitovoi khoreohrafii v ukrainoznavstvi," *Ukrainoznavstvo* 1, 42 (2012): 120–25.

10 "Chuperchuk, Iaroslav Markianovych," Barvinochok—Natsionalna studiia ukrainskoho tantsiu, http://barvinochok.com.ua/index.php/uk/dance/556-2011-02-04-23-40-45?start=3>.

11 Alexandra Pritz, "The Evolution of Ukrainian Dance in Canada," in Manoly R. Lupul, ed., *Visible Symbols: Cultural Expressions among Canada's Ukrainians* (Edmonton: Canadian Institute of Ukrainian Studies Press, 1984), 87–101.

12 "Herman, Michael, and Mary Ann Herman," in Mark C. Carnes, ed., *American National Biography: Supplement 2* (New York: Oxford University Press, 2005), 247–49.

13 *New York Times,* 5 April 2004; *Los Angeles Times,* 6 April 2004; *Ukrainian Weekly,* 18 April 2004; *The Guardian,* 24 April 2004; and *Encyclopedia Britannica 2005 Book of the Year* (Chicago: Encyclopedia Britannica, 2005), 137, published John Taras's obituary.

14 Andriy Nahachewsky, "Avramenko and the Paradigm of National Culture," *Journal of Ukrainian Studies* 28, 2 (2003): 31–50.

15 Norman Davies, *Europe: A History* (Oxford: Oxford University Press, 1996), 53–54.

16 "301.81 Narcissistic Personality Disorder," in *Diagnostic and Statistical Manual of Mental Disorders, 4th edition, Text Revision* (Arlington, VA: American Psychiatric Association, 2000), 714 ff., provides the definition adopted.

17 Joy S. Kasson, *Buffalo Bill's Wild West: Celebrity, Memory, and Popular History* (New York: Hill and Wang, 2000), especially 265–73.

18 Matthew Avery Sutton, *Aimee Semple McPherson and the Resurrection of Christian America* (Cambridge, MA: Harvard University Press, 2007).

19 Harlow Robinson, *The Last Impresario: The Life, Times, and Legacy of Sol Hurok* (New York: Viking, 1994), especially 205–11.

BIBLIOGRAPHY

Archival Collections

LIBRARY AND ARCHIVES CANADA (LAC), OTTAWA

Vasile Avramenko Collection, MG 31 D 87

Julian Stechishin Collection, MG 30 D 307

Paul Yavorsky Collection, MG 31 D 123

UKRAINIAN CULTURAL AND EDUCATIONAL CENTRE ARCHIVES (UCECA), WINNIPEG

Vasile Avramenko Collection

Ivan Bobersky Collection

Alexander Koshetz Collection

Mykyta Mandryka Collection

Lev Sorochynsky Collection

Mykhailo Seleshko Collection

Newspapers

The Advertiser (New York)

Baltimore Sun

Boston Evening Transcript

Boston Globe

Brooklyn Daily Eagle

Dilo (The Deed [Lviv])

Edmonton Journal

Fort William Times Journal

Jerusalem Post

Kanadyiskyi farmer (Canadian Farmer [Winnipeg])

Los Angeles Daily News

Montreal Daily Star

Montreal *Gazette*

Narodna volia (People's Freedom [Scranton, PA])

Narodne slovo (The People's Word [Pittsburgh])

New York American

New York Evening Post

New York Herald-Tribune

New York Times

New York Tribune

New York World-Telegram

Novoe russkoe slovo (New Russian Word [Brooklyn])

Novyi shliakh (The New Pathway [Saskatoon])

Philadelphia Public Ledger

Pravda (The Truth [Winnipeg])

Svoboda (Liberty [Jersey City, NJ])

Toronto Daily Star

Toronto Evening Telegram

Ukrainian Weekly (Jersey City NJ)

Ukrainska dumka (Ukrainian Thought [London, UK])

Ukrainskyi holos (Ukrainian Voice [Winnipeg])

Variety (New York)

Washington Evening Star

Winnipeg Evening Tribune

Winnipeg Free Press (*Manitoba Free Press* until 1931)

Websites

Harvard Ukrainian Research Institute in Cambridge,http://hollis.harvard.edu/?itemid=%7Clibrary/m/aleph%7C009499647

Internet Encyclopedia of Ukraine, http://www.encyclopediaofukraine.com/default.asp

Internet Movie Data Base (IMDb), http://www.imdb.com

Syzokryli (Ukrainian American Dance Ensemble), http://www.syzokryli.com/roma.php

Turner Classic Movies (Deslaw's *Montparnasse*), http://fan.tcm.com/_Montparnasse-1929-Eugene-Deslaw/video/1657676/66470.html?createPassive=true

YouTube (Avramenko's film *The Tragedy of Carpatho-Ukraine*), http://www.youtube.com/watch?v=iS1U3RcUQSY

YouTube (Kowal's film *The Incredible Two-Headed Transplant*), http://www.youtube.com/watch?v=u3ysiREoxFI

Films

The Black Cat. DVD. Directed by Edgar G. Ulmer. 1934. Universal City, CA. The Bela Lugosi Collection. Universal Studios Home Entertainment. 2005. 66 min. B&W.

Cossacks in Exile (Zaporozhets za Dunaiem). DVD-R. Directed by Edgar G. Ulmer. 1938. Avramenko Film Company Limited. Research copy from Ukrainian Cultural and Educational Centre (Oseredok), Winnipeg. 2004. 78 min. B&W.

The Incredible Two-Headed Transplant. DVD. Directed by Anthony M. Lanza. 1971. American International Pictures, Hollywood. MGM Midnite Movies Double Features. 2004. 88 min. Colour.

Man with a Movie Camera (Chelovek s kinoapparatom). DVD. Directed by Dziga Vertov. 1929. VUFKU, Kyiv. Ninja Tune. 2003. 68 min. B&W.

Natalka Poltavka. DVD-R. Directed by Edgar G. Ulmer. 1936. Avramenko Film Productions Incorporated. Research copy from Immigration History Research Center, University of Minnesota, Minneapolis. 2004. 92 min. B&W.

People on Sunday (Menschen am Sonntag). DVD. Directed by Robert Siodmak and Edgar G. Ulmer. 1930. Filmstudio, Berlin. The Criterion Collection. 2011. 73 min. B&W.

The Scarlet Empress. DVD. Directed by Josef von Sternberg. 1934. Paramount Pictures, Hollywood. The Criterion Collection. 2001. 104 min. B&W.

Books and Articles

Abramson, Henry. *A Prayer for the Government: Ukrainians and Jews in Revolutionary Times, 1917–1920.* Cambridge, MA: Ukrainian Research Institute and Center for Jewish Studies, Harvard University, 1999.

American Psychiatric Association. *Diagnostic and Statistical Manual of Mental Disorders, 4th edition, Text Revision.* Arlington, VA: American Psychiatric Association, 2000.

Anonymous. "Avramenko Exhibit Marks Provincial Centennials." In *Centrepieces: A Publication of the Ukrainian Resource and Development Centre,* 3–4. Edmonton: Grant MacEwan College, 2005.

———. "Chuperchuk, Iaroslav Markianovych." On *Barvinochok—Natsionalna studiia ukrainskoho tantsiu* website, http://barvinochok.com.ua/index.php/uk/dance/556-2011-02-04-23-40-45?start=3.

———. "Herman, Michael, and Mary Ann Herman." In *American National Biography: Supplement 2,* edited by Mark C. Carnes, 247–49. New York: Oxford University Press, 2005.

———. "Kinomystetstvo." In *Ukrainska radianska entsyklopediia,* vol. 5, 2nd ed., 192–94. Kyiv: Vyd-vo Akademiï nauk UkrRSR, 1977–85.

———. "Woman's World's Fair 1925." In *Encyclopedia of Chicago,* http://encyclopedia.chicagohistory.org/pages/1374.html.

Artibise, Alan. *Winnipeg: An Illustrated History.* Toronto: James Lorimer and Company, 1977.

Avramenko, Vasyl. *Ukrainski natsionalni tanky: opys.* Winnipeg: Shkoly ukrainskoho natsionalnoho tanku, 1928.

———. "Ukrainskyi natsionalnyi tanok." In *Klenovyi lyst: kanadiiskyi almanakh.* 11–17. Winnipeg: T-vo opiky nad ukrainskymy pereselentsiamy im. Sv. Rafaila v Kanadi, 1929.

———. *Ukrainski natsionalni tanky muzyka i strii.* Winnipeg: the author, 1947.

Balan, Irka, researcher, compiler, and curator. *Vasile Avramenko: A Legacy of Ukrainian Dance.* Winnipeg: Ukrainian Canadian Foundation of Taras Shevchenko, 2006.

Balan, Jars. "Backdrop to an Era: The Ukrainian Canadian Stage in the Interwar Years." *Journal of Ukrainian Studies* 16, 1–2 (1991): 89–113.

Baxter, John. *Von Sternberg.* Lexington: University of Kentucky Press, 2010.

Berg, A. Scott. *Goldwyn: A Biography.* New York: Riverhead Books, 1998.

Berger, Carl. *The Sense of Power: Studies in the Ideas of Canadian Imperialism, 1867–1914.* Toronto: University of Toronto Press, 1970.

Blanchard, Jim. *Winnipeg 1912.* Winnipeg: University of Manitoba Press, 2005.

Blumhofer, Edith L. *Aimee Semple McPherson: Everybody's Sister.* Grand Rapids, MI: William B. Eerdmans Publishing Company, 1993.

Bogdanovich, Peter. "Edgar G. Ulmer: An Interview." *Film Culture* 58–60 (1974): 189–238.

Boshyk, Yury, Wsevolod Isajiw, and Roman Senkus, eds. *The Refugee Experience: Ukrainian Displaced Persons after World War II.* Edmonton: Canadian Institute of Ukrainian Studies Press, University of Alberta, 1992.

Bradbury, Malcolm, ed. *The Atlas of Literature.* London: Prospero, 1996.

Brook, Vincent. *Driven to Darkness: Jewish Émigré Directors and the Rise of Film Noir.* New Brunswick, NJ: Rutgers University Press, 2009.

Davies, Norman. *Europe: A History.* Oxford: Oxford University Press, 1996.

Davis, Blair. *The Battle for the Bs: 1950s Hollywood and the Rebirth of Low-Budget Cinema.* New Brunswick, NJ: Rutgers University Press, 2012.

Druick, Zoë. *Projecting Canada: Government Policy and Documentary Film at the National Film Board of Canada.* Montreal: McGill-Queen's University Press, 2007.

Early, Gerald. "The Birth of Mass Culture." In *Our Times: The Illustrated History of the 20th Century,* edited by Lorraine Glennon and John A. Garraty, 146–51. Atlanta: Turner Publishing, 1995.

Ebert, Roger. "The Scarlet Empress." In *The Great Movies III*, 347–51. Chicago: University of Chicago Press, 2010.

Epstein, Daniel Mark. *Sister Aimee: The Life of Aimee Semple McPherson.* New York: Houghton Mifflin Harcourt, 1994.

Everett, William A., and Paul R. Laird. *Historical Dictionary of the Broadway Musical.* Lanham, MD: Scarecrow Press, 2008.

Eyman, Scott. *The Speed of Sound: Hollywood and the Talkie Revolution, 1926–1930.* Baltimore: Johns Hopkins University Press, 1997.

Fass, Paula S. *The Damned and the Beautiful: American Youth in the 1920s.* New York: Oxford University Press, 1977.

Foster, Charles. *Once Upon a Time in Paradise: Canadians in the Golden Age of Hollywood.* Toronto: Dundurn Press, 2003.

Foulkes, Julia L. *Modern Bodies: Dance and American Modernism from Martha Graham to Alvin Ailey.* Chapel Hill: University of North Carolina Press, 2002.

Freund, Steve. "The Birth of a Nation." In *Encyclopedia of American History*, vol. 7, *The Emergence of Modern America 1900–1928,* edited by Garry B. Nash et al., 37–38. New York: Facts On File, 2010.

———. "Movie Industry." In *Encyclopedia of American History*, vol. 7, *The Emergence of Modern America 1900–1928,* edited by Garry B. Nash et al., 214–16. New York: Facts On File, 2010.

Fried, Albert. *The Rise and Fall of the Jewish Gangster in America.* New York: Columbia University Press, 1980.

Frith, Simon. *Performing Rites: On the Value of Popular Music.* Cambridge, MA: Harvard University Press, 1996.

Gateward, Frances K. "African American Cinema." In *Schirmer Encyclopedia of Film,* vol. 1, edited by Barry Keith Grant, 59–70. Farmington Hills, MI: Thompson Gale, 2007.

Gevinson, Alan, ed. *Within Our Gates: Ethnicity in American Feature Films, 1911–1960.* Berkeley: University of California Press, 1997.

Goldman, Eric A. *Visions, Images, and Dreams: Yiddish Film, Past and Present.* Teaneck, NJ: Ergo, 1988.

Gronow, Pekka, and Ilpo Saunio. *An International History of the Recording Industry.* London: Cassell, 1998.

Hallinan, Victoria. "The 1958 Tour of the Moiseyev Dance Company: A Window into American Perception." *Journal of History and Cultures* 1, 1 (2012): 51–64.

Hartman, Michael. "Popular Culture." In *Encyclopedia of American History,* vol. 7, *The Emergence of Modern America 1900–1928,* edited by Garry B. Nash et al., 263–66. New York: Facts On File, 2010.

Herzogenrath, Bernd, ed. *Edgar G. Ulmer: Essays on the King of the B's.* Jefferson, NC: McFarland, 2009.

———, ed. *The Films of Edgar G. Ulmer.* Lanham, MD: Scarecrow Press, 2009.

Hicks, Jeremy. *Dziga Vertov: Defining Documentary Film.* London: I.B. Tauris, 2007.

Hoberman, J. *Bridge of Light: Yiddish Film between Two Worlds.* Philadelphia: Temple University Press, 1991.

Howe, Irving. *World of Our Fathers: The Journey of the East European Jews to America and the Life They Found and Made.* New York: Touchstone, 1976.

Hughes, Robert. *American Visions: The Epic History of Art in America.* New York: Alfred A. Knopf, 1997.

Isenberg, Noah. "Perennial Detour: The Cinema of Edgar G. Ulmer and the Experience of Exile." *Cinema Journal* 43, 2 (2004): 3–25.

———. *Edgar G. Ulmer: A Filmmaker at the Margins.* Berkeley: University of California Press, 2014.

James, Edward T., Janet Wilson James, and Paul S. Boyer, eds. *Notable American Women, 1607–1950: A Biographical Dictionary,* vol. 2. Cambridge, MA: Harvard University Press, 1971.

Joselit, Jenna Weissman. *Our Gang: Jewish Crime and the New York Jewish Community, 1900–1940.* Bloomington: Indiana University Press, 1983.

Kalat, David. "*Detour*'s Detour." In *The Films of Edgar G. Ulmer,* edited by Bernd Herzogenrath, 137–57. Lanham, MD: Scarecrow Press, 2009.

Kasson, Joy S. *Buffalo Bill's Wild West: Celebrity, Memory, and Popular History.* New York: Hill and Wang, 2000.

Kennedy, David M. *Freedom from Fear: The American People in Depression and War, 1929–1945.* New York: Oxford University Press, 1999.

Klymasz, Robert B. "The Fine Arts." In *A Heritage in Transition: Essays in the History of Ukrainians in Canada,* edited by Manoly R. Lupul, 281–95. Toronto: McClelland and Stewart, 1982.

Knysh, Irena. *Zhyva dusha narodu: do iuvileiu ukrainskoho tanku.* Winnipeg: the author, 1966.

Korotia-Kovalska, Valentyna. "Ukrainskyi narodnyi tanets iak nevidiemna chastyna svitovoi khoreohrafii v ukrainoznavstvi." *Ukrainoznavstvo* 42, 1 (2012): 120–25.

Korsun, Lidia. "Vasyl Avramenko—lytsar ukrainskoho tantsiu." *Chas i podii* (Chicago), 19 March 2009, http://www.chasipodii.net/article/4451/?vsid=040067543ce11ae55eb2b2b33fa4b7d8.

Koshelivets, Ivan. "Film." In *Encyclopedia of Ukraine,* vol. 1, edited by Volodymyr Kubijovic, 884–86. Toronto: University of Toronto Press, 1984.

Koshyts, Oleksandr (Alexander Koshetz). *Z pisneiu cherez svit,* vol. 1, *Podorozh Ukrainskoi respublikanskoi kapeli.* Winnipeg: Ukrainian Cultural and Educational Centre, 1952.

———. *Z pisneiu cherez svit,* vol. 2, *Iz "shchodennyka" O. Koshytsia.* Winnipeg: Ukrainian Cultural and Educational Centre, 1970.

Kovalchuk, O.O. "Avramenko, Vasyl Kyrylovych." In *Entsyklopediia istorii Ukrainy,* vol. 1, edited by V.A. Smolii, 16. Kyiv: Naukova dumka, 2003.

Kukushkin, Vadim. *From Peasants to Labourers: Ukrainian and Belarusan Immigration from the Russian Empire to Canada.* Montreal: McGill-Queen's University Press, 2007.

Kulynych, Yaroslav. *Filmova tvorchist Iaroslava Kulynycha.* New York: the author, 1994.

Kurelek, William. *Someone with Me: The Autobiography of William Kurelek.* Niagara Falls, ON: Niagara Falls Art Gallery, Kurelek Collection, 1988.

Leyda, Jay. *Kino: A History of the Russian and Soviet Film,* 3rd ed. Princeton, NJ: Princeton University Press, 1983.

Liber, George O. *Alexander Dovzhenko: A Life in Soviet Film.* London: British Film Institute, 2002.

———. "Death, Birth Order and Alexander Dovzhenko's Cinematic Visions," *Kinema: A Journal for Film and Audiovisual Media* 8, 1 (2000), http://www.kinema.uwaterloo.ca/article.php?id=306&feature.

Ling, Peter. "Sex and the Automobile in the Jazz Age." *History Today* 39, 11 (1989): 18–24.

Livesay, Florence Randal. "Songs and Dances of the Ukraine." *Canadian Magazine,* January 1927.

———. "Songs of Ukraine Preserve Spirit of Its People." *Musical America,* 12 June 1926.

Lutsiv, Volodymyr. "Nezabutnii maiestro Vasyl Avramenko u moii pamiati." In *Almanakh Ukrainskoho narodnoho soiuzu 1987,* 154–67. Jersey City, NJ: Ukrainian National Association, 1986.

Magocsi, Paul Robert. *The Shaping of a National Identity: Subcarpathian Rus': 1848–1948.* Cambridge, MA: Harvard University Press, 1978.

———. *A History of Ukraine.* Toronto: University of Toronto Press, 1996.

Makuch, Andrij. "Narodni Domy in East Central Europe." In *Continuity and Change: The Cultural Life of Alberta's First Ukrainians,* edited by Manoly R. Lupul, 202–10. Edmonton: Canadian Institute of Ukrainian Studies Press, 1988.

Mank, Gregory William. *Bela Lugosi and Boris Karloff: The Expanded Story of a Haunting Collaboration.* Jefferson, NC: McFarland, 2009.

Martynowych, Orest T. "'All That Jazz!': The Avramenko Phenomenon in Canada, 1925–1929." *Journal of Ukrainian Studies* 28, 2 (2003): 1–29.

———. *Ukrainians in Canada: The Formative Period, 1891–1924.* Edmonton: Canadian Institute of Ukrainian Studies Press, 1991.

Marunchak, Mykhailo H. *Biohrafichnyi dovidnyk do istorii ukraintsiv Kanady.* Winnipeg: Ukrainian Academy of Arts and Sciences in Canada, 1986.

May, Lary. *The Big Tomorrow: Hollywood and the Politics of the American Way.* Chicago: University of Chicago Press, 2000.

McCarten, Barry. "History and Live Theatre in Winnipeg." *Manitoba History* 16 (1988): 21–22.

McLaren, E.D. "On National Aspirations." In *Empire Club Speeches: Being Addresses before the Empire Club of Canada*, 131–36. Ottawa: Dent, 1906.

Melnyk, Olha. "Vasyl Avramenko—tantsivnyk iakoho znav tsilyi svit." *Personal-plius*, 6–12 October 2006, http://www.personal-plus.net/191/1260.html.

Merritt, Greg. *Celluloid Mavericks: A History of American Independent Film*. New York: Thunder's Mouth Press, 2000.

Morris, Garry. "Mother Russia! Von Sternberg's *The Scarlet Empress* on DVD." *Bright Lights Film Journal* 33 (2001), http://brightlightsfilm.com/33/scarletempress.php.

Morris, Peter. *Embattled Shadows: A History of Canadian Cinema, 1895–1939*. Montreal: McGill-Queen's University Press, 1978.

Myslavsky, Volodymyr. "Pershe desiatylittia isnuvannia ihrovohoho kinematohrafa v Ukraini (1907–1917)." In *Narysy z istorii kinomystetstva Ukrainy*, edited by Viktor Sydorenko, 9–52. Kyiv: Intertekhnolohiia, 2006.

Nahachewsky, Andriy. "Avramenko and the Paradigm of National Culture." *Journal of Ukrainian Studies* 28, 2 (2003): 31–50.

———. "First Existence Folk Dance Forms among Ukrainians in Smoky Lake, Alberta and Swan Plain, Saskatchewan." MA thesis, University of Alberta, 1985.

———. *Ukrainian Dance: A Cross-Cultural Approach*. Jefferson, NC: McFarland, 2012.

———. "Ukrainian Performing Arts in Alberta." In *Continuity and Change: The Cultural Life of Alberta's First Ukrainians*, edited by Manoly R. Lupul, 211–20. Edmonton: Canadian Institute of Ukrainian Studies Press, 1988.

Nebesio, Bohdan Y. "*Zaporozhets za Dunaiem* (1938): The Production of the First Ukrainian-Language Feature Film in Canada." *Journal of Ukrainian Studies* 16, 1–2 (1991): 115–29.

Novak, Mykola P. *Na storozhi Ukrainy: vlasni spohady, istorychni materiialy, dokumenty, lystuvannia, arkhiv*. Los Angeles: the author, 1979.

Obituary. "Anna Sten." *The Independent* (London), 19 November 1993, http://www.independent.co.uk/news/people/obituary-anna-sten-1505253.html.

———. "John Taras." In *Encyclopedia Britannica 2005 Book of the Year*, 137. Chicago: Encyclopedia Britannica, 2005.

———. "Shirley Ulmer: Queen of B-Movies, as Screenplay Writer and Script Girl." *The Guardian* (London), 4 September 2000, http://www.guardian.co.uk/news/2000/sep/04/guardianobituaries3.

o.H.P. "Soroklittia slavnoi diialnosty: do biohrafii prof. O.A. Koshytsia." *Dnipro* (Philadelphia), 1 and 8 March 1937.

Olender, Vivian. "The Canadian Methodist Church and the Gospel of Assimilation, 1900–1925." *Journal of Ukrainian Studies* 7, 2 (1982): 61–74.

Owen, Michael. "'Keeping Canada God's Country': Presbyterian School Homes for Ruthenian Children." In *Prairie Spirit: Perspectives on the Heritage of the United Church of Canada in the West*, edited by Dennis L. Butcher et al., 184–201. Winnipeg: University of Manitoba Press, 1985.

Paskin, Sylvia, ed. *When Joseph Met Molly: A Reader on Yiddish Film*. Nottingham, UK: Five Leaves Publications, 1999.

Pasternakova, M. "The Folk and Art Dance." In *Ukraine: A Concise Encyclopedia*, vol. 2, edited by Volodymyr Kubijovyc, 601–13. Toronto: University of Toronto Press, 1963.

Peiss, Kathy. "Making Up, Making Over: Cosmetics, Consumer Culture, and Women's Identity." In *The Sex of Things: Gender and Consumption in Historical Perspective*, edited by Victoria de Grazia and Ellen Furlough, 311–36. Berkeley: University of California Press, 1996.

Pelikan, Jaroslav. *Confessor between East and West: A Portrait of Ukrainian Cardinal Josyf Slipyj*. Grand Rapids, MI: William B. Eerdmans Publishing Company, 1990.

Pihuliak, Ivan. *Vasyl Avramenko a vidrodzhennia ukrainskoho tanku*. Syracuse, NY: the author, 1979.

Pritz, Alexandra. "The Evolution of Ukrainian Dance in Canada." In *Visible Symbols: Cultural Expressions among Canada's Ukrainians,* edited by Manoly R. Lupul, 87–101. Edmonton: Canadian Institute of Ukrainian Studies Press, 1984.

———. "Ukrainian Dance in Canada: The First Fifty Years, 1924–1974." In *New Soil—Old Roots: The Ukrainian Experience in Canada,* edited by Jaroslav Rozumnyj, 124–54. Winnipeg: Ukrainian Academy of Arts and Sciences in Canada, 1983.

Pummer, Claudia. "At the Border: Edgar G. Ulmer's Foreign Language Productions: *The Singing Blacksmith* and *Cossacks in Exile*." In *Edgar G. Ulmer: Detour on Poverty Row,* edited by Gary D. Rhodes, 41–57. Lanham, MD: Lexington Books, 2008.

Rhodes, Gary D., ed. *Edgar G. Ulmer: Detour on Poverty Row*. Lanham, MD: Lexington Books, 2008.

Robinson, Harlow. *The Last Impresario: The Life, Times, and Legacy of Sol Hurok*. New York: Viking, 1994.

Rylsky, M.T., ed. *Ukrainskyi dramatychnyi teatr: narysy istorii v dvokh tomakh,* vol. 1, *Dozhovtnevyi period*. Kyiv: Akademiia nauk Ukrainskoi RSR, 1967.

Sayers, Michael, and Albert E. Kahn. *Sabotage! The Secret War against America*. New York: Harper and Brothers, 1942.

Schaefer, Eric. *"Bold! Daring! Shocking! True!": A History of Exploitation Films, 1919–1959*. Durham: Duke University Press, 1999.

Shatulsky, Myron. *The Ukrainian Folk Dance*. Toronto: Kobzar, 1980.

Shkandrij, Myroslav. *Jews in Ukrainian Literature: Representation and Identity*. New Haven, CT: Yale University Press, 2009.

Shtohryn, Dmytro M. *Ukrainians in North America: A Biographical Directory*. Champaign, IL: Association for the Advancement of Ukrainian Studies, 1975.

Siegel, Marcia B. *The Shapes of Change: Images of American Dance*. Berkeley: University of California Press, 1985.

Smith, Gary A. *The American International Pictures Video Guide*. Jefferson, NC: McFarland, 2009.

Spoto, Donald. *Blue Angel: The Life of Marlene Dietrich*. New York: Doubleday, 1992.

Spottswood, Richard. "Ethnic and Popular Style in America." In *Folk Music and Modern Sound,* edited by William Ferris and Mary L. Hart, 60–72. Jackson: University Press of Mississippi, 1982.

Staniec, Jillian Dawn. "Cossacks and Wallflowers: Ukrainian Stage Dance, Identity, and Politics in Saskatchewan from the 1920s to the Present." MA thesis, University of Saskatchewan, 2007.

Steshenko, O.L., et al., eds. *Istoriia mist i sil Ukrainskoi RSR: Cherkaska oblast*. Kyiv: Instytut Istorii Akademii Nauk URSR, 1972.

Subtelny, Orest. *Ukraine: A History*. Toronto: University of Toronto Press, 1988.

———. *Ukrainians in North America: An Illustrated History*. Toronto: University of Toronto Press, 1991.

Sutton, Matthew Avery. *Aimee Semple McPherson and the Resurrection of Christian America.* Cambridge, MA: Harvard University Press, 2007.

Swyripa, Frances. *Ukrainian Canadians: A Survey of Their Portrayal in English-Language Works.* Edmonton: University of Alberta Press, 1978.

Thompson, John Herd, and Allen Seager. *Canada 1922–1939: Decades of Discord.* Toronto: McClelland and Stewart, 1985.

Trymbach, Serhii. "Istoriia ukrainskoho kino 1910–1920-ti roky." In *Narysy z istorii kinomystetstva Ukrainy,* edited by Viktor Sydorenko, 53–76. Kyiv: Intertekhnolohiia, 2006.

Tsuda, Margaret. "Slavic Song in New York Hills." *Christian Science Monitor,* 22 May 1990, http://www.csmonitor.com/1990/0522/uslav.html.

Ulman, Eric. "Edgar G. Ulmer." *Senses of Cinema* 24 (2003), http://sensesofcinema.com/2003/great-directors/ulmer/.

Vance, Jonathan F. *A History of Canadian Culture.* Toronto: Oxford University Press, 2009.

Verkhovynets, V.M. *Teoriia ukrainskoho narodnoho tantsiu,* 5th ed. Kyiv: Muzychna Ukraina, 1990.

Viatrovych, Volodymyr. "Karpatska Ukraina ta ii armiia u fotohrafiakh Kalenyka Lysiuka." *Istorychna pravda,* 16 March 2011, http://www.istpravda.com.ua/artefacts/2011/03/16/31888/.

Walz, Gene. *Cartoon Charlie: The Life and Art of Animation Pioneer Charles Thorson.* Winnipeg: Great Plains Publications, 1998.

Weaver, Tom, Michael Brunas, and John Brunas. *Universal Horrors: The Studio's Classic Films, 1931–1946.* Jefferson, NC: McFarland, 2009.

Wildman, Allan K. *The End of the Russian Imperial Army: The Old Army and the Soldiers Revolt, March–April 1917.* Princeton, NJ: Princeton University Press, 1980.

Wolff, Ethan. *Frommer's Memorable Walks in New York.* New York: Wiley Publishing, 2006.

Wyver, John. *Moving Image: International History of Film, Television and Video.* Oxford: Basil Blackwell, 1989.

Yanow, Scott. *Jazz: A Regional Exploration.* Westport, CT: Greenwood, 2005.

Yavorsky, Darene Roma. *"Show Them What You Can Do": Building the Ukrainian Spirit across Canada: An Illustrated Biography of Pavlo Romanovich Yavorsky.* Hensall, ON: Word and Image Studio, 2007.

Yekelchyk, Serhy. "The Body and the National Myth: Motifs from the Ukrainian National Revival in the Nineteenth Century." *Australian Slavonic and East European Studies* 7, 2 (1993): 31–59.

———. *Ukraine: Birth of a Modern Nation.* New York: Oxford University Press, 2007.

Zahaikevych, Mariia. "Mystetski paraleli: velych i paradoksy doli Oleksandra Koshytsia i Vasylia Avramenka." *Studii mystetstvoznavchi* 31, 3 (Kyiv: Instytut mystetstvoznavstva, folklorystyky ta etnolohii im. M.T. Rylskoho, 2010), 34–40.

Zhurov, Heorhii V. *Kyivska kinostudiia imeni O. Dovzenka.* Kyiv: Derzhavne vyd-vo obrazotvorchoho mystetstva UkrRSR, 1962.

———. *Z mynuloho kino na Ukraini, 1896–1917.* Kyiv: Vyd-vo Akademiï nauk UkrRSR, 1959.

Zurowsky, Jaroslaw. "Ievhen Deslav: A Forgotten Ukrainian Filmmaker." *Journal of Ukrainian Studies* 9, 2 (1984): 87–92.

INDEX

B

C

D

J

K

N

Q

R

S

T

U